Political analysis and Am

Political analysis and American medical care

Essays

THEODORE R. MARMOR
Yale University

CAMBRIDGE UNIVERSITY PRESS

Cambridge
London   New York   New Rochelle
Melbourne   Sydney

Published by the Press Syndicate of the University of Cambridge
The Pitt Building, Trumpington Street, Cambridge CB2 1RP
32 East 57th Street, New York, NY 10022, USA
296 Beaconsfield Parade, Middle Park, Melbourne 3206, Australia

First published 1983

Printed in the United States of America

Library of Congress Cataloging in Publication Data
Marmor, Theodore R.
Political analysis and American medical care.
Includes bibliographical references and index.
1. Medical policy – United States – Addresses, essays,
lectures. 2. Medical care – Political aspects – United
States – Addresses, essays, lectures. 3. Insurance,
Health – United States – Addresses, essays, lectures.
4. United States – Politics and government – 1945-
– Addresses, essays, lectures. I. Title.
RA395.A3M377   1983   362.1'0973   83-1904

ISBN 0 521 23922 2 hard covers
ISBN 0 521 28352 3 paperback

For J.S.M.

Contents

Introduction

This book is a collection of my essays on political analysis and the world of American medicine. Written during the 1970s, most were products of the latter half of that decade. They range widely in immediate topic and expected audience, method and length, generality and concreteness. The obvious question is why such a collection deserves the format of a book, given that most of the articles have already been published, albeit in a wide variety of journals and books. One reason for any book of essays is convenience. When one makes contributions to a field of inquiry but does so in quite different journals, books, and nations, there is a case for bringing together the pieces that appear enduring and useful. This case is particularly strong for applied work in the social sciences that attends to topics of public policy and diverse disciplinary interests. Such is the case with medical care, its financing, delivery, organization, and politics. No one reads all the journals. The disciplines proliferate their outlets; the interdisciplinary journals and books of public policy and particular policies further expand the range of publications. So if one has had something to say and has written in a variety of publications, there is a case for a book.

That case is further strengthened when the articles range over an intelligible but complicated field of work. This I believe to be the case here. The title, *Political Analysis and American Medical Care*, was carefully chosen. It is meant to signal both a disciplinary orientation and a common subject. As I turn to the structure of the book and its contents, I will buttress this claim of coherence. But here I want to turn to the claim itself.

The essays reflect training in political science and conviction in the importance of medical care to the modern state. Few need to be reminded that medicine is important politically. The expenditures modern societies commit to it are large (between 6 and 10 percent of gross national product across Organization for Economic Cooperation and Development, OECD, nations) and the relations between the polity and the world of medicine are contentious and often bewildering. The practice of medicine fifty years ago was largely a private matter of doctors, patients, and hospitals. Both private and public health insurance was relatively restricted, almost an infant industry. Today among the OECD nations, medical care finance is dominated by public expenditure.

The political salience of medical care is matched by its academic topicality. Medical schools seek courses to acquaint future doctors with the world of governance they will face; programs in nursing, health administration, and management include health policy and politics in their curricula. There are branches of medical care studies in the social sciences, especially sociology and economics, and a specialized cadre of philosophers and lawyers address—forbid the expression—"bioethics" and health law. Health planners and insurance officials seek guidance about the proper and likely role of government in redistributing access, financing care, and regulating its practice and quality. Once an infant industry, medical care is now a growth center, financially, intellectually, and politically. The proliferation of books, journals, and conferences mirrors, with a lag, the growth of governmental intervention in this world.

With this growth has come the expected outpouring of work on the politics of particular parts of the medical world. Public officials publish their views on the politics of health, exemplified by Enoch Powell's trenchant book on the British National Service in the 1960s.[1] Journalists cover particularly dramatic confrontations, as with Richard Harris's book on the Kefauver drug legislation of 1962.[2] Legal scholars take up the question of how state medical regulation operates, as with the classic 1954 *Yale Law Journal* article on the power of the American Medical Association (AMA).[3] And scholars of American health politics seize on one topic after another, explaining who got what, where, and when: the advent of Medicare and Medicaid in 1965, the origins and fate of health planning legislation, the closures of particular hospitals, the struggles over municipal hospitals, the regulation of physicians through the Professional Standards Review Organizations (PSROs), the play of state commissions charged with regulating hospital expansion or reimbursement, and so on. Components of the industry, particular policy struggles, program implementation, and the pressure group actions of various organizations—all provide ready subjects for political analysis.[4]

But the discussion of particular political struggles in medical care can be misleading. This is so for two reasons. First, particular cases of politics *in* medicine do not add up to the politics *of* medicine. The stakes, contestants, and forms of policy struggle vary. Conflicts over hospital closures, for instance, differ greatly from those occasioned by the regulation of the drug industry or the subsidy of medical care for the poor. The undeniably truthful claim that there are politics in the world of medical care does not entail that there is a uniform politics of medical care.

There are, in fact, many ways to regard politics in medicine. One can emphasize the institutional setting of the struggle (Congress, the Department of Health and Human Services, state government), the players (AMA, state licensing boards, city councilmen), the topic at issue (budgets, social insurance claims, professional privileges), the character of the fight (muted or noisy), the nature of the contest (how much local aid to a particular hospital or the scale of redistribution in welfare state battles), and so on.

Political scientists group political struggles more generally by their institutional setting, their policy stakes, or forms of dispute. Naming politics "medical" is but one way of describing politics in the medical care industry. The relevant considerations in disputes about medical care are the same as those in conflicts

• about any public policy: the distribution of expected costs and benefits (concentrated vs. dispersed), the geographical location of conflict and the pattern of organized interests (balanced vs. imbalanced political marketplaces), or the type of gains and losses that policies appear to generate (zero sum vs. positive sum).[5] It may well be that, in medicine, there is a distinctive distribution of political conflicts. But that has to be maintained on evidence, not by simply invoking the industry in which the politics occur. This point applies to transportation, agriculture, steel, and education as much as it does to medicine.

Thinking of "a politics of medical care" is misleading in a second respect. Such a view subordinates both constitutional arrangements and the socioeconomic structures that constrain what is thinkable and hence politically possible. Both the modes of political representation and the range of political ideologies shape the fate of a nation's policies on health. In the United States, a constitutional orientation toward dispersion of authority conditions governmental intervention into any industry.[6] Interest groups adapt to this fragmentation. In federal–state programs like the subsidy of hospital construction, this federalism encourages positive-sum games in which the tax-paying losers and the subsidized winners hardly have to confront one another. Likewise, a culture that idealizes liberal individualism and capitalist modes of economic life shapes the medical care options its polity takes seriously. State ownership of medical care institutions— and direct salaried payment of its medical care providers—continues to be a highly unlikely option in American politics, whatever its appeal in Britain and elsewhere.[7] Such constraining factors affect all American politics. And, for that reason, understanding what shapes politics in American medicine is aided by studies of these national characteristics, even when the illustrations only marginally if at all touch on medical care.

These two points suggest, then, a widened focus for any work on medical care in American politics. First, one begins with the structure of American political life and its implications for particular policy struggles in medical care. Here, the issue is what one learns from political studies generally that bears on American medicine's political life. Second, using the approaches of political inquiry, one can investigate particularly salient instances of a nation's medical care politics. Here, the question is both explanatory (why the outcome and what are the prospects?) and illustrative (what is the study a case of?). Depending on one's concerns, applications of this sort can be used to support generalizations about classes of political conflicts or the generalizations can be brought to bear on the particular instance. That is, the work can function as a window on a nation's politics or as a case example of one of its recognizable forms of struggle and resolution. Finally, political analysis is part of sensible policy appraisal. The political conflicts over policy options shape their implementability and hence their desirability, as all practitioners understand. Policy analysis without politics is like a hotel without people. The political opposition and support a policy will command is analogous to expenditure and revenue in a budget; political benefits and costs vary, just as fiscal ones do, with the particular formulations of policy options. Moreover, putting policies into effect extends political struggle. And where operational policies sharply diverge from stated ones, appraisals of the latter are misleading substitutes for judgments of the former. Forecasts of implemented policies are the necessary preconditions of realistic policy appraisal.[8]

The essays that follow are grouped into these three classes. The first part addresses the perspectives of political science and asks how its general findings illuminate our medical care disputes. The second part discusses several instances of political conflict in the world of American medicine. The five applied studies range from problems of inflation to consumer roles in health politics, from paying doctors to an overview of the health programs of the Kennedy and Johnson administrations. Not exhaustive, they nonetheless cover a diverse range. And they do so with historical material, cross-national evidence, and comparisons with analogous concerns in other sectors of American life. In this respect, they illustrate both the substantive range of American medical politics and the use of the different approaches to political analysis itself.

The third group of essays addresses a number of questions about national health insurance. The historical legacy of conflict over government health insurance was the starting point. But any national health insurance program would have to deal with the whole of the medical care industry. So the question was what one could learn from American experience with government health programs and from foreign experience with national health insurance. And that meant asking how these lessons would illuminate the shape of struggles an American national health insurance program would face. All of the third part's essays share a prospective and prescriptive emphasis; they connect different sorts of political analysis to the appraisal of national health insurance in the contentious 1970s. In the early 1980s, it is obvious that national health insurance has receded as a topical political subject. But the role of government in the medical care industry will continue to be controversial. And so the epilogue discusses the debate over competition in American medicine, the alternative, in the minds of many, to the long-standing dispute over national health insurance.

A word about the origins of these essays. For twenty years, my major interest has been the politics of the welfare state in America. But my initial topic of study was government health insurance, particularly why it was that the United States turned to the aged and the poor as the constituencies for its Great Society initiatives in medical care, the Medicare/Medicaid programs of 1965.[9] No doubt that interest in health insurance was stimulated when I became a surgeon's son-in-law in 1961. And my book on *The Politics of Medicare* (1973)[10] was in part an attempt to settle some extended family discussions. But that book also set the stage for the essays that follow. It was directed at understanding, not prescribing. It meant to make sense of an important watershed in American politics, to address retrospectively what led the nation to take the course it did during the Johnson administration. The result, however illuminating, was an insufficient guide to *future* disputes over the government's role in American medicine. I wanted to write a book on the debate over this question, the *likely* options, and, more importantly, the *likely* effects of these options. So I set for myself an agenda of preparation. I asked what I would need to know to write a useful, prospective book on national health insurance. As it happens, that book, written with a group of collaborators at both the University of Chicago and the Urban Institute, was published in 1980.[11] What this set of essays represents are the intellectual precursors of the 1980 national health insurance book.[12]

The epilogue's combination of historical summary and political forecasting completed the agenda I set for myself years ago. Students of American politics or health policy will find in these pages diverse essays, but not disconnected themes. It is to the particular essays I now wish to turn.

The first chapter, "Political science and health services administration," addresses the question of what one might learn about politics in American medicine by reviewing the work of political science. Previously unpublished in this extended form, the essay reflects the tremendous growth of interest in health politics that followed the introduction of Medicare and Medicaid in the mid-1960s. Before then, medical care politics and policy were a specialist's domain, a small part in the agenda of American politics and political study. As public program after program emerged in the 1960s and 1970s, particular analyses abounded but few general overviews.

This long essay supplies such an overview. Moreover, it was intended as a guide to newcomers—both to politics and to health—and draws out the different modes of interpreting politics in medicine. It reviews the subjects regarded as the domain of politics, the concepts political analysts employ, the main approaches they take, and the conclusions about American domestic politics that illuminate medical care. There have been few other such disciplinary surveys; indeed, Herbert Kaufman's 1969 monograph for the Public Health Service is the only one I know of with the same scope.[13]

The essay on comparative politics and health policies (chapter 2) begins as well with a methodological and disciplinary subject. It questions both what cross-national political studies can tell one about medical care politics and how medical issues can inform comparative politics, so long an area of institutional emphasis and psephological preoccupation. It deals with the broad topic of comparative policy studies but uses medical care to illustrate the costs, benefits, and limits of such inquiries. As such, the essay provides the intellectual underpinnings for three uses of cross-national evidence in the rest of the book: comparisons that set the context for American disputes, parallel studies of how different politics deal with comparable tasks (like paying doctors), and discussions of how the experience of one regime can illuminate the options of another (as with the Canadian national health insurance experience and its lessons for America). The first part, then, provides the disciplinary and methodological models of which the essays that follow are particular instances.

Chapter 3 is a political scientist's view of the internationally common problem of medical care inflation. It takes as its central focus not the causes of inflation but American government's special difficulty in coping with them. For, although all industrial nations have experienced inflationary pressures in this sector during the postwar period, America's troubles since the mid-1960s have been comparatively acute.[14] Why should this continue to be so, especially when all acknowledge that widespread insurance, restraints on price competition, and fragmented financing institutions are recipes for inflation? Why has agreement on these causes not led to significant amelioration? Chapter 3 argues that the answer lies largely in the very structure of America's political "market." With inflation's benefits relatively concentrated and its costs diffused over many patients, insurance funds, and governmental agencies, the interest in controlling inflation is much less than the concern to shift costs. The theory of concentrated and diffuse interests parsimoniously illuminates America's comparative difficulties.[15]

Chapter 4 applies the same theory to a policy fashionable in the late 1960s and the early 1970s: the idea that enhanced consumer representation in the corridors of medical power would right the wrongs of American medicine. The ambitious and conflicting aims of America's experiment in health planning constitute the essay's initial focus. The discussion then turns to the varied conceptions of representation that, by comparison, highlight the American form of consumer representation: "mirroring" local communities in the institutions of health system agencies (HSAs) all over the country. And the review of experience since the HSA program's origins in 1974 illustrates how political structures—imbalanced political markets—doom naive hopes for such planning programs.

Chapter 5 also addresses these dilemmas of American health planning but from the vantage point of comparative experience. By looking at the experiences of other nations—both similar to and different from the United States—it suggests how peculiar our own planning has been and provides guidelines our planners might follow when trying to reshape American medicine in the real world of clashing interests, scarce political resources, and competing incentives.

Chapter 6 moves away from planning but employs the methods of cross-national comparison. It takes up the topic of how governments chose methods of paying physicians and what generalizations the comparative historical evidence supports. Its aim is mainly explanatory: to sketch the factors that explain why physicians are almost always paid by the methods they prefer rather than those reformers insist are best. But the policy implications of such findings are highlighted as well. The politics of paying doctors suggest that modern governments have narrow choices regarding major reforms in the paying of most physicians.

This in turn suggests that the administration of payment schemes is crucial and that other measures to achieve the ends of favored methods of payment have to be found.

Chapter 7 surveys the fate of health programs in the Kennedy and Johnson administrations. It employs the conceptual tools of Part I to understand the character and consequences of the quite diverse programs initiated between 1960 and 1968. Its categories are those of politics, not industrial economics. So the discussion centers on the forms of welfare state politics illustrated by Medicare and Medicaid; the pork barrel bargains in programs like health research, hospital construction assistance, and community mental health centers; and the regulatory struggles within different agencies. What the federal government does in medical care is the major topic, but the central point is that the federal government's policies affect medical care but do not constitute a medical care policy.

Part III shifts the focus from politics in American medicine to a particular cluster of issues; namely, those involving the role of American government in health insurance. Chapter 8 leads off by assessing the historical record, reviewing in particular the different political fates of the two major financing innovations in 1965, Medicare and Medicaid. "Welfare medicine" here means health financing programs for the poor, in particular the federal–state Medicaid program. The puzzle posed by the Medicare/Medicaid comparison is why the two programs, simultaneously launched, should have produced such similar results medically and economically but had such different political fates. Both programs redistributed access in the intended direction (toward the old and the poor, respectively), both contributed substantially to medical inflation, and both put considerable pressure on government budgets at the federal and state levels. Why should Medicaid be regarded as a political scandal and subjected to programmatic instability and Medicare remain so stable and, broadly speaking, legitimate? The answer lies in the political constituencies they affected and the ideological claims they excited. And, more important for national health insurance, their fates reveal the profound political significance of the different welfare state conceptions government health insurance proposals can express.[16]

Chapter 9 turns to Canada and thus shifts from asking what the past of American government's role in health insurance means for future changes to what we can learn from Canada's experience with universal government health insurance. It compares the postwar developments in both countries and then, on the basis of similarities in economic structure, medical arrangements, and social stratification, inquires about the effects and fate of Canada's experiment in socialized health insurance. As such, the essay differs from the comparative design of chapter 6. Rather than testing a proposition across many regimes—as with doctors' pay—it treats Canada as a natural experiment for the United States. In that sense, the essay is both an instance of comparative political analysis and a special way to forecast the likely policy effects of a major program untried in the

United States. It stands as a check on extrapolating how American politics would deal with national health insurance from how we have historically handled partial government involvement in the health market of the Medicare and Medicaid form.

Chapter 10 reconsiders the 1970s' debate over national health insurance in the light of these national and international findings. On the one hand, it places the struggle at the center of American contentions about decent forms of social welfare policy. It highlights the special place such divisive issues have in the partisan and ideological composition of the American polity. But it also seeks to contribute to that debate by suggesting how far ideological struggle is likely to distort realistic policy forecasts.

Chapter 11 continues that effort at policy forecasting on a level devoted to patient cost sharing under various national health insurance plans; it takes up the traditionally contentious question of what role ability to pay should play in the receipt of medical attention.[17] But it emphasizes how cost sharing will, in fact, operate rather than its theoretical advantages and disadvantages.

The last chapter, "Medical care and procompetitive reform," is historical, analytical, and predictive. It reviews the current trends in American medicine and government health programs and foreshadows possible futures. For the purpose of this collection, the epilogue's distinctive role is partly a detailed analysis of proposals for increased competition in American medicine during the 1980s. But it also suggests how political and economic circumstances condition the fate of proposals like those collected under the procompetitive banner. The essay predicts that procompetitive arguments will politically rationalize the attack on contemporary health regulations without fundamentally reforming the industry.[18]

The publication of a collection of essays provides the occasion for personal acknowledgment as well as summary arguments. A diverse set of people and institutions stimulated, assisted, and encouraged me during the decade in which these essays were written. The universities where I taught—Wisconsin, Minnesota, Chicago, and Yale—all provided an atmosphere in which scholarship was taken seriously and thus stimulated. Particular research centers within these universities, however, gave the most crucial assistance, materially and intellectually. I have a particular debt to the Institute for Research on Poverty at the University of Wisconsin, which, in 1967–1969, supported my work on the politics of Medicare and, by generous aid to me as a visitor in 1971, made full-time writing possible. At the University of Chicago, I was the fortunate recipient of the Center for Health Administration's (CHAS) scholarly encouragement and financial assistance. Most research centers in American universities are paper organizations in a profound but pathetic sense; their letterheads exhaust their intellectual collegiality and misleadingly suggest a community of scholars. CHAS, as its affectionate admirers call Chicago's center, was different. Odin

Anderson made Chicago a mecca for those writing about medicine and society. His workshops attracted a seemingly unending series of visitors, both from America and abroad, stimulating its fellows and nurturing an environment in which serious work was taken seriously. Now, as the Chairman of Yale's Center for Health Studies, I know well how hard it is to create and to sustain such an atmosphere. Many of the essays collected here bear the imprint of colleagues from my six years at Chicago. However, it would be wrong to express my gratitude evenhandedly. Odin Anderson made a crucial difference to my work, and I want to thank him warmly.

There is a final group that contributed even more to these essays, my coauthors. All too often senior authors claim more credit than candor should permit. The coauthors are all acknowledged on the title pages of the essays they helped write. Many are former students whose research found initial expression in joint papers. However, they must know their contribution was greater than the individual pieces on which they worked. There is an informal, loosely organized, and continuing seminar that links them and extends the range of topics I have been able to address. Andrew Dunham, now of Colorado College, initially learned about politics and American medicine by working on the opening chapter of this book. He was the first of a series of graduate students who became colleagues and in their own right have contributed to the literature of this field. Jim Morone, now of Brown University, was the second of these gifted students. His work on the health programs of the Kennedy–Johnson years set the stage for a thesis on American health planning, parts of which are incorporated here in the chapter on the politics of consumer representation in American medicine. Amy Bridges of Harvard, the third of "the Chicago crew," made the chapter on America's peculiar forms of health planning more literate and acute than it would otherwise have been. At Chicago these students helped create an unusually stimulating workshop between 1975 and 1979, a place where articles, books, reviews, and daily exchanges emerged in exciting and seeming disorder. Their contributions are only partly revealed by particular joint articles; they all worked more anonymously on the national health insurance project that culminated in the 1980 book on national health insurance.

Other colleagues participated in the Chicago workshop and contributed substantially to the atmosphere out of which most of these essays emerged. They read drafts, contributed suggestions, and made the place and its writing more lively. All have gone on to productive scholarly careers of their own: Beth Kutza at the University of Chicago, Fay Cook at Northwestern, Will White at the University of Illinois–Chicago Circle, and Doug Conrad—the coauthor of chapter 11—at the University of Washington.

Yale's Center for Health Studies has been a congenial setting in which to select and to edit these papers. Two of its members have particularly helped to produce this book, Julie Greenberg and Terry Eicher. They manage the flow of scholarship that now is edited here, *The Journal of Health Politics, Policy and Law*, and have contributed skillfully to the readability of what I have written. Finally, I want to acknowledge the impact of Ed Lindblom on both the center I chair and the scholarship I have finished at Yale. He is a scholar whose own work on politics and public policy, as one of his readers has put it, "does for the mind, what the can opener does for the can." Moreover, he made possible at Yale, with the support of the Kaiser Family Foundation, the continuing work of the Center for Health Studies. The center, and its staff, helped turn the essays of the past decade into this book.

T. R. MARMOR

Yale University
January 1983

Notes

1 E. Powell, *Medicine and Politics* (London: Pitman Books, 1966). Other examples include David Owen's reflections as Health Minister in Britain's 1974 Labor government in D. Owen, *In Sickness and in Health: The Politics of Medicine* (London, Quartet Books, 1976), and Joseph Califano's 1981 review of his experience in the Carter administration in J. Califano, *Governing America: An Insider's Report from the White House and the Cabinet* (New York: Simon & Schuster, 1981).
2 R. Harris, *The Real Voice* (New York: Macmillan, 1964).
3 Note, "AMA: Power, Purpose and Politics in Organized Medicine," *The Yale Law Journal*, 63: 938–1022, 1954.
4 For more examples of these particular topics, see the following: Medicare—T.R. Marmor, *The Politics of Medicare* (Chicago: Aldine, 1973), and R. Harris, *A Sacred Trust* (Baltimore: Penguin Books, 1969); Medicaid—R. Stevens and R. Stevens, *Welfare Medicine in America* (New York: Free Press, 1974); health planning—N. Anderson and L. Robins, "Debate on Health Planning in the United States," *International Journal of Health Services*, 6:651–690, 1976, and A. Atkisson and R. Grimes, "Health Planning in the United States: An Old Idea with a New Significance," *Journal of Health Politics, Policy and Law*, 1:295–318, 1976; local health politics— R. Alford, *Health Care Politics* (Chicago: University of Chicago Press, 1975); PSROs— B. Decker and P. Bonner, *Professional Standards Review Organizations* (Cambridge, Mass.: Ballinger, 1973); implementation and pressure groups—E. Redman, *The Dance of Legislation* (New York: Simon & Schuster, Touchstone edition, 1973), and E. Bardach, *The Implementation Game: What Happens after a Bill Becomes a Law* (Cambridge, Mass: MIT Press, 1977).
5 The most widely cited typology of policy conflicts—redistributive, regulatory, and distributive—is T. J. Lowi's *The End of Liberalism*, 2nd ed. (New York: Norton, 1979). For discussion in this book, see especially chapters 1, 3, 4, and 7.
6 For a discussion of this theme, see chapter 1.

7 For America's peculiarities, see R. Klein's essay on American health planning, "Reflections on the American Health Care Condition," *Journal of Health Politics, Policy and Law*, 6(2): 188–204, 1981.

8 For discussion of political feasibility, see E. Bardach, *The Implementation Game*; J. Pressman and A. Wildavsky, *Implementation* (Berkeley: University of California Press, 1973).

9 The peculiarity of America's path to government health insurance is discussed, in contrast to Canada's, in R. Kudrle and T. R. Marmor, "The North American Welfare State," in P. Flora and A.J. Heidenheimer, eds., *The Development of Welfare States in Europe and America* (New Brunswick, N. J.: Transaction Books, 1981), pp. 81–124.

10 Marmor, *The Politics of Medicare*.

11 J. Feder, J. Holahan, and T. R. Marmor, eds., *National Health Insurance: Conflicting Goals and Policy Choices* (Washington, D.C.: The Urban Institute, 1980).

12 Different inducements and audiences attended each of these essays, but the common motivation was understanding politics in the world of medicine to help appraise proposals to shape that world.

13 H. Kaufman, "The Political Ingredient of Public Health Services: A Neglected Area of Research," *The Milbank Memorial Fund Quarterly*, 4:13–34, 1966.

14 R. Evans discusses America's relatively acute medical inflation problem in the 1970s in his essay, *Is Health Care Better in Canada Than in the U.S.?*, a paper presented at the University Consortium for Research on North America seminar, December 2, 1980, Cambridge, Mass., pp. 3, 11.

15 For a similar argument about the contrast of British and American experience with government's control of medical inflation, see R. Klein's essay, "Reflecting on the American Health Care Condition."

16 The differing conceptions of the welfare state in theory and practice are discussed at length in Flora and Heidenheimer, eds., *The Development of Welfare States in Europe and America*, especially Chaps. 1–3, 11.

17 The most extensive recent treatment of patient cost sharing is M. L. Barer, R. G. Evans, and G. L. Stoddart, *Controlling Health Care Costs by Direct Charges to Patients: Share or Delusion?*, Occasional Paper 10, Ontario Economic Council, 1979.

18 The tendency to confuse wishes with forecasts is particularly acute in proposals to enhance "competition" in the medical market place. For a discussion of this problem, see D. Mechanic, "Dilemmas in Health Care Policy," *Health and Society*, 59(1): 10–14, 1981.

I. The perspective of political science

1. Political science and health services administration

THEODORE R. MARMOR, ANDREW DUNHAM

Political science, the study of who gets what and how, is concerned with conflict, influence, and authoritative collective decision making in both public and private settings. The substantial expansion of government programs in health and medicine since 1965 makes political analysis increasingly important for health services research.

The public sector in 1976 provided 42 percent of the health expenditures in this country (compared to 26 percent in 1965 and 13 percent in 1930),[1] and activities of the state have been extended to determining the appropriateness of facilities, manpower training, accreditation, fee schedules, and even the quality of medical care. Because government is too heavily involved in the health care industry (injecting $50 billion in 1975 and creating innumerable programs and regulations), its actions affect everyone working in it. Anne Somers reported, for example, that in 1968 there were "sixty-eight different hospital programs or facilities affected by direct government controls";[2] both the number and the significance of these controls have increased since then. Hospital administrators must include probable governmental behavior in their own planning: What effect will certificate-of-need have on their services and facilities? What will manpower programs or licensure do to the availability of staff? How will insurance regulations or Medicaid reimbursement schedules affect hospitals' cash flow? Clearly, the job of health administrator is highly political, in both the narrow and broad senses of that term. This is no less the case for others in the medical care industry.

This chapter is designed to provide newcomers to politics or medical care with some tools of political analysis and a sense of their uses and limitations. It first sketches a broad array of political science concepts, beginning with the subject of politics and the perspectives of political scientists and continuing with a brief

This chapter was written in 1976 to be part of a multivolume handbook on health and the various academic disciplines, sponsored by the Association of University Programs in Health Administration (AUPHA). In the end, the AUPHA did not publish the series. The interest in the topic has, however, continued and partial versions of this essay have been published. It was the continuing interest in the relation between political science and health that prompted going back to the original monograph for this collection. Although the chapter was specifically designed as a primer in political science for health services administrators, its review of the discipline applies to many arenas, public and private.

outline of American government. It examines in detail the conceptual models that analysts and practitioners use in assessing political activity in both governmental and nongovernmental settings and then summarizes the major explanatory paradigms in political science. The chapter proceeds to evaluate politics in the health industry, depicting the varied nature of its political conflicts and the typical patterns of American health policy and concludes with a detailed application of political analysis to a particularly revealing health care struggle—the proposed expansion of Cook County Hospital in Chicago during the 1950s.

Conceptions of political science

The life of politics

The narrowest and most common approach to political science concentrates on conflict and decision making in government: who gets what and how in the public arena.[3] Such analysis emphasizes the direct influences on government ("inputs"), how governmental institutions convert ("process") those influences into decisions or actions ("outputs"), and the impacts of actions ("outcomes"). Outputs and outcomes become part of the influences on government ("feedback") and, thus, the circuit is completed.

This approach has produced a substantial literature on public opinion and the role of parties, voting, and other forms of political participation. Political scientists with this perspective have emphasized the importance of interest groups in politics, not just in elections or the passing (or blocking) of legislation but also in the administrative implementation of programs. They have also argued that the internal organization and processes of government themselves have a profound effect on decisions and actions.

Simply finding out what the government is actually doing, moreover, is not easy. Indeed, a major task of political science has been descriptive, to identify and clarify government action. These efforts have yielded numerous studies of governmental structure, legislative arrangements and rules, public administration and bureaucratic behavior, and judicial process. This conception of political analysis, concerned with what one might term the "life of politics"—the activities in the governmental or public sector—is now the conventional approach of American political scientists.

The politics of life

A broader but rarer approach to political science examines the "politics of life" —conflict and collective, authoritative decision making in general, not just in government settings. This approach recognizes that politics occur everywhere: in hospitals, universities, relations between private organizations, and offices. This approach concentrates on organizations, nongovernmental as well as governmental, and on situations in which the destructive consequences of collective choices are central. It deals with the micropolitics of everyday life.

Social structure and political settings

The broadest approach to political science begins with social structure, political culture, and ideology. This perspective emphasizes the context within which the life of politics and the politics of life take place. The values and social arrangements of every society create systematic biases that favor some interests, promote certain types of action, and affect whether some issues and policies are even placed on the political agenda. Studies that include cross-cultural and cross-national comparisons often embody this approach. Such comparative studies can be valuable in showing new alternatives, the probable consequences of choices, and the limits of effective choice.[4]

Nondecisions and the political agenda. Many important issues do not reach the level of collective choice but are settled outside of the public realm by what have been termed *nondecisions*.[5] The fact that national health insurance proposals never received serious attention during the depression of the 1930s reflects a nondecision. In 1935, President Roosevelt excluded national health insurance from his Social Security proposals because he feared vitriolic and powerful political opposition. There was virtually no serious congressional consideration of health insurance because one individual's decision on a political agenda tacitly determined the extent of public consideration on the issue.

There are innumerable instances of a prolonged lack of recognition of issues by decision makers. Such issues are outside the contemporary politics of life or the life of governmental politics, and yet they are significant both because the biases of a system are revealed as much by what is not done as by what is done and because they may become politically salient. Politics may well be the "art of the possible," but it is important to understand what makes something possible and how and why that circumstance changes. There are few political and sociological analyses of the important subject of how, when, and why political "possibilities" change over time.

The social setting of politics. The social system places limits not only on what is seriously considered but also on what can be accomplished. The structural approach in political science locates health (or any other sector) within the larger society, focuses on the incentives for coherence and compatibility with society, and assesses the impact of society on the behavior of the health care system. Consider, for example, a society with a barter economy contemplating a national health insurance that includes deductibles payable in cash. Such a policy is simply incompatible with the social system. Although simplistic, the example draws attention to the fact that every society has limits that are vitally important for the formation and implementation of social policies.

A more realistic example is the constraint on egalitarian policies in a society based on individual material incentives. It is obvious that the basic problem of the poor in America is that they do not have enough money. Massive redistribution of cash in an economic system based on wage labor, however, would weaken the incentive to work. Even public services—education, public housing, food stamps, medical care and so on—if provided at "too high" a level might diminish such incentive.

This is not to say that such a limit is approached in America today, only that there is a ball park within which social welfare policy is played out. The ball park perimeter, of course, can and does change; every industrialized nation has developed a variation of the welfare state over the last fifty years. The structural approach in political science tries to understand, explain, and predict such basic societal changes.[6]

Politics as channeled social behavior. The social structure not only sets the boundaries within which social behavior occurs, it also directly affects that behavior. Characteristic incentives, constraints, and possibilities in a society channel behavior in predictable directions. For example, the undersupply of physicians serving poor or isolated areas is part of larger social processes. Merely increasing the number of physicians will do little to bring medical care to these areas since existing incentives and other social and medical opportunities continue to channel most physicians elsewhere. This example stresses the importance of the structural approach. It indicates that many problems related to health services are part of larger social problems and that effective attempts to deal with them must account for the social context. This context, too, changes over time. Thus, a political analyst must be concerned not only with the feasible short-run solutions to immediate problems but also with the way those solutions will interact with, and possibly alter, basic social features.

Appraising alternative approaches

Political science obviously considers a vast area of behavior, ranging from conflict over minor, day-to-day, collective decision making to major governmental actions and ultimately to social structure and values. There are disadvantages to this broad range of subject matter. Any field that can range from office politics to broad Marxist theories of historical development must of necessity often appear (and sometimes be) unfocused or contradictory. But there are also major advantages to be gained from this wide scope.

On the first level, all of us face the politics of life in the course of our daily work. We are constantly embroiled in issues of conflict and power, both with other organizations[7] and within our own.[8] Although effectiveness in such situations is to some extent an art—and can, in any case, only be truly mastered through experience—political science can help to sensitize workers, administrators, clients, and citizens to typical inter- and intraorganizational political problems and processes. Merely alerting many people to the fact that most problems they face are partly political is a major first step. By explaining what is typical and why, political science can point to ways to achieve desirable but untypical results.

On the next level, increased and increasing governmental involvement in medical care means that health care actors are affected more significantly by government. They must, in short, be able to predict governmental behavior and impact, foresee uncontrollable factors, and act more efficiently within the constraints they impose. Also, in order to achieve their ends, they often want or need to become involved in politics. Political science may help them be more efficient and effective in their dealings with government.

On the final level, political science is a consumer—and, at its best, a synthesizer—of the full range of social sciences. It is concerned not merely with governmental affairs but with the distribution of all types of social benefits and burdens—for example, perceptive and sensitive work on the development of Medicare would include a variety of approaches: sociological analysis of the changing role of the family and the plight of the elderly in industrial societies; psychological discussion of the needs and fears of the elderly and the response of the rest of the population; historical study of events and processes that led to the current situation; economic breakdown of the supply, demand, cost, and benefit distribution of services under alternative health insurance programs; consideration of the political struggle and the organizational character of the various proponents and the bureaucracies that would administer the program; and description of the stakes and personalities involved in decision making and implementation.

General applications of political science

The American governmental system

Branches of government. It is important to understand the governmental structure in which political activity takes place. The American system is sometimes described as incorporating a separation of powers. This is inaccurate—its central feature is a sharing of authority. The executive, legislative, and judicial branches do not have distinct arenas of legitimate power as much as they have overlapping jurisdictions. The bureaucracy has grown so large and influential that it is now often considered a fourth branch of government that also shares power.

The budget process is a good example of how power is shared among the branches. Although the Constitution grants Congress the "power of the purse," the budget is actually formed through a long, complicated, interorganizational process: Executive agencies make requests for what they need (want, hope) to get; this is modified by the president's Office of Management and Budget before the budget message is sent to Congress, though presidential involvement continues after submission; various committees again change it and the Senate and House as a whole may have to compromise on its terms; Congress sends the appropriation back to the president who may veto it; the courts may force the president to spend money, if any is impounded, or may forbid certain expenditures; and finally, the bureaucracy administers—and often alters—expenditures. Thus, the executive, legislative, judicial, and bureaucratic branches are all involved in important, intermingled ways.

Federalism. The federal nature of the American system also produces a substantial degree of shared, overlapping authority. Though federal, state, and local governments are often viewed as hierarchical and separate, as in a layer cake, they are more accurately regarded as a marble cake, mixed and swirled together.[9] This is partly because federal legislators have strong regional ties. More importantly, most programs are a complex mixture of federal, state, and local action.

The federal government provides categorical grants for a vast number of specific projects and sets standards that the state and local governments meet to some degree. Many "federal" programs, such as neighborhood health centers, are administered exclusively by local units and are altered significantly to fit the political and social features of the area. Conversely, even a basically "local" function such as elementary education is strongly influenced by federal grants and regulations.

This sharing of and struggling over authority—both horizontally among the branches and vertically among the units of the federal system—means that most governmental activity involves complex interaction among the components of the system. The complexity is vastly increased because of the many agencies with overlapping responsibilities and programs. Legal structures, programs, and political settings vary immensely among the fifty states, three thousand counties, and tens of thousands of local governments and special districts.[10] Those interested in the health industry, however, should have a knowledge and understanding of at least the basic components of the American governmental system. This information can be acquired from an introductory political science course or textbook. A more specific knowledge of the governmental agencies and programs that directly affect work will, and indeed can, only be learned on the job and must be learned anew in each new position. The wealth of specific information—personalities, past histories, programs, legal rules, and so on—required to operate effectively cannot be taught in a classroom, but understanding the importance of learning these facts can be.

Certain aspects of politics, such as basic ways of looking at political activity, the key determinants of political behavior, and typical patterns of results, are more universal and will always be useful. The greatest contributions of political science are analytic models and explanatory paradigms that can be applied in both governmental and nongovernmental settings.

The politics of health: how distinctive?

The politics of health depends not so much on the substantive sector—the medical care industry—as on political factors that also commonly affect other sectors. Many of the specific issues and actors are, of course, unique to the field of health, but the nature of the politics of health is not obviously distinctive. This can be most simply explained by the fact that the health industry faces the same governmental arrangements as most other industries. There is the same mixing and balancing between public and private responsibility; the same marble cake of local, state, and federal authorities; the same voting alignments and party systems; the same federal legislature representing local interests and divided into contained committees; and the same political culture and social structure. This subject will be covered in more detail later, the underlying premise being that the political arena of health fits into the general pattern of American politics.

Perspectives of political analysts

Before we turn to the current state of political science, it will be helpful to look at the current state of political scientists. Allison[11] has persuasively argued that analysts—and practitioners—tend to use one or more of three conceptual models in thinking about the actions of government and other political actors. The models are usually only implicit, but each focuses attention, often unconsciously, on different facets of a situation, accentuating different problems and facts. The models are not so much theories of how or why events occur as conceptual "lenses" that direct what one looks at and what one looks for. Since observers can have many perspectives, it is important to be aware of these distinguishable models, or lenses, and their use. The three models, termed *rational actor*, *political bargaining*, and *organizational process*, are all used to answer the question, Why did or why will the government (or hospital or planning agency) take a particular action? Since each uses unique units of analysis and causal connections, each has an important but dissimilar angle on the total picture.

Rational actor. This model examines governmental action as the product of the rational choice of a single policymaking center. It assumes that government acts as a single unit facing problems that it purposely tries to solve. Someone using this model focuses on the goals and objectives of "the government," looks at possible alternative means to achieve those ends, analyzes their probable consequences, and then identifies the optimal solution as the predicted action (or explains an action as being a solution to the problems the government is facing). A statement such as "the Hill–Burton Hospital Construction Program was instituted because there was a shortage of hospital beds in the United States" is a good example of an application of this mode of analysis. A problem is identified— here, a shortage of beds—and governmental action is explained as a rational response to that problem.

Political bargaining. An analyst using this model perceives governmental policy as a result—not necessarily rational—of bargaining between various individual and group actors, each with its own interests, stakes, resources, and political skills. It recognizes that "the government" and groups trying to affect policy consist of many different agencies, groups, and individuals almost never sharing exactly the same goals and priorities. Analysis focuses on the players or actors in various positions and on the rules of the game that order the process. Actors have their own parochial perceptions and priorities, for it is recognized that people's positions affect their viewpoint—"where you stand depends on where you sit." This is true both horizontally (the secretary of Health and Human Services, HHS, has different concerns from the secretary of Housing and Urban Development, HUD) and vertically (the president has different stakes and a different perspective on matters concerning health than the secretary of HHS).

There is, thus, not one set of problems but many, with the players bargaining, compromising, competing, and forming coalitions with others to try to achieve their ends. The result of this maneuvering is determined by the political skill of the players, the kinds of resources (money, time, staff help, information, access to or personal ties with other players, official authority) they can command, and their stake in the outcome. The result is often one that no one really desired. According to this model, the characteristics of the Hill–Burton Program would be viewed as the product of many different forces: hospitals seeking money, but only for nonprofit hospitals; sponsors in the Senate seeking political recognition; states struggling over the formula to apportion money; and planners and state health officials attempting to acquire and control their part of the largess from Washington.

Organizational process model. This model interprets governmental action primarily as the output of large organizations. What is termed *governmental action* is mostly what goes on in such large bureaucracies as the Social Security Administration and the Internal Revenue Service. In order to deal methodically with the vast number of cases, the personnel of such organizations must of necessity have rules, repertoires, and standard operating procedures (SOPs). Such SOPs contribute, no doubt, to the organization's ability to function smoothly and perform its normal tasks, but they are often neither particularly innovative nor adaptable to new or unusual circumstances or changes in goals and responsibilities. Anyone who has ever worked in or been affected by a bureaucracy is intuitively aware of the importance of routines, but the point is that they are systematic and can be analyzed rigorously with fair predictability.

A central assumption is that large organizations change slowly and incrementally. If the government is doing something today, it usually means that the output was already in the bureaucracy's repertoire and that the government was behaving similarly yesterday. However innovative a plan may have been when it was conceived, it is usually implemented by a bureaucracy that continues to do things as they were done in the past, at least in the short run. (This is one reason for creating new agencies to administer new programs.) Finally, in complex programs involving more than one agency, problems of coordination become immense. Each agency follows its own SOPs and deals with its own area of jurisdiction, often leaving no one responsible for the overall result.

The organizational process model, then, incorporates a triple restriction on governmental behavior. First, recognition and definition of problems and suggested solutions often reach a top decision maker from within a bureaucracy and so are shaped and altered by the way a bureaucracy typically processes information. Moreover, the bureaucracy, in performing its normal functions, has often helped to create the very problem the decision maker faces, and its behavior has foreclosed certain alternatives. Second, there is a gap between "choice" at the top and actual implementation by an organization. The decision maker's real options are, as a result, still further constrained. Third, the decision maker is faced with a problem of coordination between different branches of the organization, each doing its own task in its own way.

The interpretation of the Hill–Burton Program from an organizational perspective highlights factors that are subordinate in the other models. Organizational analysts emphasize that the problem of inadequate health care for many Americans, especially in rural areas, was redefined and generalized as inadequate medical facilities and, in particular, as a shortage of hospital beds. They stress that the Hill–Burton Program was not new but was similar to other categorical grants to states. In evaluating the program, one is not surprised to find that, since at first the critical shortage was in rural areas, bureaucratic rules were established to channel funds there. However, even when central cities had the most pressing need for modernized hospitals, the bureaucratic rules continued (partly because of the success of the program) to channel funds to rural areas until a 1964 amendment.

Directed by the model to look for gaps between "policy decisions" at the top and actual organizational behavior, the analyst finds that, although hospitals receiving Hill-Burton funds were supposed to devote 5 percent of their resources to charity cases, this provision was simply not enforced by the bureaucracy. Finally, an analyst using this model looks for evidence of poor coordination and may find the Small Business Administration giving loans to new proprietary hospitals, which were not included in the Hill–Burton Program, to build in the same areas as established hospitals receiving Hill–Burton funds.[12]

It should be reemphasized that these models apply to nongovernmental as well as governmental behavior. The actions of a large hospital can be seen as its rational adaptation to the problems it faces; as the result of the procedures and bureaucratic rules of various departments within the hospital; or as the outcome of bargaining or adjustment between trustees, medical staff, and administrators.[13]

Conceptual models emphasize that what one sees depends partly on how one looks at political actions. The central task is to use them systematically and consciously and not to allow the model that comes to mind first to dominate. Using only one lens will usually give an incomplete and inaccurate picture; some combination of all three models is usually necessary to understand an organization's behavior. In this respect, the organizational process model should be emphasized since there is a tendency to assume that once a decision is made— whether through struggle and compromise or some "rational" choice—the issue is resolved. Use of this model ensures that the problems and distortions of implementation will be anticipated.

Types of explanations: sources of influence and who benefits

It is helpful to follow a discussion of how political scientists and political actors view the world with one concerning the ways in which political scientists attempt to explain its features. To understand who gets what and how, political scientists have produced several broad theories about the relationship between political systems and their social settings. Various paradigms in political science locate power in a variety of sources and places and regard governmental action as dominated by distinct actors and processes and benefiting distinctly different interests. Although these paradigms are not mutually exclusive, they do rest on divergent assumptions about government and society.

Popular rule through elections. The first paradigm emphasizes the role of elections in public policy, focusing on the undeniable fact that the American electorate has the ultimate formal power to select and discard many top officials. Since these leaders themselves choose a considerable proportion of the nonelected officials, it can be argued that government is ultimately accountable and responsive to the needs and desires of the citizens. Governmental policies are thus understood as expressing the "will of the people."

Any simple version of democratic theory applied to American government, however, encounters grave difficulties. In the first place, voting for a candidate does not imply that the voter is making a statement of policy on each of the many issues of the day, especially when candidates are ambiguous about their positions. Respected public opinion surveys indicate that a majority of the American population does not consider politics particularly important and that the general public is uninformed about most political issues, personalities, and facts.[14]

When politics and government are especially salient, for example, during the upheavals of the 1960s and the Vietnam War, citizens become more knowledgeable. Most citizens, however, do not consider it worthwhile to understand the government's actions, especially since they can have so little impact on most. It is hard enough for, say, operators of nursing homes to keep abreast of governmental programs and regulations that affect their livelihood, much less ordinary citizens who usually have little stake in the issues.

Between a quarter and a third of the adult American population never engages in political activity, whereas another quarter does nothing except vote every 2 years. Perhaps 10 percent of the population can be considered aware and deeply involved in political activity. It should be noted that those who do vote or are active tend to be wealthier, with views that are not representative of the whole population.[15] It is still possible, however, that the general public influences the tone or direction of governmental policy, if not the specifics, by *not* voting for officials when "things go badly."

Most voters identify themselves as either Democrats or Republicans, and that identification is the strongest determinant of whom they vote for, stronger than issues or personalities. To the extent that parties formulate different programs, the public, though unaware of specific political issues, may exercise some choice and control over policy by voting for the party whose basic stance they prefer. Still, it is certain that governmental policies are not a direct expression of popular views and that what government does and will do cannot be explained or predicted simply by public opinion and the electoral will of the citizenry.

Interest groups. The group process model, probably the dominant paradigm in political science, claims that large organizations, not individual citizens, are the vital force in American politics. These organizations raise issues, lobby for positions, help select officials, and influence the administration of governmental programs.[16] The vital importance of organizations stems from their possession of the resources—time, information, and expertise—necessary for effectiveness in the political process.

One version of this approach holds that organizations produce the democracy that the electoral system does not because, even though individual workers or doctors may not be politically active, the union or the American Medical Association (AMA) represents their position and promotes their interests. However, not all people are members of organizations, professional or otherwise, and many who are do not agree with their organization's political positions.[17] There are also problems in assuming that the individual's interests and opinions are independent of the issues. Changes in public opinion often are known to follow events or official statements; perhaps governmental action creates public opinion, not vice versa.[18] Interest groups expend much of their political effort in convincing their own members; thus, it is possible that unions *create* labor opinion as much as they express it.[19] Regardless of these qualifications, the paradigm centers on the influence of interest groups, not on their democratic nature.

Pressure on governmental officials is one of the least used—and least effective—means of influence despite the common usage of the term *pressure group* to denote organizational participants in the political process. Interest groups are rarely in a position to pressure an official. Few groups control enough votes to threaten a recalcitrant official with electoral defeat, and their use of money or other resources is not consistently adequate to impose their will. The influence of interest groups comes, therefore, partly from the good relations they maintain with officials. For example, since congressmen simply cannot keep abreast of all issues, interest groups provide information, write speeches, and even help congressmen draft bills. Interest groups usually work at helping their supporters rather than converting their opponents.

It is difficult for a congressman or any other official to ascertain his constituents' or the public's thoughts. If, however, those he sees most often are violently opposed to some policy, it is likely that he will also have doubts about it. Officials, like the rest of us, want to work in an environment that is pleasant, nonconflictual, and secure. They prefer to avoid decisions that generate political controversy and offend major groups with whom they must work. Trying to control their environment through conciliation, however, leads to an orientation toward the status quo and implies a pattern of policies that typically benefit, or at least do not harm, the most active interest groups. Thus, mutually beneficial relations and extensive contacts are the typical basis of an interest group's influence.

Yet, to the extent the influence of an interest group rests on its good relations with officials, its power is problematic. Marmor [20] has pointed out that much of the AMA's reputed power and ability to block Medicare rested upon the large number of congressmen who agreed with the AMA and were themselves opposed to a major new governmental health insurance program. When Johnson's election landslide in 1964 put new congressmen with different beliefs into office, the limited "power" of the AMA was revealed. The AMA was unable to pressure those new congressmen into opposing Medicare. The AMA clearly has influence on some policies, but their form is shaped more by an American ideological bias toward private control of medicine than by electoral pressure. In this case, the results the AMA wanted were not the ones they produced through pressure.

Even if organized groups seldom have the political power to force a favorable outcome, they are, nonetheless, deeply involved and influential in the political process. However, all interests are not equally well organized; hence, groups have unequal access to political influence. First, because money is required to organize and engage in political activity, there is a bias in favor of wealthy organizations. Schattschneider concluded in his classic study of interest politics that "the business or upper-class bias of the pressure system shows up everywhere."[21] Second, there is a bias against large groups with relatively diffuse interests and small stakes, especially those whose interests relate to public goods, such as clean air or conservation. Public goods are essentially available to all, so that beneficiaries cannot be adequately charged for activity on their behalf.

Assume, for example, that each American could save an average of five dollars a year if drugs were prescribed by generic name only. Although this implies a total saving of over $1 billion a year, few individuals have a large stake in the issue. Since most individuals have little to gain, few are likely to work hard for or contribute money to a group advocating a law making dispensing of generic drugs mandatory. In addition, if such a group were organized, noncontributors would gain as much as contributors, so there is no economic incentive for people to join or to help, even though they might favor the law. This is the "free rider" problem. Mancur Olson has shown, in fact, that under some conditions groups will not form and policies will not be promoted even when the policy is in everyone's interest.[22]

To carry the example further, let us assume that the drug companies oppose the plan. They are already organized, both as individual firms and as an industry. Because of their large financial stake in the outcome, they have considerable economic incentive to be actively opposed. They also have the resources to employ skilled personnel who can work full time lobbying, and their expertise and information are hard to challenge. Indeed, they often have a virtual monopoly on data. Few people can disagree if an official of a drug company testifies that "our figures show that the law would cut profits 8.2 percent, reduce the amount of research on new drugs 22 percent, and so retard the discovery and production of seventeen new lifesaving drugs each year." A congressman or governmental bureaucrat trying to serve the wider public interest might find it difficult to advocate a law with such punishing economic consequences, especially in the absence of reliable countervailing information.

American political culture. A variant of the group process model emphasizes the distinctiveness of American political culture.[23] Americans tend to distrust power, particularly governmental power and compulsion, and to prefer voluntarism and self-rule in small homogeneous groups with limited purposes. However, the problem of compulsion and avoidance of governmental power typically leads to the capture of public authority by private groups.[24] In many states, for example, it is doctors themselves who establish the standards for licensing physicians; public authority is, in effect, wielded by a private group.

There is an implicit American assumption that self-rule in small groups maximizes freedom. The importance of this ideology of self-rule is both expressed in, and reinforced by, the federal nature of American politics. Even programs initiated and financed largely by the national government are often run by state and local interests. The belief in self-rule is not, of course, restricted to the medical field. Agricultural policy, for example, is made by congressional committees composed of members of agricultural districts working in close collaboration with representatives of the Farm Bureau. Self-rule is a cherished American belief, but when hospitals make hospital policy and wheat farmers make wheat policy, their particular interests are represented at the expense of other, more general, citizen interests.

American distrust of power produces general opposition to increases in the scope of governmental authority. Efforts by American government in the area of social welfare have been much more limited than those in other industrialized democracies, and they have tended to be decentralized and piecemeal.[25] American politics has been characterized as incremental, with programs growing only slowly through time. Lindblom argues that policy is more the result of accretion than of broad decisions; it is not made as much as it evolves.[26] Wildavsky found this same incrementalism in the budgetary process, arguing that programs typically receive the funding of previous years with only marginal changes.[27] Lindblom, in particular, asserts that incremental policymaking is ideal in a pluralist democracy, for it ensures mutual adjustment and restrains authoritatively imposed policies in situations of uncertainty and conflicts of values.[28]

Elite rule. Elite theory is the most common of the paradigms discussed. Its advocates stress that there are a relatively few large and immensely powerful institutions in this country and that these institutions are controlled by a few men in top positions. C. Wright Mills has more forcefully presented this view, arguing that there is a power elite in the commanding positions of society that controls vast resources and makes decisions that dominate the country's activities. Mills maintains that the few hundred who run the key institutions—such as the president of the United States; the heads of General Motors, Exxon, and CBS; the Joint Chiefs of Staff—in effect run the country.[29] Although most political scientists are skeptical of Mills's extreme formulation, there is no denying the immense importance of a relatively few public and private institutions.

Most of the debate in political science over the role of elites has centered on studies of community power. Elitists have argued that there are only a small number of powerful people in each community or city. Pluralists agree that there is an iron law of oligarchy—that relatively few actors are directly involved in public decision making—but they disagree with the elite theorists on the size of this oligarchy, its homogeneity, and its openness to citizens' pressures. It is obvious, for example, that not all of the 6 million people in Chicago participate in decision making; the real question concerns the responsiveness and accountability of the few who do.

Robert Dahl, in his classic study of New Haven, argued that different leaders were influential on different issues—that is, there was not *one* power elite, but *different* elites in school policy, urban renewal, and so on. He argued also that the actual decision makers were responsive to and influenced by a larger public, partly through anticipated reactions (especially of election results) and that it was possible for newcomers to become influential and affect decisions.[30] Dahl also argued that these elites were not restricted to the rich but extended to middle and even lower income groups.

The debate about the role of elites is still unresolved among political scientists, partly because different cities have different power structures, but mostly because methodological and ideological issues seem to dominate the arguments.

Marxism. A Marxist variant of elite theory asserts that key decision makers are either wealthy themselves or make decisions for the benefit of the capitalist class. On a more general level, Marxists see government in capitalist countries as serving the interests of capitalism, sometimes muting conflict, but primarily perpetuating the dominance of the propertied classes. This dominance is maintained in part by ameliorative programs for the lower classes that reduce the most disruptive consequences of capitalism without eliminating its basically unequal class structure. Thus, for example, old people are not thrown out of hospitals onto the street just because they have no money, and unemployed workers are "bought off" by subsistence allowances. Other governmental programs socialize costs so that the government pays for the education or health programs required by capitalism for greater productivity and profits.[31]

At its strongest, this paradigm attempts to explain why the needs of capitalist development have led all industrial democracies to some form of welfare state and why this trend seems to be inevitable. It is noteworthy that education is seen not simply as an individual right but as a social duty. The young are required by law to attend school because society needs educated citizens. Some of the arguments in favor of national health insurance are also based on this line of reasoning, stressing the social more than the individual benefits of improved health.

Public finance. It is interesting to compare Marxist paradigms with a traditional theory of public finance. There are striking similarities, except, of course, for the final evaluation. Theorists in public finance argue that the state should provide certain key services that cannot be, or are not, provided efficiently by the private sector. Defense and environmental protection are obvious examples, but so are education and vocational training programs. An individual firm may not be able to provide the latter two because workers are mobile, and citizens may not be able to provide them for themselves because of the expense. Since such services ultimately benefit the whole society, the government should step in. Government, then, augments or corrects the private sector's services.[32]

Statist theory. A small but growing body of literature can be called *corporatist* or *statist* theory—works that see the state itself and the top governmental functionaries as the source of the majority of decisions and the most powerful influence on public policy. Reacting to the greatly increased role of the government, particularly at the federal level, and the shift in power from the legislature to the executive, several theorists have pointed out that the government now has far more resources at its command and a much wider influence than any other sector. The secretary of defense, after all, is the head of a far larger enterprise than the chairman of General Motors, and many government officials control more resources than the individuals or nongovernmental organizations with which they deal. Much public policy originates with these officials, who reflect their own view of the public interest or meet their own personal or organizational needs. Although statist theory was developed in studies of authoritarian governments, it is also increasingly recognized as relevant to the United States and other democratic countries.[33]

Paradigms and the 1965 Medicare bill

These paradigms have been found useful in explaining, and predicting, what the government did or might do since they help identify the forces that shape and influence governmental behavior. Although they do not allow analysts to predict with great certainty, they can at least direct attention to the right issues and the right questions. They should also help analysts avoid surprise at governmental behavior or concern over unlikely events. Table 1 sketches an application of these paradigms to the 1965 Medicare bill.

The paradigms provide different interpretations of the reasons Medicare passed and of its impact. Their relative value depends somewhat on the level of generality desired. For example, the actual passage of Medicare cannot be fully explained without reference to the Democratic election landslide of 1964, and yet, elections and party ideology give little insight into the specific provisions of the bill. If the question concerns the reasons why the United States was so slow, compared to Western Europe, in initiating a major governmental health care program, then the political paradigm is very useful. However, that paradigm does not explain why a program was finally enacted in 1965. Thus, the aspects of governmental behavior in which one is interested affect which paradigms seem most useful.

Emerging areas of political science relevant to the health sector

Implementation

Domestic public policy has only recently become a popular field within political science. Two areas of study in particular should be especially useful to practi-

Table 1. *Political science paradigms and the 1965 Medicare bill*

Paradigm	Application
Public rule through elections	The public was "permissive," not directive: It favored "action" but did not specify what action or when. There was no public agreement on provisions. Public views did not determine when Medicare passed; there had been general support for several years with no legislative enactment. The Democratic party, loosely allied with labor in ways similar to the social democratic parties of Europe, scored large gains in the 1964 election and passed social welfare legislation.
Interest groups	There were many bills before Congress, but most had no chance of passage. The "serious" bills had strong backing of important groups: labor, AMA, and American Hospital Association. These groups had a significant effect on specific provisions of bills. In particular, efforts were made to ensure the participation of providers by including provisions they desired such as non-interference with the practice of medicine and payment of usual and customary fees.
American political culture	There is minimal governmental involvement in the medical industry, and it is largely restricted to financing. The program is developed through accretion: Beneficiaries are the same as in other programs, and the program is run through existing structures, such as Blue Cross and the Social Security Administration, using existing methods, such as payment by usual and customary fees.
Elite rule	The president gave vital support and worked for the passage of a bill, and he and the majority of Congress belonged to the same party. One individual, Wilbur Mills, played a crucial role, such as expanding coverage of doctors, with the inadvertent assistance of committee Republicans. There was a change in elites because the electoral landslide eliminated many opponents and added supporters. Even though there was no change in public opinion, a changed elite led to passage.
Marxism	Medicare socializes the cost of labor and lessens pressure on corporations for retirement benefits. It shifts costs to regressive Social Security tax and widens the gap in disposable income. Some benefits go to the old and the poor, but the major benefits go to providers.
Public finance	The private system was not providing the desired care to the elderly and the poor. Government acted to correct this. The poor and aged are rational target groups since they have high medical costs and little income. The private system works for other groups.
Statist theory	Strategy is developed largely by governmental officials in the executive branch. They decided to have a limited program, to use the Social Security system, and to focus on the aged.

tioners. First, political scientists are focusing more on implementation of programs, realizing that policy goals and legislation can be greatly altered when they are actually administered. So far, most of the work has simply documented this fact, showing differences between programs as conceived and as carried out.[34] We can expect more understanding of the key variables in implementation and, it is hoped, better understanding by policymakers of what their alternatives actually are and what a program will really look like in practice. For example, it is now clear that simply establishing commissions to regulate industries will not by itself achieve desired public goals and that much closer attention to the practices of regulators is required. Allison makes an excellent first step in this direction. However, such research is still largely in the future. A number of young scholars are pursuing this implementation topic.[35]

Correlates of policy

A second research area that should prove useful lies in the "correlates of policy" studies that have been conducted both on American state and local programs and on international programs. These studies have analyzed the factors associated with the existence and success of different kinds of public programs. The early studies on America indicated the importance of socioeconomic variables in determining policy. For example, the wealth of a state has been found to be the best predictor of the extent of its welfare program. They showed, too, that there is often no clear relationship between inputs into programs and outcomes. For instance, money spent on education does not necessarily affect its quality. These preliminary studies have often been crude.[36] More sophisticated, detailed, reliable, and useful data are emerging.

The expansion from American cases to international comparisons is another fairly new but important development in these studies. Some have examined the correlates of social welfare policy by comparing nation-states throughout the world. Others have looked at only a few nations to investigate in depth their similarities and differences.[37] International comparisons of this sort can use the natural science experiment approach to analyze and predict in some detail the consequences and impact of specific policy options.[38]

Formal models and political behavior

Modeling is quite a different area that is also growing. Modeling employs rigorously constructed theories of behavior, draws predictions from these assumptions, and tests them against data. This method has been used with remarkable success in studies of voting and electoral behavior, and it is just beginning to move into other areas, such as public policy. When coupled with empirical work, it will be fruitful in generating explanations of governmental behavior and the impact of programs.

An application of political science to the field of health

The preceding discussion of general paradigms leads naturally to the question of what political science has to say about governmental behavior in the field of health. As the "Introduction" suggests, there is no single "politics of health"; there is, rather, politics throughout the health industry, its character depending on the particular policy arena. Lowi[39] has argued that different policy issues exhibit different types of political processes. There are different actors, styles, and locations of conflict, and typical outcomes. In a single substantive area, such as health, the dispute varies depending on whether it falls into what can be termed the *redistributive, regulatory,* or *distributive* arenas of American politics.

Redistributive arena

Redistributive programs have broad impacts on economic classes or large demographic units of the population. But a proposal or program can fit into this arena even though, objectively, it is not redistributive in impact since participants' perception determines the nature of the political arena. For example, what matters is not so much whether Medicare actually redistributed medical care or income as whether it was depicted as redistributive and "socialistic."

In the field of health, redistributive politics confront such issues as the proper role of government in organizing, financing, and redistributing health services. Although government involvement is often described as a takeover or restriction of private initiative, this is no zero-sum game. Increased governmental involvement can, and often does, produce an increase in private authority. For example, the creation of Professional Standards and Review Organizations (PSROs) led to increased authority for private medical organizations.

Certain variables of political conflict—such as site, contestants, and argument—are common to redistributive policies regardless of the substantive field. Large national organizations tend to be opposed to one another, sides are relatively stable over time, disputes are normally ideological in nature, and political battle is centralized, usually in the federal legislature. The struggle over Social Security, the long dispute over federal aid to education, the fight over Medicare, and most recently the struggles over national health insurance are typical examples of redistributive politics.

The scope of conflict—or who is involved—has been called "the most important strategy of politics."[40] It is obvious that the arena of dispute has a major impact on what kinds of policies emerge and whom they benefit. Redistributive political conflict takes place on the state and local levels, but, because of larger constituencies, it is more salient and more common at the national level. McConnell,[41] and Madison before him,[42] argued that the larger the constituency actively involved in conflict, the closer the result will be to the interests of the mass public. Small constituencies, in this view, make it easier for private power to appropriate public authority for its own interests. Federal programs, according to McConnell, tend to favor private interest less and to be more progressive than state programs.

Resolutions of national redistributive conflicts do appear to distribute benefits to groups that normally benefit less from American politics and society, yet clear decisions about redistributive conflicts are relatively rare. The politics of Medicare was fought out, with varying intensity, from Truman's administration until passage in 1965. Because of the stable cleavages involved in redistributive policies, an unusual or dramatic event is normally necessary for political resolution. In this case, the Johnson landslide in 1964 created the conditions for the immediate passage of Medicare as well as Medicaid and federal aid to education. Stable cleavages associated with redistributive politics are one reason for the cyclical nature of American politics—periods of relative stability followed by periods of major innovation in programs.

Regulative arena

When decisions are finally made about the proper scope and role of government, new conflicts emerge over the administration and financing of the programs and over the effects of such programs on the industries involved. Most political controversies over finance and administration conform to the pattern Lowi terms *regulative politics*. Regulative politics does not involve broad social groups but rather a sector, industry, or organized set of producers or consumers. The groups are not class based. Conflict is less ideological and tends to center in the executive branch. Regulative politics is not confined to what are officially called *regulatory commissions* or *agencies* but occurs whenever decisions are made that change the burdens or benefits of an industry or sector.

It is typical for producer groups with relatively better organizations, more resources, and greater stakes in the outcome to dominate the struggles in the regulative arena. For example, the general public was very concerned about the enactment of Medicare in 1965 but was much less actively interested in the way hospitals and physicians would be paid under the program. As discussed previously, this is a case where there is less public attention to issues because they do not affect the public directly and, although the overall impact may be large, each individual has only a small stake in the outcome. Yet the payment question in Medicare was of vital importance to hospitals and doctors. This created "unbalanced interests." In cases of unbalanced interests, stakes are vital to producer groups; they have the resources with which to fight for these stakes, and, as a result, they can normally achieve their ends.[43]

The regulative policy arena is often characterized by what Edelman has called *symbolic politics*: "the rhetoric to one side and the decision to the other."[44] For example, in the midst of popular demand to control the rising costs of medical services, a regulative commission might well be created to decide on rate increases. This satisfies the public that "something is being done," but the commission may actually have little control over the industry and may even assist it.

Thus, in the political market of unbalanced interests, the public may receive symbolic benefits, but the producers usually get most of the material benefits.

Distributive arena

Involved in the distributive arena are issues that can be divided into small units and decisions that can be made without general rules that apply to a whole sector or industry. Questions about the supply of services—where to build a new hospital, how to divide up the funds for a program between different localities or functions—typically fall into this arena. The key characteristics are that beneficiaries are separated from those who bear the burdens and that decisions are discrete and can be made with little obvious relation to other decisions. This is not to say that there are no interconnections; because of finite resources, a research grant to one medical center means that another will get less. However, since decisions can be made on a case-by-case basis and the affected parties may never have to come face-to-face, one group's winning does not obviously point to another group's losing. Rules need not apply universally. An overall policy emerges, of course, but it is the aggregate of a large number of discrete decisions, not a consciously planned and coherent policy. Decisions are often arrived at through logrolling, in which everyone directly involved gains. Actors in this arena tend to be individuals, committees, and planning commissions, rather than classes, national organizations, or large groups of producers or consumers. Struggle is usually nonideological, and results depend on the specific circumstances of each case.

When such issues are decided at the local level, the outcome depends on the local power structure, the importance of the issue, and the attitudes and skills of the individuals involved. Outcomes in this arena vary by community and may change with time, but, in general, the dominant local elites and notables win. Robert Alford gives an insightful and stimulating analysis of such conflict in New York City.[45] He describes the health policies of the city as largely the result of decisions made by the professional monopolists, although those he calls the "corporate rationalizers" are beginning to challenge the established medical powers and privileges. He feels that "equal health advocates" are not, at this time, a significant factor in urban health policy and concludes that "dominant, challenging, and repressed structural interests" are not restricted to local politics or even to health but are representative of American politics in general.[46]

The proposed expansion of Cook County Hospital: a case study of health politics

The last part of this chapter applies political analysis to a set of general administrative tasks. A case study is used to make the applied political analysis as specific and as clear as possible. The case—the 1950s' struggle over whether to expand Chicago's Cook County Hospital—is taken from Edward Banfield's classic work, *Political Influence: A New Theory of Urban Politics*.[47] The administrative tasks include: planning, decision making, and organizational change; developing an information base; moderating costs; accountability; interprofessional communication and personnel-related activities; ethical considerations; leadership; legislation and public policy; coordination among other interests; public relations and community involvement; and developing personal ties.

Background of the case

Cook County Hospital, on the West Side of Chicago, even with 3,400 beds, was overcrowded. The obstetrical ward, designed for 6,000 births a year, had over 16,000. Dan Ryan, president of the Cook County Board, which had formal responsibility for the hospital, announced in late 1954 that a bond issue would be presented to the voters in order to raise money both for an 800-bed addition and for needed renovations to the West Side hospital. Ryan's proposal was framed by Dr. Karl Meyer, the medical superintendent of Cook County Institutions (since 1914!), who had an extraordinarily wide range of contacts: president of the Board of Trustees of the University of Illinois, private doctor to "boss" John Duffy of the Nineteenth Ward, and so on. Meyer argued that, since the West Side hospital already had existing facilities (heating plant, available land), it would be quicker and cheaper to expand there than to build a new hospital.

Everyone agreed that the county's hospital facilities needed to be expanded, but the question was where. Leaders of the Welfare Council of Metropolitan Chicago, an organization of 253 constituent welfare and public health agencies, argued that the West Side site was too far from the rapidly growing South Side. Over the years, several studies by public agencies had recommended building a South Side branch hospital. The Welfare Council's health experts studied the problem again in 1955 and recommended a 700-bed hospital on the South Side. Meyer agreed that there should be a South Side hospital but said it should have 1,500 beds, not 700. He argued, however, that the need on the West Side was pressing and, thus, facilities should be added there immediately.

In the spring of 1955, the Welfare Council met with Ryan to give him a prepublication copy of their study. He agreed to form a citizens' committee to look into the question and asked the council to supply him with a list of people to serve on the committee. They gave him a list of "blue ribbon" people, not just council supporters. However, when Ryan finally got around to appointing the committee—a year and a half later—he assumed they were all council supporters and so added other names to ensure "balance." Forty-nine invitations were sent out but many people declined to serve; as a result, the committee actually ended up stacked *against* the council position. Ryan picked a "representative" subcommittee (one black, one woman, one labor leader, etc.) to gather information. The council sent experts to testify before the subcommittee, but it was clear the members of the subcommittee trusted their own judgment as much as the expertise of those testifying.

The newspapers in Chicago, meanwhile, came out against the West Side expansion and for the South Side branch. Michael Reese, a nonprofit voluntary hospital on the South Side, also favored a county branch on the South Side and contributed money to a group working to defeat the West Side bond issue at the polls. (Reese was losing more than $1 million a year in unpaid or charity work.) However, Dr. Nathaniel Calloway, president of the Chicago Urban League and of the South Side branch of the Chicago Medical Society, announced that he was opposed to a South Side branch. (Although he was only speaking for himself, the newspapers assumed he was presenting the position of the Urban League.) He attributed the problem not to insufficient hospital facilities on the South Side but rather to racism by the existing hospitals. Calloway was too busy to campaign, however, and neither he nor any other participants tried to enlist the support of William Dawson, the black political boss of the South Side, or of the black newspaper, *The Defender*.

Ryan's committee ended up making recommendations substantially similar to the original proposal. The Welfare Council threatened to campaign *against* the bond issue (which required a vote in the upcoming election). Ryan, worried that the opposition by the council and the newspapers might not only defeat this proposal but also lead to the defeat of other bond issues dear to the Chicago political machine, decided a compromise was necessary. He offered to appropriate $250,000 to study the purchase of a South Side site. The council was not enthusiastic. When the next day a *Tribune* editorial attacked the recommendations of Ryan's committee, Ryan agreed to *drop the expansion* of the West Side hospital while the council agreed to *support a bond issue for West Side renovation*. As Meyer remarked, "We got nothing and they got nothing."

Health services administration tasks

Planning, decision making, and organizational change. The separation of planning, decision making and managing organizational change is not clear-cut for a political scientist. The value of planning without regard for decision-making problems is questionable; most important decisions involve organizational change or innovation. Since very few decisions are self-executing, it is not possible to "decide" very much without attending to organizational change. Policies can be understood as predictions of behavior: if X is done, then Y will follow. This conventional policy analysis is applicable to many fields: If we vaccinate against swine fever, fifty thousand lives will be saved at the cost of $135 million. Political science asks whether the policy can or will be implemented, as well as whether, if implemented, it will have the predicted effect. In the Chicago hospital case, one of the policy predictions was that if a South Side branch is built and operated, more and better service will be delivered to residents. Traditional policy analysis looks at an alternative (X) and evaluates the costs and benefits that follow (Y).

What is usually left out is an examination of the implicit assumption that X actually can or will be done. Can or will a South Side branch actually be built and operated even if Ryan "decides" to build it? Will community protests block or delay acquisition of a site? Will the Cook County Hospital administration put adequate resources into a South Side branch when they favor the West Side addition? These are obviously crucial questions for evaluating the South Side alternative, but such implementation questions are not stressed in conventional policy analysis. To choose wisely, a policymaker must be aware of, and make predictions about, how organizations and individuals will actually behave— how they will implement and react to policies.

The problem is partly one of language and conceptualization. We ordinarily use "policy" in different and somewhat contradictory ways.[48] There are three main usages that, although overlapping, are conceptually separable: policy statements or positions, policy action, and policy outcomes. Many political science studies have established that the gap between plans, decisions, action, and results can be very substantial.[49] A policy statement may be only symbolic, with no intended action or material outcome; it may express a real intent but, for various reasons, produce no action; the stated policy may be altered in action; or the stated policy may actually be carried out but the desired results not achieved.

Planning unrelated to feasibility, decision-making problems, and organizational change produces policy statements with no necessary relation to policy action or results. The record of the Comprehensive Health Planning agencies illustrates this problem. As long as the planners were removed from decision-making power, they were unable to affect American medical care significantly.[50] If the "best" plan is unacceptable or unworkable, it is not the best. Likewise, the best decision must be workable to count as a policy decision. Congress, despite legislating the Early and Periodic Screening, Diagnosis and Treatment Program, did not meaningfully "decide" to have the program. They did not pay careful attention to the necessary conditions for organizational change and program implementation. The program "took five years to begin even partial operation."[51] A formal decision was made in the sense of a policy statement and even a legislative action, but there was no decision in the sense of policy action or policy results.

The Chicago branch hospital case also illustrates these difficulties. Meyer planned an addition to the hospital, but he did not adequately consider the political and organizational problems involved in the decision and adjust his plan accordingly. Ryan made a decision to build the West Side addition, but he too failed to account for the political controversy that forced him to reverse himself. In the end, there was no policy change because the planning and decision making had not included the political and organizational considerations.

Collective decisions are not simply rational choices in the classic sense of consistent, value-maximizing action in pursuit of stated goals. Although collectivities can often usefully be thought of as single units, collective choices and collective action also display characteristics that are different from the choices and behavior of a unitary rational actor.[52] In particular, collective choices often result from bargaining and mutual adjustment, and collective action displays characteristics associated with organizational processes such as incrementalism,[53] bounded rationality,[54] and others. In the Cook County hospital case, the final result, no additional hospital facilities, occurred even though everyone agreed more facilities were needed. That result is incomprehensible without the realization that political choices are more complex than the simple question of whether more facilities were needed.

A realistic view of decision making pays attention to the political issues and stakes involved. Effective decision makers are aware of and concerned about their personal power and the stakes in the decisions they make. They estimate the impact of policy alternatives on their power and include that impact in weighing the alternatives. Ryan favored the West Side expansion but he decided it was not worth the risk of losing the vote on other bonds. To maintain his control over other issues, he compromised on the hospital controversy.

As we have already noted, politics is the art of the possible. Policymakers in any field calculate what is possible as well as what is desirable. They evaluate the forces that are or might be involved in an issue; they consider who is affected and how much they are affected, what they *can* do in support of or against a policy, and what they are *likely* to do. The political science theories discussed earlier point to the factors that should be considered: voters, interest groups, elites, and so on.

Policymakers calculate not just what is possible but also the cost of achieving the possible. Policies are not simply possible or impossible: A greater expenditure of resources increases the likelihood of success or at least increases what can actually be achieved. This leads decision makers to consider ways of increasing the likelihood of achieving their goals, either by lessening opposition or by increasing support.

Ryan might have been able to win approval of bonds for a hospital addition. He would have had to expend the effort to organize a campaign in support of the bond vote to counteract the council and the newspapers. If he had been more attentive, he would have considered ways to defuse council opposition before they took a position against the bond issue. He should immediately have tied the West Side expansion to acquisition of a South Side site, thus giving a little something to everyone (logrolling is a common and effective political tactic). The council should have tried to mobilize support for the South Side branch so that they could have an impact beyond merely stopping the addition. They should have looked to see who would benefit from the branch and tried to activate their support. Particularly, they could have focused on key elites—Dawson, the *Defender* editor—and on organizations with a potential interest in the issue. Perhaps other hospitals besides Reese would have pressed for a South Side branch as a means of solving their own problems. Interest group analysis (and some common sense) would have told them who their potential supporters were, and political sensitivity would have made them aware that they had to do more than say "the South Side branch is the best choice." They also had to gather political support for the best choice.

Before making a general decision about what to do, one needs to delineate specifically the steps required to implement each alternative. If many steps are required, involving many independent actors with limited agreement on the policy, then the likelihood of delay, alteration, or outright failure is great.[55]

Building a South Side branch required picking a site (certain to arouse strong opposition in the community chosen because of urban removal, disruption of the neighborhood, and the eventual influx of the "undesirable" county patients); getting money from the legislature to help operate it; getting residents to staff it (which in turn would require accreditation as a teaching hospital and, therefore, physicians to teach the residents). Each of these steps required time and effort to achieve the cooperation of other actors.

Including these implementation problems as part of the decision-making process significantly changes the value of the South Side alternative. The need was pressing, but acquiring a site and constructing facilities would take five or six years.[56] It was not certain legislative support could even be obtained, and operating a teaching hospital would be very expensive (the West Side branch was staffed largely by the adjoining University of Illinois Medical School). Decision makers should make estimates of the implementation problems a program will face and, in the light of the estimates, reevaluate the alternatives; their relative value is often quite different when examined in this fuller, more realistic manner.

Once a decision has been made, plans should be devised to implement the decision effectively and efficiently. Sensible administrators realize that programmatic compliance with official decisions is subject to many problems, that merely "making decisions" and "issuing orders" do not automatically produce results, and that organizations are unwieldy instruments for achieving change.

Kaufman lists three major problems in achieving policy compliance: communication, capability, and disposition.[57] He points out that subordinates often do not know what they are supposed to do. This can be because the directions from above are unclear ("costs are too high"), contradictory ("control costs, improve quality, and increase output"), or not obviously applicable to the specific case at hand. Even if subordinates know exactly what they are supposed to do, they may be incapable of doing it. The technology may simply not exist; there may be insufficient resources on hand; the subordinate may be too busy, inexperienced, incompetent, and so on. Capability is especially relevant in innovative programs— at the very least there will be a start-up period in which the subordinates do not perform well since they are learning new procedures. Finally, even if the subordinates know what they are supposed to do and are able to do it, they may simply *not* do it. The required behavior may conflict with their own goals and interests, violate their values or professional norms, or simply be too much trouble.

The problem of disposition becomes especially important when the ability to compel compliance is reduced. Although this discussion referred to subordinates, the problem of compliance is even greater when the authority lines are weak or unclear. Effective coordination of two federal agencies that share programs and authority,[58] for example, local administration of federally mandated programs,[59] creates problems that go beyond compliance by subordinates. Local officials have independent constitutional authority and responsibilities and are not subordinate at all. In this respect, hospitals are similar to government, with their separate but shared authority and responsibility. If communication, capability, or disposition is a problem (and at least one usually is), then compliance may not occur. These are general problems common to all collective action; it is, however, possible to analyze—and anticipate—the form they take in a specific organization or program.

No organizational structure or process is neutral. Organizational arrangements affect decisions, behavior, and results. Perrow, for example, argues that the multiple leadership and segregated decision making found in hospitals (between trustees, medical staff, and administrators) favor action on consensual areas, even if they are not top priority areas. Short-term harmony, according to Perrow, is given more weight than long-term consequences. The power of one group to make minor decisions without consultation often accumulates to major effects, and important values outside the interest area of the key groups are not well served.[60] Perrow's conclusions about hospitals replicate the findings about disaggregated governmental decision making in general.[61]

The effective administrator, aware of the bias in organizational arrangements, understands how organized structure affects policy. This requires, first, appreciating the structure of organizational rewards and sanctions and estimating how that structure influences behavior. This involves looking at the recruitment process in the organization, the skills represented, the existing professional norms, the career rewards, and the expectations of security and autonomy. These estimates of organizational characteristics are not dependent on the particular personnel involved. In Chicago, the incentives for the superintendent of the County Hospital were to expand on the West Side, both because it would ease his organizational problem (overcrowding) and because it would expand his own bailiwick. The council should have expected—and tried to head off—the recommendation for organizational expansion in the existing hospital.

Second, estimates can be made from the past history of the organization: how it has behaved, what tendencies it has shown, and what strengths and weaknesses it has displayed. Past behavior gives indications of the organization's real, not just stated, goals.[62] Organizations change slowly, and the best estimate of what the organization will do tomorrow is what it is doing today. The Welfare Council had repeatedly stated its support for a South Side hospital. Ryan should have expected that the council would oppose any choice that did not give priority to a South Side branch.

Finally, estimates of organizational behavior can be derived from evaluations of specific key personnel—their goals and their past experience and behavior. Ryan was sixty years old in 1955; he had been a member of the Cook County Board for thirty years (his father had been president of the board before him); he was independently wealthy and not in good health. Although he was certainly interested in the health care of the city, "he would look for the course of action that promised to make the least trouble."[63] Thus, when a fight developed over the hospital addition, Ryan made little effort to try to persuade the opposition or to reach a compromise, and, in the end, he chose to avoid a major battle. If the choice had been made for a South Side branch, Meyer would still have been medical superintendent of Cook County institutions, and, hence, responsible for establishing the branch. Given his past record of support for expansion on the West Side, there would be reason to expect that his performance in building the South Side branch would be unenthusiastic. An added cost to Ryan of choosing the South Side branch, therefore, was the possibility that Meyer would do a bad job of supervising construction, adding to costs and delay. Meyer might even have to be replaced to get the branch built.

Estimates of bias help one anticipate organizational behavior and improve the implementation of decisions. Proposals for programs of utilization review (UR) to control health costs and quality provide a useful illustration of how such estimates can help. A sketch of who would be adversely affected highlights UR's potential threat to physicians' autonomy, particularly if nonprofessionals review the judgments of physicians. Strategies to lessen this adverse effect (review is only triggered in cases where length of stay is abnormal, for example, and only physicians are on the review committee) and to provide compensating benefits (malpractice protection) could be devised. Although this might prevent physicians from refusing outright to cooperate with the UR program, they still have other commitments and priorities that could interfere with their cooperation. Although there are incentives to produce quality care, for example, there are fewer incentives to produce the quality medical records that allow review. Many doctors find writing legible records a definite burden. Physicians, therefore, are unlikely to change unless faced with strong incentives or sanctions. Even if physicians can be persuaded to cooperate, they have little training or experience in evaluating whether a procedure is really worth the financial cost for a particular patient, and so their capability to control costs is limited. Of course, it is not clear exactly what they should be doing in terms of altering quality or service to control costs. The administrator who has determined the potential effects of a policy on organizational behavior is better able to assure successful implementation.

Developing an information base. Information is a form of power. It can be used to promote a desired policy or to discredit an opposing position. Information itself may be neutral, but its use is not. Recognition of this fact directs attention to the kinds of information that will be needed for particular issues. First, possible opposition to a policy should be anticipated so that information can be gathered to counter potential arguments or to assuage concerns. It is possible that the information base will actually lead to better policies, for decision makers may realize that the concerns are justified.

Second, information that bears directly on the problems to be faced by the decision makers should have high priority. It is impossible to gather all the facts; selection is inevitable. Selection makes an implicit choice. Different people consider different issues important and thus selectively employ information. Special attention must be paid to the issues and problems faced by the eventual decision makers and an effort made to secure the most critical and useful information.

In Chicago, the Welfare Council merely emphasized the "need" for accessible facilities on the South Side. It did not try to get information that could diffuse opposition or that related to Ryan's special problems. If, for example, they had demonstrated that a South Side hospital could have been in operation as quickly (and as cheaply) as the West Side addition, or shown Ryan an obtainable site, then their information would have been relevant and perhaps persuasive. Since they did not provide the information that mattered to Ryan, their expertise was irrelevant and they missed the opportunity to win their case.

Recognizing information as a form of power directs attention to the sources of information. The producers of information gain advantages and can easily present the facts in a way favorable to their interests. For example, any system of state cost controls that allows hospitals to use their own accounting systems is virtually unworkable administratively. The resultant bias of information occurs quite naturally and requires no dishonesty. Producers of information gather the facts that matter to them and ignore information that others consider important. For example, hospitals may have excellent records on who has received treatment for hypertension and adequate information on the effectiveness of the treatment. However, most hospitals have an inadequate idea of the extent of hypertension in the community since they have little incentive to gather such information. That information is important for someone concerned with treating the problems of hypertension (though not important to the hospital's problem of treating their own patients). Thus, anyone considering a program to meet the problem of hypertension in the community starts with the disadvantage of inadequate information. In developing an adequate information base, attention must be paid to who has the incentives and the resources to get important information and, especially, to what are their stakes in the information and their "slant" or bias.

Although information is an important source of power, the limits to the value of information and facts in decision making must also be recognized. Information is less the way to "make" decisions than it is another way to "argue" over decisions. Facts seldom, if ever, speak for themselves; there can be honest disagreement over interpretations, priorities, and the facts themselves.

All the participants in the Chicago hospital dispute agreed that an expansion of the County Hospital was needed, but they disagreed over priorities. More information might have focused the argument a little more, but information alone could not settle the trade-offs among costs, time, and needs on the West versus South Side. The council believed in their own expertise and the compelling case for the South Side hospital. They thought the facts determined the issue and felt their study report would carry the day. However, Ryan never even read it. He "would not think of taking home [the council's] lengthy memoranda for study. He did not even own a brief case. He never put anything in writing when he could avoid it. He did his business by talking, and he talked as little as possible. Very often his conversation consisted of a grunt, an expressive stare, and a wave of the hand."[64] By failing to recognize the limit of facts and expertise in decision making, the council failed to get a South Side branch. The other disputants, although they respected the expertise of the council, felt that the issue was one of judgment as much as of expertise and that their judgments were at least as valid.

Beyond these general comments on the role of information in policymaking, political science suggests the relevance of three types of information. The first is public opinion. A democratic society expects policies to "reflect" the judgment of the governed. Since many decisions are based as much on values as on expertise, it is important that the values of citizens be taken into account. Yet, it is difficult to ascertain the will of the people. The general public is neither particularly attentive to nor very informed about issues, and it is impossible to determine accurately what the public thinks without expensive random surveys (in which many will respond "Don't know"). Those active citizens who do speak up are not always representative of the general public, since they are usually better educated and have different concerns.[65]

In Chicago, there was no reason to believe that Calloway, the spokesman for the Urban League, was speaking for a majority of South Siders. Similarly, only a small percentage of the electorate actually votes on bond issues, but Ryan's concern about the election was an apparent cause of not expanding Cook County Hospital. The point is that no effort was made to discover the true feelings of the population and that, without such an effort, the desires of the population remain unknown.

The second type of information important in policymaking is distributional data, for both the value of, and the support for, policies depends partly on who gets what. In Chicago, the geographical distribution of patients using the over-crowded West Side hospital was relevant to deciding where to build. If many of the patients lived on the South Side but traveled to the County Hospital because there were no available facilities nearby, then building on the South Side could ease the overcrowding on the West Side. If, however, the patients were mostly West Siders, then a South Side branch would not improve conditions in the County Hospital.

Acquisition of distributional data and the identification of target groups lead not only to better-formulated policies but can also point to potential political support for, or opposition to, policies. If most of the users of the existing West Side County Hospital lived nearby, then they could potentially have been acti-vated to vote for the bond proposal to expand on the West Side.

Finally, political science directs the administrator to develop a *personal and informal network of contacts* for information gathering. The precise content of this information cannot be anticipated: Administrators must develop a sensitivity to what they need to know and what might be useful to them.[66] What is clear is that effective administrators keep a multitude of channels open to this flow of information.

Adhering to a strictly hierarchical chain of command may turn out to be less effective than overlapping responsibilities and bypassing communications be-cause a strict hierarchy does not facilitate the flow of information so essential for the administrator. The head of the nursing department, for instance, may not tell (or know) of dissatisfaction among nurses that is causing inefficiency and a high turnover rate, or the government may not announce new auditing procedures until the regulations are officially set. With an established network of informal sources of information, administrators are more likely to know how the organiza-tion is really operating, what other organizations are planning, what problems are developing, who the influential members of organizations are, and so on, and so have a better chance to do their job effectively.

Moderating costs. The benefits and burdens of policy decisions are not borne equally and so costs are not easily or clearly assigned. Recent cutbacks on Medicaid eligibility, benefits, and payments certainly lessen costs to the states but probably increase costs to poor patients, to doctors who do more charity work, and to higher income patients who are charged more through cost shifting. Whether such cutbacks then count as moderating costs or increasing costs de-pends on one's perspective. The incentives—costs and benefits—of a system are usually different than for a subunit within it. Benefits for one unit may be burdens for another. The most effective way to moderate overall costs is to ensure that the decision-making subunit has the same cost incentives as the system as a whole. Economists often argue that if patients bore the costs of medical care directly (out-of-pocket), they would have an incentive to keep their own costs down, and this, in turn, would keep total costs down. Although such a system is reasonable, it inevitably creates financial barriers to access. Alternatively, if the government were to pay for all health care out of a single and fixed budget, as in England, the government would then have a concentrated interest in controlling costs.[67] In either case, the decision-making unit has incentives that conform to the goal of moderating system costs.

Costs are not only monetary. Closing an underutilized or inappropriate hospital may save money for a "region" but will probably increase costs in patient travel time. Although these trade-offs *can* be worked out, it is important to recognize that there are also political costs. A public agency that is responsible for closing a hospital must bear the political costs of that decision (protests, bad will from local providers and consumers, a reduced appropriation next year, etc.). The agency is forced to weigh the monetary gains against the potential political losses—it may actually be cheaper not to close the hospital. On the other hand, if the agency also reaps political or monetary gains from the closing (credit for moderating costs, keeping taxes down) or bears some of the burdens of not closing (e.g., budget responsibilities), then it is more likely to make the decision to close. Here again it is important to ensure that the decision-making subunit has the same incentives as the system as a whole and to recognize that, particularly with public or nonprofit agencies, the important incentives are *not* necessarily monetary.

Accountability. Decision makers can be accountable to many different constituencies. Government officials may be accountable to the general public, the voting public, the attentive public that follows their actions, their political party, a particular interest group, other officials, and so on. Accountability is not the same for all issues all the time; it depends somewhat on the issue and its importance. The basis for accountability is control over the resources the decision maker or organization needs. In theory, a decision maker responds to the needs and preferences of a constituency that can hold him accountable for his action. Although responsive government is possible without accountability, accountability mechanisms are designed so that decision makers are, at times, dependent on constituents and so have an incentive to be responsive. Constituents can evaluate the decision maker and punish or remove him if *they* decide he is not serving their interests.

Democratic theory argues that elected officials will be accountable to the public because the public controls the most important resource—the job—at election time and so can reward or punish the official. However, low voter turnout, limited electoral competition, candidate ambiguity, high campaign costs, and so on can all erode that accountability. Ryan was eventually constrained by the upcoming bond election. He feared that the council could defeat the hospital (and other) bond issues and, to avoid that, he dropped the West Side addition. The council then was able to hold Ryan accountable at the polls, just as in theory. However, it is clear that Ryan was not accountable to other affected groups. He was not responsive to the poor (mostly black) South Siders who would have gained from more hospital facilities because he did not fear them at the polls.

Decision makers are not only accountable to specific groups, but this accountability can be quite specific and limited in scope. Ryan was not accountable for everything he did, just for the bond issue that was up for a vote. He gave in on that, but the council could not make him build the South Side branch they wanted. He was essentially unaccountable on that issue. Studies in political science, in general, are pessimistic about achieving accountability. There is only weak evidence that voting does, in fact, lead to accountability and responsiveness.[68] The more common findings support the iron law of oligarchy: Organizations, both public and private, eventually are controlled by only a few members. Certainly the evidence is conclusive that formal accountability—elections, consumer representation—is insufficient to produce results. Consumer representatives are unlikely to have the expertise or incentives to counterbalance effectively the power of producers. Merely putting a housewife on the board of a health agency does not produce accountability. Some form of competition (to give the constituency a choice) and realistic control of needed resources (to give the constituency the power and the incentives to exercise the choice) are necessary supplements to the formal accountability mechanisms. Political science tends to emphasize these considerations of power as necessary for accountability. Although power is important and, in the long run, over a wide range of incumbents, situations, and issues, probably necessary, other factors are often more important in the short run. For example, internalized norms of democracy and the ideal of serving the public often produce responsive policies even when the public has no available accountability mechanisms. Given the difficulty of achieving accountability, such norms are perhaps the best means of assuring responsiveness.

One of the best ways to reduce accountability to the general public is to restrict participation in the decision-making process by "keeping health out of politics." Health issues involve politics in the largest, best sense of the term *politics*: an activity in which important values are discussed, fought over, and resolved. Health issues will be political issues: The only question is how large a constituency will be involved. The smaller the constituency involved in the political process, McConnell has argued, the less the larger public interest is represented.[69] Questions that seem technical or of minor importance to the public (such as a formula for needed hospital beds in an area or the specific provisions in a prospective reimbursement program) do not generate wide interest or participation and, even though the general public *is* affected, the constituency actually involved is quite small—usually only the providers who are directly affected.

Removing health from general issues in the public eye (cost, access, equality) to a multitude of smaller issues in less visible arenas (PSROs, reimbursement schedules) tends to decrease effective participation by the public and allow the interests of smaller constituencies to be better served.

Interpersonal communications and personnel-related activities. Power is a central concern in all personnel relations. Crozier argues that power in organizations is measured by the degree of uncertainty in important behavior: Uncertainty allows control over and, hence, manipulation of variables that are important to others. The more rationalized and routinized the job, the less power involved. He focuses on two sources of power available to administrators: making rules (thus limiting the power of others) and ignoring their own rules.[70] There are, however, usually several competing sources of uncertainty in an organization, and so competitive power roles exist. These roles are almost never played out to their fullest since the occupants must continue to live with each other. Power is not, after all, the only element in organizational behavior. Furthermore, individuals have motives that are not totally defined by their roles—but this fact increases management's power by allowing manipulation of these individual goals. Although individuals whose jobs are largely controlled by rules have little leeway and, so, little power, the very proscription of their tasks lessens their dependence on others—so managers have less power over them. Although there are many other political analyses of public administration and of power within organizations,[71] such topics are more usually dealt with by organizational theorists than political scientists.

Obviously, supervising interprofessional working relations and managing personnel-related activities are a part of decision making and organizational change. Political science has many examples of their operational significance but few scholarly prescriptions.

Ethical considerations. Political science has embarrassingly little to say about creating an ethical environment. Political science, after all, teaches the importance of manipulation and of compromise. Machiavelli is not usually considered a great ethical thinker. Still, getting things done inevitably raises ethical issues.

In the Chicago case, nothing was accomplished partly because the participants were not adequate manipulators; a greater concern for the workings of politics would have allowed a greater concern for community health as demonstrated by additional hospital facilities. There is, of course, a limit to the morality of ultimate ends. Some values ought not to be compromised and manipulation should go only so far. However, within the limits of the Chicago case political efficacy would have represented ethical improvement.[72]

Leadership. Richard Neustadt's argument that presidential power is the power to persuade is applicable to other leaders. A leader does not "command" as much as he "persuades" others that it is in their own interest to do as he wants. The ability to persuade is determined by the leader's "vantage points." The council's vantage points were the prestige and influence it had with the newspapers and the voters. Using these vantage points, the council was able to persuade Ryan that it was not in his own interest to risk a vote on the bond issue for the West Side expansion. These vantage points can be either formal authority or effective control over important resources. Position, however, is not enough. Power also depends on the ability and will to use those vantage points. Power is thus related to past behavior and decisions. Ryan was persuaded partly because he had seen the effects of newspaper recommendations on bond issues in the past: He felt it was worth as much as fifty thousand votes.[73] Power is protected (and created) by the decisions a leader makes, the choice of "measures and men."[74] Ryan's power was protected by his careful selection of a subcommittee that eventually recommended substantially what he had originally proposed. The council, on the other hand, did not do as well: Their nominations to the committee were not as carefully selected, and they did not monitor the final formation of the committee so it ended up stacked against them. When this committee recommended the West Side addition, the council lost its last hope of getting a South Side branch. More careful consideration of its power stakes in the committee selection might have maintained the council's ability to achieve its ends.

In general, others will react according to their judgment of a leader: what his past actions show he can, and will, do. Thus, actions are the building blocks with which actors construct future power. Through his actions he shows that others can support him and not be left with their neck out and that they cannot go against him without at least weighing the risk. As the old saying goes: "Don't get mad, get even."

In the Chicago case, Ryan could not completely disregard the council position without the risk of a bond defeat, so he chose to give in on the West Side addition. Influence here is, as usual, reciprocal. A leader needs to persuade other people who have their own vantage points from which they try to persuade him. In the bargaining in Chicago, *both* sides gave up what they wanted: Neither the West Side nor the South Side got additional hospital beds.

The recognition that power is created and maintained through the decisions a leader makes leads to an awareness of a leader's own, personal power stakes in any decision. The analogy implicit here, of power as capital that can be squandered or invested wisely to accumulate more capital, has value only if it is remembered that accumulation of power is not an end in itself. Accumulation of power is a means to other ends, and those ends may require the forfeiture of power—as, for example, when an official publicly resigns in protest over policies he considers unacceptable. Most decisions are not based on a leader's power stakes: Other stakes are more important. Leaders, however, should at least be aware of their power stakes, both to try to improve and protect their positions through present decisions and to consider the possible effects on their future influence as a benefit or cost of a decision.

Legislation and public policy. Numerous political science studies describe the life of governmental politics; they cover all aspects of governmental activity, from legislative behavior to the role of mayors to budgeting processes. These descriptions, even if they are not specifically related to health, give a general idea of how American government operates. Studies of Congress that include descriptions of the committee system are relevant to health administrators even if the studies do not mention health. They demonstrate, for example, that the administrator's local congressman will not be very influential on health bills unless he is on the relevant committee. Such basic background information is a prerequisite to effective action in governmental politics.

Descriptive accounts of governmental behavior also acclimatize administrators to the nature of political activity and give them a sense of the importance of rules and details. Bardach's account of the reform of the mental commitment laws of California tellingly demonstrates the value of knowing the rules and of understanding the actors involved. California has a deadline in each session for introducing bills; when it became obvious that the mental commitment bill would not be ready by the April 1 deadline, the sponsors introduced a bill that consisted only of a title: "The California Mental Health Act of 1967." "The full text, inserted as 'author's amendments,' did not appear in print until April 28."[75] The key swing vote in conference committee was elicited from a member of the John Birch Society by showing him a letter of support for the bill from the Santa Ana Freedom League—a letter that just "happened" to have been written by an old friend. Knowing and using details like these can make the difference between victory and defeat.

The average administrator with a full-time job will obviously not be able to learn all the available tricks and important information for functioning in the governmental sector. Working with a specialist in governmental politics will greatly increase an administrator's impact on events. The specialist may be a lobbyist for a professional organization or a friendly legislator or government official. These contacts can also provide administrators with essential and timely information. The general public often learns about a bill when they read in the paper that it has been passed or defeated.[76] Obviously, it is too late at that point to have an impact on the legislation. Administrators with a communication network of peers and specialists can get the timely information they need to influence public policy.

Contacts with government officials are especially useful since they facilitate a continued impact on policy. Legislation is not the end of the policymaking process. Many laws are vague enough that the officials implementing policy are, in fact, making it.[77] Even when clearly worded, legislation is modified in implementation. Attending to the implementation and administration of programs is, therefore, an essential part of influencing public policy.

Many political science studies are attempts to go beyond description to explain public policy. They have produced various theories, discussed earlier, that identify the major causal factors affecting public policy. These theories should provide an understanding of why the government behaves as it does and improve estimates of what government is likely to do in the future. However, it should be noted that these theories are often of only minor value to administrators trying to affect public policy. After all, the major causes of a policy are not always controllable. Administrators typically attempt to increase state spending on, and reimbursement levels for, Medicaid services. Political science research in this area suggests, however, that the major determinants of state welfare spending are levels of economic development and the degree of competition between political parties. This knowledge may keep administrators' expectations in bounds, but it does not help them increase spending even within the limits of the possible. The variables that political scientists see as important are often not variables that can be controlled by administrators and, thus, are not very useful in attempts to affect policy.

Coordination with other interests. Coordination can occasionally benefit organizations and arise through voluntary compliance. However, "groups are usually reluctant to yield rights and privileges that they have already exercised, and will resist significant restructuring unless it appears that there is something in it for them."[78] Where organizational benefits from coordination are lacking, no substantive coordination will be achieved without selective incentives or sanctions to induce organizations to change their past behavior.[79] Coordination with other interests requires the same attention to organizational bias and to problems of compliance discussed under decision making.

Public relations/community involvement. Administrators have a large impact on the amount of citizen participation and involvement. First, administrators can reach out and actively solicit and organize citizen participation. However, even beyond that, there is evidence that leaders actually exert control over who will contact them and become active politically.[80] An administrator's attitude is an important determinant of citizen involvement.

The community can be thought of as several different and overlapping publics, and maintaining good relations with one does not necessarily mean good relations with the others. In the Chicago case, the citizen group most affected—the poor and the users of Cook County Hospital—were almost totally excluded from the controversy. In America, political participation is related to socioeconomic status; administrators should be aware of the differential involvement of publics.

Developing personal ties. The development of personal ties and informal networks of communication should be a major part of improving an administrator's ability to operate effectively. Even if the contacts are not in the same field, they can be useful, and numerous studies have shown that the politically active and influential tend to be joiners who are involved in many different activities. Few health administrators will have the personal ties that Meyer had developed in his years of service (he was twice offered the Democratic nomination for governor!) and that gave him such tremendous influence in Cook County, but general contacts will be valuable to any administrator.

Conclusion

The Cook County Hospital case is now over twenty-five years old. Obviously, the medical industry has changed dramatically since then, and if the struggle were to take place now, more groups would be involved. A federally mandated and funded Health System Agency granting a certificate-of-need would be the most obvious addition. The community served by the hospital would quite certainly be more active now. However, although the specific actors and organizations involved would have changed, the basic political analysis needed for a complete understanding of the struggle would be the same.

Change in the medical industry and the government's role in health is extremely rapid. Thirty years ago there was no federally mandated planning or regulation at all. First, the Hill–Burton Program was developed and then, in 1967, the Comprehensive Health Planning and the Regional Medical Programs were added, resulting in three overlapping agencies with some planning responsibilities. In 1974, Health Systems Agencies (HSA) were legislatively authorized to consolidate those programs. Within two years, Congress was seriously considering amendments to change HSA functions even though not all authorized agencies were yet in operation.

The point is that simply learning the contemporary structure and organization of government health programs is not going to be very useful to health service administrators. What is needed is a sensitivity to the political nature of their job and some approaches and analytical tools with which to look at and understand the political situations they are in. Health services administrators must become political analysts.

Although political science can help administrators become better political analysts, more sensitive to and with a better understanding of the political world around them, acting in a political environment is more an art than a science. No one can provide a checklist or a recipe that guarantees that, if an administrator does X, Y, and then Z, success will follow. Political science can help instill in administrators an awareness of the political problems they face and give them some ways of looking at those problems. Political action, however, remains an art and, although political science may help with the technique, it cannot by itself make administrators talented artists. There is no substitute for experience and talent.

Notes

1 M. Mueller and R. Gibson, "National Health Expenditures," *Social Security Bulletin*, 39:3–22, 1976.

2 A. Somers, *Hospital Regulation: Dilemma of Public Policy* (Princeton, N.J.: Princeton University Press, 1969), p. 16.

3 H. Lasswell, *Politics: Who Gets What, When, and How* (New York: McGraw-Hill, 1936).

4 K. Altenstetter, "Medical Interests and the Public Interest: West Germany and USA," *International Journal of Health Services*, 4:29–48, 1974; A. Heidenheimer, "The Politics of Public Education and Welfare in the USA and Western Europe," *British Journal of Political Science*, 3:315–340, 1973.

5 P. Bachrach and M. Baratz, "Two Faces of Power," *American Political Science Review*, 59:947–952, 1962.

6 H. Wilensky, *The Welfare State and Equality* (Berkeley: University of California Press, 1975).

7 R. Elling, "The Shifting Power Structure in Health," in J. McKinley, ed., *Politics and Law in Health Care Policy* (New York: Prodist, 1973), pp. 83–107.

8 C. Perrow, "Goals and Power Structures: A Historical Case Study," in E. Freidson, ed., *The Hospital in Modern Society* (Glencoe, Ill.: Free Press, 1963), pp. 112–146.

9 M. Grodzins, *The American System* (Chicago: Rand McNally, 1966).

10 R. Stevens and R. Stevens, *Welfare Medicine in America* (New York: Free Press, 1974).

11 G. Allison, *Essence of Decision* (Boston: Little, Brown, 1971).

12 J. Lave and L. Lave, *The Hospital Construction Act* (Washington, D.C.: American Enterprise Institute, 1974).

13 Perrow, "Goals and Power Structures."

14 A. Campbell, *The American Voter* (New York: Wiley, 1964).

15 S. Verba and N. Nie, *Participation in America* (New York: Harper & Row, 1972).

16 E. Banfield, *Political Influence* (New York: Knopf, 1961); R. Dahl, *Who Governs?* (New Haven, Conn.: Yale University Press, 1961).

17 J. Colombotos, C. Kirchner, and M. Millman, "Physicians View National Health Insurance," *Medical Care*, 13:369–396, 1975.

18 M. Edelman, *The Symbolic Uses of Politics* (Urbana: University of Illinois Press, 1964).

19 R.A. Bauer, I.S. Pool, and L.A. Dexter, *American Business and Public Policy* (New York: Atherton, 1963).

20 T.R. Marmor, *The Politics of Medicare* (Chicago: Aldine-Atherton, 1973).

21 E. Schattschneider, *The Semi-sovereign People* (New York: Holt, Rinehart & Winston, 1960), p. 31.

22 M. Olson, Jr., *The Logic of Collective Action* (Cambridge, Mass.: Harvard University Press, 1965).

23 L. Hartz, *The Liberal Tradition in America* (New York: Harcourt, Brace & World, 1955).
24 G. McConnell, *Private Power and American Democracy* (New York: Knopf, 1966).
25 Heidenheimer, "The Politics of Public Education, Health, and Welfare in the USA and Western Europe."
26 C. Lindblom, "The Science of 'Muddling Through,' " *Public Administration Review*, 19:79–88, 1959.
27 A. Wildavsky, *The Politics of the Budgetary Process* (Boston: Little, Brown, 1964).
28 Lindblom, "The Science of 'Muddling Through.' "
29 C.W. Mills, *The Power Elite* (Oxford: Oxford University Press, 1959).
30 Dahl, *Who Governs?*
31 R. Milband, *The State in Capitalist Society* (New York: Basic Books, 1969); J. O'Connor, *The Fiscal Crisis of the State* (New York: St. Martin's Press, 1973); V. Navarro, "Health and the Corporate Society," *Social Policy*, 5:41–49, 1975.
32 R. Musgrave, *The Theory of Public Finance* (New York: McGraw-Hill, 1959).
33 Navarro, "Health and the Corporate Society"; T. Lowi, *The End of Liberalism* (New York: Norton, 1969).
34 J. Pressman and A. Wildavsky, *Implementation* (Berkeley: University of California Press, 1973); M. Derthick, *New Towns in Town* (Washington, D.C.: The Urban Institute, 1972); A. Foltz, "The Development of Ambiguous Federal Policy: Early and Periodic Screening, Diagnosis and Treatment (EPSDT)," *Milbank Memorial Fund Quarterly*, 53:35–64, 1975.
35 Both G. Allison ("Implementation Analysis") and E. Bardach (*The Implementation Game: What Happens after a Bill Becomes a Law*, Cambridge, Mass.: MIT Press, 1977) directly address the implementation subject. R. Katzman's study of the FTC is a good example of detailed accounts of regulatory practice (*Regulatory Bureaucracy: The Federal Trade Commission and Antitrust Policy*, Cambridge, Mass.: MIT Press, 1980).
36 H. Jacob and M. Lipsky, "Outputs, Structure, and Power: An Assessment," *Journal of Politics*, 30:510–539, 1968.
37 Altenstetter, "Medical Interest and the Public Interest"; Heidenheimer, "The Politics of Public Education, Health, and Welfare in the USA and Western Europe."
38 S. Andreopoulos, *National Health Insurance: Can We Learn from Canada?* (New York: Wiley, 1975).
39 T. Lowi, "American Business, Public Policy, Case Studies, and Political Theory," *World Politics*, 16:677–715, 1964.
40 Schattschneider, *The Semi-sovereign People*, p. 31.
41 McConnell, *Private Power and American Democracy*.
42 J. Madison, "Federalist 10," in *The Federalist Papers* by A. Hamilton, J. Madison, and J. Jay (New York: New American Library, 1961), pp. 77–84.
43 Marmor, *The Politics of Medicare*.
44 Edelman, *The Symbolic Uses of Politics*.
45 R. Alford, *Health Care Politics* (Chicago: University of Chicago Press, 1975).
46 Most of the work in political science on the judicial process is not directly relevant to this discussion. The courts certainly do not easily fit any of Lowi's three arenas of politics. R. Dahl ("Decision-making in a Democracy: The Role of the Supreme Court as a National Policy-maker," in *Readings in American Political Behavior*, R. Wolfinger, ed., Englewood Cliffs, N.J.: Prentice-Hall, 1966), in his study of the Supreme Court, pointed out that since justices are appointed by the President with the consent of the Senate, they tend to be part of the dominant electoral coalition. He went on to show

that only rarely have court rulings thwarted the strong desires of the other branches. In an intensive study of a single judicial doctrine, Sorauf found wide local variations in the impact of a ruling of the Supreme Court and concluded: "To rephrase the old saw,... the Constitution in reality consists of what influential partisans and decision-makers say the Supreme Court says it is" (F. Sorauf, "Aorach versus Clauson: The Impact of a Supreme Court Decision," ibid., p. 225). These studies seem to indicate that the effect of legal struggles will usually not be markedly different from the results of other political conflicts but exactly when and how the results do differ are simply not known.

47 E. Banfield, ed., "The Branch Hospital," in *Political Influence: A New Theory of Urban Politics* (New York: Free Press, 1961), pp. 15–56. Presentation of the case is based on Banfield's account. Direct quotes are indicated with page numbers in the text.
48 H. Eulau and K. Prewitt, *Labyrinths of Democracy* (Indianapolis: Bobbs-Merrill, 1973).
49 R. Neustadt, *Presidential Power* (New York: Wiley, 1962); Pressman and Wildavsky, *Implementation*; Derthick, *New Towns in Town*; Foltz, "The Development of Ambiguous Federal Policy"; M. Crozier, *The Bureaucratic Phenomenon* (Chicago: University of Chicago Press, 1964).
50 A. Dunham and T. Marmor, "Health Planning: A Comment," *International Health*, 6:667–670, 1976.
51 Foltz, "The Development of Ambiguous Federal Policy," p. 35.
52 Allison, *Essence of Decisions*.
53 Lindblom, "The Science of 'Muddling Through.' "
54 J. March and H. Simon, *Organizations* (New York: Wiley, 1958).
55 Pressman and Wildavsky, *Implementation*.
56 Banfield, *Political Influence*, p. 27.
57 H. Kaufman, *Administrative Feedback* (Washington, D.C.: Brookings Institution, 1973).
58 Pressman and Wildavsky, *Implementation*.
59 Derthick, *New Towns in Town*.
60 Perrow, "Goals and Power Structures."
61 McConnell, *Private Power and American Democracy*.
62 A. Etzioni, *Modern Organizations* (Englewood Cliffs, N.J.; Prentice-Hall, 1964).
63 Banfield, *Political Influence*, p. 18.
64 Ibid., p. 24.
65 Verba and Nie, *Participation in America*.
66 Neustadt, *Presidential Power*; E. Bardach, *The Skill Factor in Politics* (Berkeley: University of California Press, 1972).
67 See chapter 3 and also T. Marmor, T. Heagy, and D. Wittman, "The Politics of Medical Inflation," *Journal of Health Politics, Policy and Law*, 1:69–84, 1976.
68 Verba and Nie, *Participation in America*; Eulau and Prewitt, *Labyrinths of Democracy*.
69 McConnell, *Private Power and American Democracy*.
70 Crozier, *The Bureaucratic Phenomenon*.
71 See, for example, Etzioni, *Modern Organizations*; R. Elling, "The Shifting Power Structure in Health," in J. McKinley, ed., *Politics and Law in Health Care Policy* (New York: Prodist, 1973), pp. 83–107; Kaufman, *Administrative Feedback*; A. Downs, *Inside Bureaucracy* (Boston: Little, Brown, 1967).
72 M. Weber, "Politics as a Vocation," in H. Garth and C. Wills, trans. and eds., *From Max Weber: Essays in Sociology* (Oxford: Oxford University Press, 1958), pp. 77–128.

73 Banfield, *Political Influence*, p. 55.
74 Neustadt, *Presidential Power*, p. 57.
75 Bardach, *The Skill Factor in Politics*, p. 123.
76 R.A. Bauer et al., *American Business and Public Policy* (New York: Atherton, 1963).
77 Lowi, *The End of Liberalism*.
78 D. Mechanic, *Public Expectations and Health Care* (New York: Wiley-Interscience, 1972), p. 6.
79 B. Mott, *Anatomy of a Coordinating Council* (Pittsburgh: University of Pittsburgh Press, 1968); Alford, *Health Care Politics*.
80 Eulau and Prewitt, *Labyrinths of Democracy*, chaps. 15 and 16.

2. Comparative politics and health policies: notes on benefits, costs, limits

THEODORE R. MARMOR, AMY BRIDGES,
WAYNE L. HOFFMAN

Interest in the cross-national study of public policy has increased in the 1970s. Whether one uses conferences or special journal issues and books as a guide, the incidence of efforts including the words comparative and policy is greater than a decade ago. [1] Crudely, one can take a jaded or an optimistic view of these developments. One might regard this as simply the internationalization in American political science of what is called policy studies. With more resources available for policy studies, the ordinary market for academic output adjusts appropriately. The supply of efforts reflects the supply of funds. Hopefully, one can show that studying policies across nation-states is intellectually interesting in its own right. More compelling justification of cross-national policy studies is what comparative policy research teaches us. This essay focuses on comparative research about health policies to illustrate the difficulties and advantages of comparative public policy research.

Comparative research and policy learning

Policy research provides an additional vantage point for traditional political scientists. Consider the following questions about health policy, for example: Who benefits from alternate arrangements of publicly financed medical care services? What notions of distributive justice prevail in the distribution of access and treatment? Who dominates in the health policy subsystem? What, particularly, are the consequences of a particular administrative and fiscal structure for

Abridged from Theodore R. Marmor, Amy Bridges, and Wayne L. Hoffman, "Comparative Politics and Health Policies: Notes on Benefits, Costs, Limits," in Douglas E. Ashford, ed., *Comparing Public Policies; New Concepts and Methods*, pp. 59–80, © 1978 by Sage Publications, Beverly Hills, Calif., with permission. (Sections on the Canadian cost experience are deleted here but appear in chapter 9 of this volume.)

References to publications included in this collection have been changed from their original source to the appropriate chapter number in this book. Insofar as it was possible, references which were in press or forthcoming at the time of original publication have been completed.

national health insurance and its implementation according to the social values of the political market? What stimulation does a policy alternative give to prospective group or sectoral demands on government? What will policy alternative X do to the capacity of government to govern or to change at a later date to another policy if X fails? (Lowi, 1973:61–67).

Moreover, policy studies provide a viewpoint from which to study political processes. Lowi's work (1964), for example, has focused on the political alliances which policies create. Charles Anderson (1977:19–41) suggests that public discourse about policy alternatives serves as a key to the understanding of political culture. When we examine policies as outcomes, and look for their determinants, research focuses on the "input" side of political processes.[2]

Finally, policy research may focus on public policy itself. Here, the "input" of the political process serves to illuminate constraints on policy alternatives. Or we may want to make conditional predictions about the effects of given policy options. And politics in the broad sense will serve to explain what happens to policies during what is deceptively referred to as "implementation."

Cross-national policy studies facilitate these kinds of learning. First, they allow the researcher to weigh the social determinants of policy more carefully and especially to distinguish culturally specific from more general determinants of policies. The latter distinction suggests means for distinguishing manipulable policy activities from those relatively immune to manipulation. Second, comparative policy analysis provides material for evaluating alternatives by looking at their probable effects. Third, comparative research helps the researcher identify the ways that institutional arrangements for implementing policy structure the politics of administration. Each of these tasks requires somewhat different research designs. The discussions which follow illustrate the kinds of learning comparative policy studies facilitate, and the difficulties in the research design for each.

Diverse political systems and micro-policy focus: the politics of doctors' pay

Comparative policy studies, we argued above, allow the researcher to weigh the social determinants of policy and, in particular, to distinguish culturally specific from other determinants of policy outcomes. Individual country studies cannot logically test the explanatory power of hypotheses which emphasize distinctive features of individual political systems, for example, explanations which rest on "political culture." These were the arguments Marmor and Thomas [chapter 6, this volume] addressed in a research review of Eckstein's classic *Pressure Group Politics*. Eckstein traced doctors' bargaining victories over the British government to the physicians' success in privatizing the bargaining process; this, in turn, rested on institutional arrangements specific to Britain.

Neither internal nor external evidence supports Eckstein's view that bargaining structures determine much of the British Medical Association's effectiveness. The internal evidence—remuneration disputes over time—indicates that intimacy of negotiatons is not a crucial factor in accounting for BMA success on pay. External evidence is another check on this causal scheme. Three countries were chosen for intensive study—Great Britain, Sweden, and the United States—and their policy decisions about how doctors are to be paid by the state were examined: (a) the changes in methods of remuneration following the general practitioner crisis (1965–1966) in Great Britain; (b) the fee-for-service policy of the National Health Insurance Act in Sweden (1955); and (c) the Medicare "reasonable charge policy" in the United States.

We should make clear two features of this type of comparative study at the outset. First, the countries differ markedly in the setting and atmosphere of negotiations for medical remuneration.[3] Second, the policy decisions in each case are strikingly similar when measured against the intentions of the medical organizations. That is to say, methods which the respective medical organizations were known to prefer were, broadly speaking, what the government policy became in each of the three examples. Here we have a common burden on a political system—the requirements to settle physicians' remuneration in public programs—and three different decision-making structures to cope with it. The existence of a common outcome suggests that the causal factor lies in the nature of the pressure group and the resources which doctors, as opposed to other producer groups in the society, share. Why doctors in different national settings prefer different methods is a separate issue in the history and sociology of professions. For present purposes, it is enough to know that knowledge of their preferences is the single best predictor of policy decisions in this area.

The evidence gathered in the testing of this hypothesis was of two sorts. First, the pattern of payment-method decisions since World War II in three Western industrial countries—Sweden, Great Britain, and the United States—was investigated. Data from these countries include broad patterns of medical payment methods during the postwar period, as reported in the secondary literature, and Marmor and Thomas's analysis of the extraordinary controversial instances of payment-method decisions in the three societies. The second major types of data collected were secondary analyses of payment methods used in other industrial countries, notably the Netherlands, West Germany, France, Switzerland, Spain, Italy, Canada, Greece, Poland, the Soviet Union, and Israel (Abel-Smith, 1963:27–35; 1965:33–40; Glaser, 1970; Schnur and Hollenberg, 1966:111–119; Badgley and Wolfe, 1967). This evidence revealed that as producers of a crucial service in industrial countries for which governments can seldom provide short-run substitutes, physicians have sufficient political resources to influence decisions regarding payment methods quite apart from the form of bargaining their organizations employ. The hypothesis thus directly links physicians' economic and political power to public policy outcomes, asserting that intervening bargaining variables are not central in explaining public policy decisions in this area.[4]

The policy implications of these findings are important. First, the most important thing for governments to understand is both the nature of medical power and the limits of that power. We conclude that certain features of payment-method controversies are, in fact, not negotiable, however many of these disputes arise in the course of medical-government confrontations. The reason for governments' inability to control medical-payment methods emerges from the different priorities and economic power of the bargaining antagonists. That is, doctors can, by withholding services, impose higher political costs than governments are willing to pay simply to rearrange methods of paying them. The same kind of reasoning about priorities and political power will show that doctors cannot impose their will on governments in all cases—doctors almost everywhere resist NHI, for example.[5]

Knowing what governments cannot do and what outcomes will occur is obviously important to government officials involved in controversial negotiations. In health policy, such knowledge may permit concentration on alternative means to the goals toward which traditional government payment-preferences aim. There are two alternatives to continued dispute over the choice of payment methods. One is to concede the choice of method to physicians and concentrate on administrative techniques to make these methods less undesirable. The other is to seek alternative ways to accomplish the goals which payment methods were to serve: reward of quality education, limits on excessive services, and so on.

This kind of inclusive research design, focusing on the industrial nations of the West as a group, is akin to a "most different systems" approach, although it does not strictly meet its requirements. As Przeworski and Teune (1970) suggest, use of a multination research design offers a basis for more valid results than, for example, two-nation designs. But the multination design also incurs the risk of uncontrollable complexity. Increases in "N," that is, expansion of the number of cases, involve the addition of numerous variables that ought to be controlled for a valid comparison. Only a very limited number of national cases exist for most policy comparisons. Tentatively, we suggest that multiple country designs are best used to identify the parameters or limits of social choices—invariant relationships across a variety of political structures and cultural values.

There are dangers in the kind of policy research which allows us to identify broad system characteristics as determinants of social policies. First, what exists may too drastically curtail our view of what is possible. After all, there was a time when no one had NHI. Second, the appeal of the "certainty" of this kind of knowledge may distract researchers from asking more important questions. So, for example, Newhouse (1976) shows with some certainty that per capita expenditures on medical care vary over a broad range, according to per capita GNP. Yet, since neither the quality of medical care nor the mix of medical care services is determined by per capita expenditures, it is not clear that we learn anything crucial about *medical care* when we explain per capita expenditures.

Policy evaluation and similar systems

Comparative policy research can address the consequences as well as the constraints of policy choice. Research following a "most similar systems" approach facilitates appraisal of the effects of policy options. This paradigm requires that the nations compared share a number of features that causally relate to the policy consequences of analytic significance. More simply stated, one country may serve as a "laboratory" for another's policy choices. Deborah Stone, for example, argues that the United States can learn from the German experience of regulating physicians under national health insurance, because "of all the European countries, West Germany's system is most like that of the United States" (Stone, 1976: personal communication). Both countries use contributory public financing programs to allow individual patients to purchase care from private physicians and physicians receive pay on a fee-for-service basis. While Stone rightly argues that pure transplantation of other national policies is usually impossible, she emphasizes that cross-national examples have mostly served as negative warnings. Yet, her own work shows that we can learn from West Germany how physicians supply services when they are subject to pricing and volume restrictions; this information can make American policy planning about peer review more realistic (Stone, 1981).

Canada's current program, which resembles some leading American proposals, can serve as a "natural experiment" for the United States, a guide both to the impact of national health insurance and the reactions of policymakers and the public to this impact. The Canadian national health insurance experience is especially applicable because both Canadian society and its health concerns are strikingly similar to America's [chapter 9 in this volume]. Public officials of both countries worry about the increased proportion of national resources expended on medical care and wonder what health improvement it has bought. They also want to assure more equal access—financially, geographically, socially. A vocal minority in each country wants major reorganization of medical care providers. Finally, after many years of expansion, both Canadian and American officials are trying to reduce the use of expensive hospital service and stabilize the number of hospital beds and, to a lesser extent, physicians (Andreopoulos, 1975; [chapter 9]).

Politically, socially, economically, and culturally, the United States is closer to Canada than to any other nation.[6] Canadian political authority is decentralized. Its tradition of dispute over federal power resembles the United States'. The structure of the health industry is strikingly similar, as Table 1 makes plain. American and Canadian hospitals are largely "voluntary" and physicians in both

Table 1. *Selected statistics on health resources, utilization, expenditures and inflation in Canada and the U.S.*

	Canada	U.S.
Resources		
Hospital beds/1,000 population, 1971	7.0	7.5
Short-term hospital beds/1,000 population, 1971	5.6	4.2
Physicians/100,000 population, 1971	151.0	174.0
*Short-Term Hospital Utilization**		
Percent occupancy, 1971	80.1%	76.7%
Length of stay, 1971	9.9	8.1
Patient days/1,000 population, 1971	1552.0	1199.0
Expenditures		
Per capita hospital expenditures, 1970	$132.53	$135.41
Per capita physician expenditures, 1970	48.25	70.13
Average Annual Change in Health Care Expenditures		
Total personal health care, 1965–1971	13.3%	12.3%
Total personal health care, 1969–1971	13.6	11.6
Institutional care, 1965–1971	13.6	15.0
Professional services, 1965–1971	13.8	10.5

* For U.S., data are for nonfederal short-term hospitals. For Canada, data are for nonfederal, nonproprietary general hospitals.
Sources: Canada Health Manpower Inventory 1973; Annual Report 1972–1973; Hospital Insurance and Diagnostic Services; National Health Expenditures in Canada 1960–1971 with Comparative Data for the United States, Health and Welfare, Canada. *Statistical Abstract, 1973*, U.S. Census Bureau.
Cited in Lewin & Associates, Inc., Government Controls on the Health Care System: The Canadian Experience, p. v.

countries are still typically paid under a fee-for-service system. The two countries similarly adjusted to the growth of health insurance, which was largely private at first, becoming increasingly public in character in the postwar period.[7]

Despite using the language of "natural experiment," we recognize that cross-national research seldom allows for really scientific experiments. Such designs would permit the researcher to hold some variables constant while manipulating the experimental ones. Not even two nations can be matched on all but a few policy-related factors; results thus run high risks of invalidity. One response to this difficulty is to despair of social science's capacity to produce valid results from cross-national policy research of a quasi-experimental sort (see Teune, 1978; Zaltman, 1973). This response might be termed the fallacy of comparative difference. Because we cannot have controlled experiments across nations, we cannot learn from the experiences of other nations at what Teune calls the micro-policy level. Here fascination with the natural science paradigm leads to despair. Yet we can learn by reasoned and plausible exclusion of national differences which appear distantly related to major research that "negative evidence" from cross-national research suffices to evaluate their probable consequences. This is the case with the discussion in chapter 9 of the relevance of Canadian experience to incentive reimbursement policies for American hospitals. Finally, the Canadian study led to the formulation of a broad hypothesis about the relationship between levels of health expenditures and the degree of dispersal of budgetary and regulatory authority in health financing [chapter 3 in this volume].

Cross-national research in health, then, permits awareness of new alternatives, anticipation of what might not be expected, and confirmation of relationships between policy choice, action, and consequences (Teune, 1978). It is to this last topic that we want to turn in the final section, to discuss research on the administration of health programs cross-nationally.

Implementation and cross-national research in health

There is now broad scholarly acceptance of the view that administrative implementation matters enormously in the achievement of public policy purposes. As Pressman and Wildavsky (1973) note in connection with American social policies of the 1960s, there is "widespread concern about the inability to implement governmental programs" (Pressman and Wildavsky, 1973:166). But the study of implementation is hard to do; part of the difficulty is methodological and professional. The process of implementing complex programs is unwieldy and messy, extending over long periods of time, unmarked by discrete, grand decisions or congressional roll calls or election results. The participation of pressure groups is continuous; there are fewer public hearings in which the stakes and actions of the interested parties are clear. Policy choice centralizes government action for analytic purposes; implementation disperses policy objectives, spreading the subject matter geographically, temporally, and intellectually. When the issues of policy direction are uncertain, political incentives press actors to mobilize supporters, not to design operational measures to ensure policy compliance. And when policy choices are deeply controversial—as with many health issues—implementation estimates are part of the arsenal of policy warfare, not aids to policy design.

If the task is difficult, the inclination to attempt it in health matters is nonetheless growing. And the effort to use cross-national research in the process is evident. This partly results from concern about the costs of medical care in advanced industrial countries, as expressed in a profusion of royal commissions in the 1970s seeking to structure public programs to moderate the rapid escalation of medical-care expenditures. This worry about the increased proportion of national resources going to medical care is becoming even more widespread as expenses in Sweden, Canada, the United States, and West Germany approach or exceed 8 percent of GNP. Health expenditures constitute one of the most powerful sources of strain within contemporary welfare states, making matters of change and choice both urgent and important. Increases in the proportion of public expenditures spent on social welfare policies may make a preemptive claim upon government resources or, by straining the capabilities of states to meet them, may even trigger political transformations. It is this context that lends urgency to the evident international preoccupation with the structure of public health programs.

The organizational model of medical-care delivery is at the center of reconsideration. Attempts to shift from inpatient to outpatient care are widespread, as is emphasis on preventive medicine to reduce disease and costs. Planners give attention to innovative use of existing medical manpower and to the redefinition and reallocation of professional functions. The result is widespread adoption of controls over hospitals and other health facilities (Bridgman and Roemer, 1973; Altenstetter, 1976). Despite the nationalization of medical-care financing, stringent control of the health sector has been the exception in Western Europe, with Great Britain and, to a lesser extent, Sweden atypical. In most of the continental countries, private providers continue to deliver medical services, subject to financing constraints. Changes in political regimes during the postwar period, however dramatic their impact on other sectors, have not transformed the delivery and regulation of medical care.

Two developments in this sector have dominated the cross-national research agenda. Decisions dealing with the allocation of financial resources (through third party payment, central government subsidies, or combinations) are becoming increasingly centralized (Maynard, 1975; Maxwell, 1975). At the same time, these countries are regionalizing medical institutions. This usually entails a decentralization of administrative functions from the top down and a centralization of finance from the bottom up. With decentralization has come the hope for democratization of control over medical care delivery (Klein and Lewis, 1976).

The central research question is whether differing structural arrangements have discernible effects on health expenditures. There is some empirical support for the view that the dispersal of finance—private-public, public-public, public with quasi-state organizations—and the separation of finance from administrative responsibility are associated with higher costs relative to other administrative structures ([chapter 3 in this volume]; Evans, 1974; and Van Langendonck, 1976).

The question is whether governments are able and willing to reshape health administration radically. Fragmentary cross-national research suggests three points. One is that it takes power at the center to produce administrative change at the periphery. Strong unitary states have a greater capacity to implement even what is unwise, weak, or ineffective than federal states. Secondly, federal states with sharing of authority—as distinguished from administrative deconcentration—are better able to share financial responsibility than to reshape administrative arrangements. Canada illustrates the ease of health revenue sharing; the German *lander* likewise adopted fiscal sharing more rapidly than federal administrative regulations (Evans, 1976; Altenstetter, 1976; Bridgman, 1976).

Corporate elements in all of these societies (local elites, medical groups, hospitals, and unions) will balance or restrain unitary or federal governments' capacities. The health industry is technologically similar from industrial nation to industrial nation, which means one finds great similarity of medical issues everywhere.

One hypothesis is that the ratio between corporate resources and resistance is higher for the medical professions at the periphery than at the center of national politics. Professionals generally seek decentralization of authority only when the scope of conflict narrows, when the professional interest groups are already in place and have paid all their organizational overhead, and when they can concentrate their marginal resources on overtaking the public authorities. At the national center the same professional groups have to deal with large mobilized political parties and mass organizations.

What can one say about governmental motivation to change administrative arrangements? We often talk about government in a very unrealistic way. We speak as if governmental behavior were always purposive. When we find governmental action—administrative reorganization, for example—we assume there must have been a large problem to which the government was directing its efforts. Or we assume that if there is a large problem out in the world, it must be the case that the government is going to do something about it (Allison, 1973). Yet a good deal of what government does pertains to the internal maintenance needs of people within it. One of the things occurring in discussions of administrative decentralization in health is that people whose job it is to run the government (or who claim to be running the government) have to find something to do. What they have to do is shuffle back and forth between the periphery and the center to make administrative arrangements. Administrative reorganization is thus an attractive response to bureaucratic needs. Reorganization has imprecise effects, takes much effort, and produces symbolic benefits from the appearance of action (Alford, 1976). This may have little to do with bringing medical-care needs closer to the public so that the patient can use resources more appropriately.

Reflections on cross-national policy research in health

Sometimes comparative research reveals what is possible, not what is desirable or transportable, providing illumination, not indoctrination. Sometimes such research produces seemingly transplantable policies, but the effects are so hard to disentangle from other forces that learning whether such a policy would be appropriate is difficult. This is a case of temptation without satisfaction. A third lesson is that cross-national research work is difficult, costly and time-consuming (Andersen, 1976). Only compelling, expected returns justify both the costs and the difficulty of identifying comparable circumstances and similarities. But sometimes the expected benefits are policy learning; then the issue will be whether the policy choice is clear enough to warrant the expected costs. In other cases, the benefits will be significant tests, impossible within a single-nation framework, of social science theories. Cross-national research in health suggests there is a place for both types of work.

In this essay we have reviewed three types of cross-national studies in health policy politics. Several areas of research have not been discussed. Most important, although we have alluded to them, we have not discussed macro-studies of health expenditure patterns over time. In addition, we have not investigated here what effects government intervention in the health sector has had on the general problems of governance in advanced industrial societies. The current preoccupation with the fiscal strains of the welfare state has highlighted this issue as a matter of controlling health expenditures. But the political significance of that effort is not restricted to fiscal stress. Health issues are salient to citizens in all the countries discussed; government programs affect citizens' views of the capacity of public authorities to govern beyond short-run budget disputes. Finally, this essay should not be interpreted as support for the notion that there is a common politics of health across or within nations. What counts as a "health" policy, as Charles Anderson has pointed out, varies cross-culturally. What is more, there is no evidence that political disputes over health are uniform and distinctive. There are political struggles in the arena termed health, but not a politics of health. That means the arena is a microcosm of welfare-state politics, not a peculiar phenomenon. For that reason, the lessons of comparative research in health are valid for comparative policy research in general.

Notes

1 The October 1976 Cornell conference, at which the articles of this volume were originally presented, is itself an example. In the health field, there has been a burst of cross-national interest. The Fogarty Center at the National Institutes of Health held meetings in May 1976 both on cost-control issues and on center-periphery political relations in health, with the papers forthcoming in published form. The advent of the German Marshall Foundation, among others, has increased the funds available for cross-national research among advanced industrial countries; and special issues on comparative policy studies, like *Policy Sciences* (December 1975), are just beginning, almost certainly to be increased by the efforts of the Council on European Studies' research planning groups and the Ford Foundation's sponsorship of collaborative research projects on the common problems of industrial societies.

2 See, for example, Chapter 1, Heidenheimer, Heclo, and Adams, 1975; and Clark, 1976.

3 Highly structured and regular in Great Britain and Sweden; diffuse and irregular in the United States, where consultation may take place in congressional hearings or through ad hoc meetings with executive officials responsible for public medical care programs.

4 This is simply the other side of the coin of Teune's concern with invariant policy effects.

5 In sum, the limits of physicians' power depend on the issue arena in which they are struggling. There has also been some dispute on these limits. See the symposium on Robert Alford's *Health-Care Politics* in the *Journal of Health Politics, Policy and Law*, Vol. 1., No. 1, especially Flash's contribution. Heidenheimer's (1976) work has traced the relation of physicians' power to national financing of medical care services, stressing the impact of timing on the configuration of later disputes.

6 Two major differences between the American and Canadian experiences are often put forward as problematic for using Canada as a "most similar system." These are the greater constitutional and political independence of the Canadian provincial governments compared to the American states and the different route followed by Canada to national health insurance. The first means only that Canadian health insurance *had* to be decentralized. If we choose centralized insurance, we may have to rely more on European experience. But the greater the role the United States assigns to decentralized units, the more we can learn from Canadian national standards and provincial cost control (or inability to control costs).

The second major difference is historic. Canadian national insurance began with hospital coverage in 1958, followed a decade later by full-scale coverage of physicians' charges. In contrast, the United States has been extending protection to additional segments of the population, first the aged, then the poor, and perhaps in the end to everybody. This may tell political scientists a lot about the welfare state, but it should not deter health care planners from comparison. Having converged at full coverage, Canada and the United States are facing similar choices. Cross-national comparisons of a more "macro" sort may, however, be concerned with these questions. See Heidenheimer, Heclo, and Adams, 1975; Anderson, 1972; Teune, 1973.

7 Similar does not, of course, mean identical. For some purposes, the differences in the way Canadian and American health insurance policies incrementally changed are of significance. See, for example, Evans (1975:3–4). But Evans was not placing North American patterns on continuum of advanced welfare states. Had he done so, the internal North American differences would have been minimized.

References

ABEL-SMITH, B. (1963). "Paying the family doctor." Medical Care, 1:27–35.
    (1965). "The major pattern of financing and organization of medical services that have emerged in other countries." Medical Care, 3:33–40.
ALFORD, R. R. (1976). Health care politics. Chicago: University of Chicago Press.
ALLISON, G. T. (1973). The essence of decision. Boston: Little, Brown.
ALTENSTETTER, C. (1976). "The importance of organizational arrangements for policy performance." Paper presented at the International Conference on "Changing National-Subnational Relations in Health: Opportunities and Constraints," May 24–26, Fogarty International Center, Bethesda.
ANDERSEN, R. (1976). "A framework for cross-national comparisons of health service systems." In M. Pflanz and E. Schach (eds.), Cross-national socio-medical research: Concepts, methods, practice. Stuttgart.
ANDERSON, C.W. (1978). "The logic of public problems: evaluations in comparative policy research." In D. Ashford (ed.), Comparing public policies: New concepts and methods, Vol. 4, Sage yearbooks in politics and public policy. Beverly Hills, Calif.: Sage Publications.

ANDERSON, O. W. (1972). Health care: Can there be equity? The United States, Sweden, and England. New York: Wiley-Interscience.

ANDREOPOULOS, S. (ed., 1975). National health insurance: Can we learn from Canada? New York: John Wiley.

BADGLEY, R. F., and WOLFE, S. (1967). Doctors' strike: Medical care and conflict in Saskatchewan. New York: Alberton Press.

BRIDGMAN, R. F. (1976). "Hospital regionalization in Europe: Achievements and obstacles." Paper presented at the International Conference on "Changing National-Subnational Relations in Health: Opportunities and Constraints," May 24–26, Fogarty International Center, Bethesda.

BRIDGMAN, R. F., and ROEMER, M. I. (1973). "Hospital legislation and hospital systems." World Health Organization, Public Health Paper No. 50, Geneva.

Canada Health Manpower Inventory (1973). Annual report 1972–1973: Hospital insurance and diagnostic services. National health expenditures in Canada 1960–1971 with Comparative data for the United States. Health and Welfare, Canada.

CLARK, M. (1976). The comparative politics of birth control. Determinants of policy variation and change in the developed nations. Unpublished Ph.D. dissertation, University of Michigan.

EVANS, J. R. (1976). "Planning and evolution in Canadian health policy." In K. White and M. Henderson (eds.), Epidemiology as a fundamental science. New York: Oxford University Press.

EVANS, R. G. (1974). Personal communication to R. A. Berman, July 2.

GLASER, W. A. (1970). Paying the doctor, systems of remuneration and their effects. Baltimore: Johns Hopkins University Press.

HEIDENHEIMER, A. (1976). "Public capabilities and health care effectiveness: Implications from a comparative perspective." Paper presented at the International Conference on "Changing National-Subnational Relations in Health: Opportunities and Constraints." May 24–26, Fogarty International Center, Bethesda.

HEIDENHEIMER, A., HECLO, H., and ADAMS, C. (1975). Comparative public policy: The politics of social choice in Europe and America. New York: St. Martin's Press.

KLEIN, R., and LEWIS, J. (1976). The politics of consumer representation. London: Centre for Studies in Social Policy.

LOWI, T. J. (1964). "American business, public policy, case studies, and political theory." World Politics, 16:677–715.

——— (1973). "What political scientists don't need to ask about policy analysis." Policy Studies Journal, (autumn):61–67.

MAXWELL, R. (1975). Health care: The growing dilemma: Needs versus resources in Western Europe, the US, and the USSR (McKinsey Survey Report, 2nd ed.). New York: McKinsey.

MAYNARD, A. (1975). Health care in the European community. Pittsburgh: University of Pittsburgh Press.

NEWHOUSE, J. P. (1976). "Income and medical care expenditures across countries." Rand Paper Series No. P-5608. Santa Monica, Calif.: Rand.

PRESSMAN, J., and WILDAVSKY, A. (1973). Implementation. Berkeley: University of California Press.

PRZEWORSKI, A., and TEUNE, H. (1970). The logic of comparative social inquiry. New York: Wiley-Interscience.

SCHNUR, J. A., and HOLLENBERG, R. D. (1966). "The Saskatchewan medical care crisis in retrospect." Medical Care, 4:111–119.

STONE, D. A. (1981). "The limits of professional power: National health care in the Federal Republic of Germany." Chicago: University of Chicago Press.

TEUNE, H. (1973). "Public policy: Macro perspective." In G. Zaltman (ed.), Process and phenomena of social change. New York: John Wiley.

(1978). "A logic of comparative analysis." In D. Ashford (ed.), Comparing public policies.

Van LANGENDONCK, J. (1976). "Private diligence vs. public inertia?" Paper presented at the International Conference on "Changing National-Subnational Relations in Health: Opportunities and Constraints," May 24–26, Fogarty International Center, Bethesda.

ZALTMAN, G. (ed., 1973). Process and phenomena of social change. New York: John Wiley.

II. Politics in the world of medicine

3. The politics of medical inflation

THEODORE R. MARMOR, DONALD A. WITTMAN,
THOMAS C. HEAGY

The problem of inflation in medical care: introduction

In the past twenty-four years the price of medical services has risen 1.5 times as fast as the Consumer Price Index. The proportion of the gross national product devoted to health care has increased by 71 percent from 4.6 percent to 7.8 percent. Clearly, a continuation of these trends would have serious consequences. Moreover, many economists believe that the "continuing trend towards full or nearly full insurance coverage in the context of a nearly unregulated fee-for-service delivery system is likely to produce continued inflation in medical care."[1]

This paper discusses the politics of anti-inflation policy in the medical care sector and the determinants of governmental responses to problems known jointly as medical care inflation. We attempt first to clarify the issue by distinguishing between four different concepts commonly used when discussing medical inflation. We then present some of the standard solutions to the problems suggested by economists.

Of necessity, a discussion of the political "market" and the political attributes of the solutions proposed goes hand in hand with a discussion of inflation. The politics of medical inflation in our view produce persistent expressions of concern about inflation rates, but actions which at worst exacerbate the problem or at best are weak. The most decisive governmental reactions to medical inflation will continue to be reductions of medical care benefits in selected public pro-

Author's note: Written in 1975 and first published in 1976, this essay's statistical references assume the time perspective of the mid-1970s. Were it written in the early 1980s, the article would have emphasized even more the United States' continued difficulty with medical inflation and the Canadian success in controlling relative medical inflation in the late 1970s. Neither development challenges the theoretical approach of this article. Also, it should be noted, chapter 9 attends to more recent Canadian experience and chapter 12 brings the discussion of American medical inflation up to 1980.

This chapter is taken from the *Journal of Health Politics, Policy and Law*, 1(1): 69–84, 1976. Copyright ©1976 by the Department of Health Administration, Duke University. Reprinted with permission.

Other published versions include "Politics, Public Policy, and Medical Inflation," in M. Zubkoff, ed., *Health: A Victim or Cause of Inflation?* (New York: Milbank, 1976), pp. 229–316, and "The Politics of Medical Inflation," in T. Marmor and J. Christianson, eds., *Health Care Policy: A Political Economy Approach* (Beverly Hills, Calif.: Sage, 1982), pp. 61–81.

grams rather than actions to reduce medical inflation generally, until or unless the budget for health is centralized at one governmental level. We find, in general, that a decentralized payment structure reduces the government's interest in effective implementation of anti-inflationary policies.

Clarification of the problem

Considerable confusion has arisen in the discussion of controlling medical inflation because commentators have discussed at least four different problems under the common rubric of "medical inflation."

1. *Absolute price inflation.* Absolute price inflation is measured by the Medical Services component of the CPI.[2] According to this index, the annual rate of medical inflation has averaged 4.4 percent over the past twenty-four years.[3] This measure seems clearly inappropriate. What we are concerned with is medical price inflation only to the extent that it exceeds general inflation. If the inflation rates are identical, the problem is one of general inflation, not medical inflation.

2. *Relative price inflation.* The difference between the annual rate of growth of the Medical Services component of the CPI and the total CPI measures relative price inflation. By this index, the rate of medical inflation has averaged 1.3 percent per year over the past twenty-four years.[4] This may appear small, but represents a total increase of 37 percent in the relative price of medical services over the twenty-four year period.

3. *Total real expenditures growth per capita.* Measured by the percent growth in expenditures per capita on medical services deflated by the total CPI, the annual rate of expenditure growth over two decades has averaged 4.8 percent.[5] This measure is inappropriate for reasons similar to the one cited in regard to absolute price inflation: the measure incorporates the general growth of real GNP per capita. Only if the real expenditures on medical services grow at a faster rate than total real income is its growth noteworthy.

4. *Relative expenditure growth.* The increase of medical expenditures as a percent of GNP is an appropriate measure. The annual rate of growth has averaged 2.3 percent, from 4.6 percent of GNP to 7.8 percent of GNP, an increase of 71 percent. Relative expenditure growth can be divided into two components, relative price inflation (see 2 above), and relative quantity growth.[6] Over the past twenty-four years, both have been major contributors to relative expenditure growth.

Neither relative price inflation nor relative expenditure growth is a priori bad. People are concerned about relative price growth for at least two reasons. First, it redistributes income to health care providers from everyone else. Second, an increase in medical care's relative price has a disproportionate impact on the poor who spend a larger part of their income on medical care.[7] On the other hand, the assumption that relative prices are too high implies that prices can be too low. For example, a major part of the growth in the price of hospital services is explained by the increased wages of unskilled workers,[8] formerly among the worst paid workers in the economy. The relative increase in their wages may have been not only justified but insufficient.

People are also concerned about the reduced share of GNP available to other sectors. But as in the case of relative prices, growth in relative expenditures is undesirable only if relative expenditures are excessive on *Pareto optimal* or equity grounds. Critics of relative medical inflation argue that government subsidy, insurance, and other programs promote consumption of more and better quality medical services than are really needed; that expenditures on medical care bring rapidly diminishing marginal benefit; and that some of the money going to health care could be better used elsewhere in the economy.[9] It can also be argued, however, that the increase in relative expenditures has been the desirable result of increased access for the poor and better quality generally.

Despite disagreement concerning the optimal level of expenditures, it is clear that if relative expenditures increase at current rates without limit, they will soon become intolerable. For the remainder of this paper we will accept the argument that relative prices and expenditures in medical care are currently too high and that government action is justified in curtailing further medical care inflation.

It is essential to note that limiting relative expenditures requires the simultaneous control of relative prices and relative quantity. However, some proposed policies would reduce relative price at the expense of increasing relative expenditures. If the goal is simply to control relative price, these are appropriate means. But, if the goal is to control relative expenditure, they are not. Ultimately, the choice of policy tools will depend on how the medical inflation problem is defined.

The appropriate response to the problem of medical inflation depends on its causes. Some observers have diagnosed six major causes of medical health inflation [10] (whether relative prices, relative expenditures, or high prices):[11] (1) wealthier societies tend to spend a larger fraction of their resources on medical care; (2) cost-increasing technological developments in medical care in the post-war period, such as kidney machines and open heart surgery, have outweighed cost-decreasing developments such as antibiotics; (3) doctors and hospitals have monopoly power; (4) the supply of doctors has been artificially limited and substitutes legally limited in scope; (5) greater use of medical insurance has reduced the marginal cost of medical care to the patients; and (6) the government supplies a substantial subsidy of health care. Only to the extent that health inflation is caused by numbers 3 to 6 is it a "problem" requiring or responsive to government action.

Cures

There are three broad types of responses to the problem so diagnosed. The first is to improve the market; that is, to make the market for medical care resemble efficient markets in other sectors where the interplay of people seeking private gain and paying out-of-pocket for their goods and services disciplines both the consumer and the provider. Such a strategy includes making patients more informed about the market and likewise giving them greater financial stakes in acting on that information. Typically such remedies include the suggestion of patient financial participation through substantial coinsurance and deductibles. This type of remedy is exemplified by Martin Feldstein's major risk insurance proposal where families would pay up to 10 percent of their income for medical care and anything above that would be paid for by the federal government in a catastrophic health insurance plan.[12] Other critics have argued for HMO expansion as part of the market improvement strategy.[13]

A second answer to this set of problems is to compensate for the poor market structure with public utility type regulation.[14] The standard site for such regulation is the states; electrical utilities are an example of such a regulated industry. The standard subjects of such regulation are health care facilities and the prices they charge for their services. Many states are establishing commissions that deal with facility supply (Certificate of Need) and, in separate commissions, pricing (primarily for hospitals). Massachusetts, Maryland, Connecticut and other states have set up so-called rate commissions to regulate hospital prices.[15]

The third answer is to replace the economic market with a political market by effectively nationalizing the industry. In this case there is a constraining bilateral relationship between buyers and providers: the buyer is the government and the providers are the industry's constituent parts. The government bargains with the providers on price, supply, and quality, representing diffuse and decentralized consumers unorganized to influence health policy decisions. In effect, the government is dealing with the monopoly power of the providers by creating a monopsony for the consumers. The Kennedy-Corman bill (S.3, H.R. 21), for example, provides that the federal government pay for almost all medical care services and regulate the prices of those services by regional health boards in market areas throughout the country.

The response of government

For years economists have "supplied" solutions to medical care inflation, yet the government has largely ignored their advice. In some ways, as by granting tax subsidies for medical insurance, it has contributed to medical inflation. Analysis of the political "market" suggests why there is little reason to expect bold government action against medical inflation (relative price or expenditure growth) in the future.

The theory of imbalanced political interests: concentrated versus diffuse benefits and costs

The political "market" refers to institutional arrangements—the relationships among organized pressure groups, voters, authoritative governmental agencies and affected citizens—that determine what governments do. As George Stigler says of governmental *regulation*, the theory of public policy ought to explain "who will receive the benefits and burdens of governmental [action]."[16] Important is the emphasis on the natural imbalance between the interests of mass publics and health care providers on issues like inflation.

An imbalanced political market is simply one where participants have unequal power. This stands in sharp contrast with the egalitarian theory of one man–one vote, implying equal power by all participants. Of the many theories of imbalanced political markets, one is especially applicable to medical care—that of concentrated versus diffuse interests. Those with concentrated interests feel the effects of a policy (whether subsidy or tax, compulsion or prohibition) significantly. Those with diffuse interests have no important stake, great as the aggregate costs or benefits may be. A $1 per capita tax would be a diffuse cost of large aggregate magnitude in the United States as a whole.

The incentives to press claims for concentrated interests are much greater than those for diffuse ones. The prospect of having one's well-being substantially affected creates powerful incentives to act to protect one's interest. An interest marginal to one's well-being—even though large when aggregated over the class of affected parties—provides insufficient incentives to act. This distribution of incentives results, then, in a systematic imbalance of the probabilities of interest representation. It is not the case that the theory of imbalance in the political market explains the outcomes of political struggles by itself. For the outcomes are a product not simply of the representation of interests, but also of other political resources—wealth, information, skill—that fuel the representation of those interests. But the structure of interests does largely determine which groups play a role in the channels of policy action and whose preferences are likely to count most in that process.[17] The theory of imbalanced interests holds that concentrated groups, other things being equal, will be more effective in the political process than diffuse ones.[18]

There are other concepts of imbalanced political markets. One stresses inequality of information among voters. Clearly, vote maximizing candidates for political office[19] will neglect the interests of the uninformed and cultivate those of the more informed voter.

Obviously, groups differ in wealth as well. Other things being equal, the rich can exert greater influence per capita on election results and political decisions than the poor through donations.

A group with extra-political purposes (e.g., a labor union) will have greater political capability than a solely political one. The first has already paid its overhead; the second must spend much of its resources on organizational maintenance.

Since the results of most political activity constitute collective goods, the differential ability of various groups in overcoming the collective good problems of political activity creates an unbalanced power differential.[20]

These theories overlap; a cause in one may be an effect in another. For example, a group with concentrated benefits and costs has special incentives to be well informed.

In addition, there is usually a substantial correlation among the characteristics that lead to greater political influence. For example, doctors are better informed (on health regulation issues), wealthier, better organized and have more concentrated interests than do patients. This obviously makes it difficult to pinpoint the specific effect of their concentrated interests on public policy as opposed to the effect of the other characteristics. This is why the case of welfare mothers is enlightening. On the basis of every criterion of political power except concentrated interest, one would expect them to have virtually no success in the policy arena. The extent to which they have been successful in increasing benefits in the post-war period might be explained by the theory of concentrated interests.[21]

Imbalanced interests and inflation

What is the connection between the theory of imbalanced political interests and the response to the problem of relative inflation generally?[22] The theory predicts that government will respond cautiously and ineffectively to relative inflation in any sector. In the past half decade, relative inflation, indeed, double digit inflation in the early 1970's, has been a serious problem in both construction and medical care, especially since these sectors together form a very large component of GNP. Substantial relative inflation in them preempts other national and individual spending.

Yet, any effective attack on this public "bad" mobilizes the resistance of concentrated interests in the affected industry.[23] Governmental action to control relative inflation in construction costs would save the average household far less than it would cost construction workers. Control of medical care inflation likewise would cost providers (hospitals, nursing homes, physicians, nurses, etc.) much more than it would benefit patients.

How does this apply to medical care inflation?

Who will influence health care most? Doctors, hospital administrators, union officers and insurance underwriters will have power beyond their numbers; tax payers in general, and patients in particular, will be underrepresented. The reason is quite simple. The providers are very knowledgeable and concerned about health care policy since it is so important to their lives. On the other side, the expected benefits or costs of a health care policy are relatively unimportant to consumers in normal health. Their interests are diffuse, including not only health, but also food, clothing, shelter, education, recreation, and employment. It does not pay the consumer to take strong action. Consumers do have a voice, but it is systematically underrepresented in the political process.

Political leaders, then, have little incentive to follow politically controversial economic advice on how to combat relative medical care inflation.[24] If it is everybody's problem—if the burdens are widely distributed among millions of health care purchasers—political rewards for improvement will be insufficient. A 10 percent decrease in health expenditures—an average of reduction from $400 per capita per year to $360 per year—would reduce the total health bill of the United States by a striking $10 billion. But, while "society" would "save" that much, the efforts to produce such a reduction would mobilize the powerful countervailing efforts of providers.[25] A 10 percent decrease in one's average health bill is of marginal concern to citizens in comparison to the preoccupation of providers with medical care pricing policy. As a result, governments have greater pressure upon them to resist anti-inflationary policy than to act on it.

The main exception is that governments in their buying capacity have a substantial interest in reducing their own program costs. Government departments, acting as if the total government expenditures are relatively inelastic, try to reduce expenditure increases by other departments. There is, therefore, an internal government market which partially serves to put a brake on programmatic expenditure increases. This means that the form of financing is very important. For example, non-health agencies will be less concerned about increased expenditures derived from payroll deductions than those financed from general taxes. Not surprisingly, providers strongly prefer payroll deductions to financing from general revenues.

Theory suggests that the more any particular level of government pays for medical care, the more it will be concerned about price and expenditure increases. Again, there is some evidence to support the theory. Great Britain, with a centralized public finance payment structure, has a significantly lower inflation rate and level of expenditure than the U.S., Canada, and Sweden, which vary in degree of public support (with Sweden being close to 100 percent government supported) but share decentralized financing.[26] Tables 1 and 2 present the changing proportion of resources spent on health care in several western industrial nations.

Medicare and Medicaid illustrate the complex interplay of the forces we have been discussing. During the period 1966–70 total government expenditures on both Medicare and Medicaid increased very rapidly; more beneficiaries were using more expensive services more often than planners had foreseen.[27] By the 1970's, the Nixon Administration was trying to hold down these program costs, first under brief price controls with no permanent effect, then merely by reducing Medicare and Medicaid benefits rather than cost inflation as such.[28] In constant dollars Medicare payments per beneficiary stopped growing. Medicaid payments per beneficiary actually declined. Because during the 1970's the number of beneficiaries continued to rise, total real expenditures also increased in both programs, though at a much slower rate.[29]

The theory of concentrated costs and benefits appears to predict past govern-

Table 1. *Total expenditures for health services as a percentage of the gross national product, seven countries, selected periods, 1961–1969*

Country	WHO estimates[a]		SSA estimates[b]	
	Year	Percentage of GNP	Year	Percentage of GNP
Canada	1961	6.0	1969	7.3
United States	1961–62	5.8	1969	6.8
Sweden	1962	5.4	1969	6.7
Netherlands	1963	4.8	1969	5.9
Federal Republic of Germany	1961	4.5	1969	5.7
France	1963	4.4	1969	5.7
United Kingdom	1961–62	4.2	1969	4.8

Source: The Report of the Health Planning Task Force prepared under the auspices of the Research and Analysis Division of the Ontario Ministry of Health.
[a] Brian Abel-Smith, *An International Study of Health Expenditure*, WHO Public Paper No. 32 (Geneva: 1967).
[b] Joseph G. Simanis, "Medical Care Expenditures in Seven Countries," *Social Security Bulletin* (March 1973): 39.

Table 2. *Increases in relative medical expenditures, 1961–1969*

	Average annual rate of increase of medical expenditure minus average annual increase for GNP
France	4.8
Sweden	4.2
Netherlands	4.2
Canada	3.3
Federal Republic of Germany	3.3
United States	2.8
United Kingdom	2.6

Source: Adapted from Table 7, page 31, of Michael H. Cooper, *Rationing Health Care* (New York, John Wiley and Sons, 1975).

mental responses to medical inflation and the impact on Medicare/Medicaid. It has more difficulty in predicting which of the two programs would be affected the most by concern over their program costs. Medicaid payment is more decentralized (federal, state, some cost-sharing by beneficiaries) but is financed by general revenues. Medicare payment is centralized but is financed by a payroll tax. The two factors tend to cancel out. Medicaid may have lost ground not because of its financing, but because the poor are less politically attractive than the old.[30]

Applied to the politics of inflation control in medical care, the theory of concentrated interests suggests that market improvement will be an unlikely strategy. It could work, and the diffuse public would pay lower insurance premiums and lower medical prices than otherwise. But precisely for that reason, the providers would probably mobilize their concentrated interests to defeat or sabotage it. The point about the market improvement proposals is not that they are all conceptually *ineffective*, but that the greater their likely effectiveness, if enacted, the greater the opposition of the concentrated interests and, therefore, the more *politically* unlikely their implementation.

The government—which would have to improve the market—would benefit from an anti-inflationary policy for medical care as fiscal agent for approximately one-quarter of total medical care expenditures.[31] But it would also incur all of the political costs of market improvement. So, the greater the share of costs a single level of government has in the medical care market, the greater its willingness to impose an anti-inflationary policy on medical providers.

Public utility type regulation, on the other hand, is politically feasible but questionably effective. The demand for state regulation is partly a gesture towards controlling relative medical care inflation and partly an expression of the belief that direct controls of supply and price can, through state commissions, actually moderate inflation.

Certificate of Need legislation and other supply restrictions will undoubtedly apply only to facility expansion and not to current hospital bed supply. This is protective legislation for present hospitals even if supply restraints will limit total expenditure growth, and supply constraints may even exacerbate relative price inflation.[32]

Rate review—medical care price setting—as proposed in the United States would be weak because it would be independent of governmental payment in programs like Medicare and Medicaid. This separation of the payer from price regulator is likely in practice to lead to a weak price-setting mechanism. The government agency with the greatest interest in relative prices is clearly the one which pays for medical care services. Again, state regulation of medical care inflation is possible; it just won't work and isn't working in states that are trying it because states pay a relatively small share of our medical expenditures.[33]

The third strategy—restraining inflation by fiscally centralized national health insurance—presents a mixed picture. On the one hand, the concentration of governmental responsibility of health expenditures is, on the basis of our theory, likely to promote serious government interest in restraining inflation. On the other hand, the concentrated provider interests will be (and are) mobilized to resist precisely this feature of proposed national health insurance legislation. Again there is evidence to support our theory: most current providers resist the notion that health should be financed out of a single budget, whatever their views on the particular form of national health insurance. They point to Great Britain as a "starved" medical care system, where somewhere' in excess of 5 percent of GNP is expended on health care despite the fact that it is all publicly funded.[34] Yet, as Rudolph Klein points out, this can be interpreted as an international achievement:[35]

The British National Health service is remarkable for one achievement. In most other Western societies, expenditure on health care has been soaring over the past decade at a rate which has provoked an anxious search for ways of limiting the growth. In contrast, the NHS has been conspicuous for its success in containing the rate of increase in spending; in Britain the demand has been for an acceleration in the growth rate.

Health care expenditures in Sweden, Canada, and the U.S. are more than 8 percent of GNP, despite the range of financing sources from totally public (at various levels) to substantially private.[36] The Kennedy-Corman strategy makes concentrated or diffuse budgeting for health a significant issue.

To summarize, the greater the likely effectiveness of an anti-inflation policy, the less likely is its enactment. The market improvement strategy has some promise of effectiveness, but little likelihood of success. Public regulation at the state level has political appeal, but a much lower probability of effectiveness. Controlling inflation through a single national health insurance program has some chance of effective constraint, but for that reason is likely to mobilize effective opposition.

The greatest chance of controlling relative medical inflation would appear to be through the back door of a national health insurance plan that is not necessarily passed for the purpose of controlling medical inflation and does not have a strong inflation control mechanism built into it, but which increases the effective pressure for controlling medical inflation in the future by increasing the portion of medical expenditures that flows through the federal budget.

For limiting relative expenditure growth (as opposed to price inflation) in the hospital sector, supply control is both effective and politically viable because its costs fall primarily on the prospective newcomers to the industry. Their opposition to supply control is outweighed by the support of established hospitals that want to curtail competition.

Nothing illustrates the futility of most conventional cost-control proposals better than the suggestions made by the September, 1974, HEW Summit Conference on medical inflation. Nearly all were in fact inflationary and beneficial mainly to health care providers, who contributed most of the prepared papers.

The Summit Conference on inflation: illustrations

The Conference made the following recommendations:

1. Increase the federal budget for health service programs. (This action will increase the relative expenditures on health and will increase the inflationary pressures in the health care industry. While there may be, depending on the

program, some substitution from the private sector to the public thereby hurting some health care firms, increased federal activity will for the most part benefit health care providers.)

2. Keep operating costs as close to parity with increases in the Consumer Price Index as possible. (This is the goal of anti-inflationary policy, but no method of implementing it is contained in this section.)

3. Restructure reimbursement. For example, reimbursement should be on a total budget rather than a line item basis. This policy has been tried in some Canadian provinces with limited success.[37]

4. Shift emphasis to ambulatory and preventive care. (While there may be some shift from the more expensive hospital care, the main effect is to bring more health care onto the "insurance gravy train." A good example of this problem is given by Lave for dental care.[38] If the marginal costs of prevention are less than the benefits, inflation will be reduced; conversely, inflation will be increased if the reverse is true).

5. Initiate consumer education activities directed toward increasing consumer knowledge regarding what are realistic patient expectations from the health care system. (Inflationary and expenditure impact is insignificant one way or another, but it does create some jobs for health care researchers.)

6. Provide consumers with information on fees and prices. (It will probably result in a one-time reduction in prices of small magnitude. It should be noted that a footnote to the report mentioned that the providers showed considerable skepticism regarding this approach and suggested that it was, in fact, inflationary—no comment is necessary.)

7. Change the statutory definition of health maintenance organizations in order to allow for more flexibility in assembling benefit packages tailored to the needs and financial resources of particular population groups. (While this may be desirable, it is not clear what effect this will have on health care inflation. Essentially this law allows HMOs to use the optimal discrimination in pricing—a monopoly ploy to increase revenues and profits.)

8. Do not allow the quality of health care to become a casualty of zealous efforts to contain costs in the health sector. (Unfortunately, this is the crux of the matter, that increases in quality—more comfortable beds, better trained nurses, equipment which only brings very marginal increases in success rates—have been responsible for a substantial part of the increases in hospital care costs. *Not* to put a lid on quality improvement is *not* to put a lid on relative expenditure growth. On the assumption that hospital costs have risen because of increases in both quality and quantity demanded, then the desire to reduce relative expenditure increases without having any effects on quality improvement is a desire not to stop relative expenditure growth.)

9. Monitor the impact of the contribution to inflation in the health care sector. (This is a chance for the self-interested researcher to get in on the "anti-

inflation gravy train." The main effect will be to increase trivially the relative amount of expenditures devoted to health care.)

10. Encourage comprehensive health planning coupled with regulatory power to reduce duplication of facilities via the innovative use of Certificate of Need and rate setting mechanisms. (This is essentially the hospital supply proposal we have already discussed.)

11. Increase supply of primary care providers and, in particular, third party reimbursement for the services of non-physician providers should be encouraged. (Economic theory predicts the first part of the suggestion would work but Canadian experience suggests the opposite.)[39]

12. Reconsider wage and price controls. (It was noted that a wide array of provider groups dissented from this view.)[40]

Conclusion

Economic theory suggests that the economic market will systematically underproduce public goods. This conclusion is often used as a justification for governmental intervention. But the implication of this paper is that moving from the economic marketplace to the political marketplace does not necessarily solve problems. In the absence of some concentrated interest, the political market is unlikely to adopt a policy simply because it constitutes a public good.[41] The political market (like the economic one) will systematically underproduce public goods (and over-produce public "bads"). The political process is unlikely to right the distributive wrongs of the economic marketplace when a similar set of actors dominate both.[42]

The application of this theory to national health insurance suggests sober estimates about the government's ability to restrain national health care expenditures, which are increasing at the rate of more than $10 billion a year. The experiences of Canada and Sweden suggest that government financing on a large scale alone does not reverse the upward spiral in prices and expenditures. Certainly this has been the case when the government uses an insurance mechanism in which financing is diffusely shared among patients and different units of government. There is evidence that where financing is concentrated and service providers are directly budgeted (rather than reimbursed retrospectively by insurance) expenditures and the rate of medical inflation are lower. This has been the case in Great Britain, with its National Health Service. While one would not expect the United States to legislate a national health service, the experience of Great Britain has important implications for the degree of financing concentration desirable in a future national health insurance program.

Notes

1 Joseph Newhouse, "Inflation and Health Insurance," in *Health: A Victim or Cause of Inflation*, ed: M. Zubkoff (New York: Milbank Memorial Fund, 1975).

2 Some analysts (including the authors of this paper) believe that the medical services component of the CPI overstates medical inflation because it does not fully take into account improvements in quality. However, since this assertion (if true) would not affect any of the conclusions of our paper, we will not consider it further.

3 Bureau of Labor Statistics, *Monthly Labor Review*, various issues.

4 Ibid.

5 U.S. Department of Health, Education, and Welfare, *The Health, Education and Welfare Income Security, Social Services Conference on Inflation Report* (Washington, D.C.: Government Printing Office, 1974).

6 Relative quantity growth is that growth in medical services as a percent of GNP that would have occurred in the absence of any change in the relative price level of medical services. It includes both quantity changes (in the strict sense) and quality changes.

7 Karen Davis, "The Impact of Inflation and Unemployment on Health Care of Low Income People," in Zubkoff, *Health.*

8 Lester Lave, "The Effect of Inflation on Providers," in Zubkoff, *Health.*

9 Joseph Newhouse, "Inflation and Health Insurance," in Zubkoff, *Health.*

10 For example, U.S. Department of Health, Education, and Welfare, Social Security Administration, *Community Hospitals: Inflation in the Pre-Medicare Period*, by Karen Davis and Richard Foster, Research Report No. 41 (Washington, D.C.: Government Printing Office, 1972); Martin Feldstein, "A New Approach to National Health Insurance," *The Public Interest* 23 (Spring 1971); Lave, "The Effect of Inflation;" and Newhouse, "Inflation and Health Insurance."

11 Numbers 2 to 6 cause *high* relative prices (and/or expenditures) not *increasing* relative prices (and/or expenditures). For them to cause relative inflation they must increase in magnitude or effectiveness over time.

12 "A New Approach."

13 Newhouse, "Inflation."

14 Fredric L. Sattler, "Hospital Prospective Rate Setting, Issues and Options," working paper, SSA Interstudy Hospital Prospective Payment Workshop (Minneapolis: Interstudy, 1975). For a survey of the extent of state rate review and certificate-of-need agencies see L. Lewin & Associates, *Nationwide Survey of Health Regulation*, NTIS Accession No. 236660-AS (September 1974) and *An Analysis of State and Regional Health Regulation* (February 1974). For analytical commentary on these developments see L. Lewin, Ann Somers and Herman Somers, "Issues in the Structure and Administration of State Health Cost Regulation," *Toledo Law Review Symposium* (June 1975).

15 Sattler, "Hospital Prospective Rate Setting."

16 George Stigler, "The Theory of Economic Regulation," *The Bell Journal of Economics and Management Science 2* (Spring 1971).

17 These concepts are taken from the work of Graham Allison, *The Essence of Decision* (Boston: Little, Brown, 1971), especially the discussion of the organizational process model of politics. It further uses teaching materials prepared by Allison on "The Massachusetts Medical School Case," Public Policy Program, Harvard University, 1973.

18 Compare the similar, but not identical views of George Stigler, "The Theory of Economic Regulation," and Richard Posner, "Theories of Economic Regulation," *The Bell Journal of Economics and Management Science 5* (Autumn 1974): 335–58 for further discussion of economic approaches to the study of public policy policies.

19 Donald Wittman, "Political Decision-Making," in *Economics of Public Choice*, eds: Robert D. Leiter and Gerald Serkin (New York: Cyrco Press, 1975), pp. 29–48.

20 A government program to help farmers, to give a specific illustration, helps a particular farmer whether or not he has contributed to lobbying for the passage of the bill.

74   *Politics in the world of medicine*

Since the farmer's individual efforts are costly and unlikely to change the outcome, he and all other farmers are likely to abstain from political activity. This is a variant of the "prisoner's dilemma," a game theory problem where individually rational behavior results in collectively irrational behavior for the participants involved.

Which groups will be most successful at overcoming the collective good behavior? Clearly, those groups which are best capable of internalizing the rewards and external-izing the costs, i.e., making some of the good private instead of collective. For example, those who do not contribute are beaten up (a private bad to the person), while those who contribute receive a special citation or invitation to a dinner (a private good). The analysis takes on many subtle variations. Different kinds of groups are better at policing themselves for correct behavior (smaller groups versus larger and more physically concentrated groups than diffuse). See Mancur Olson, *The Logic of Collective Action* (Cambridge: Harvard University Press, 1968). A monopolistic firm in an industry is thus capable of exerting a great political pressure on behalf of the industry because first, it is the industry and, therefore, the good is a private good and second, it does not have to organize a large number of firms for political action since it is already organized. For an excellent discussion, see William A. Brock and Stephen P. Magee, mimeo (University of Chicago: Center for Mathematical Studies in Business and Economics, 1975) and for an insightful diagrammatic exposition, see John Chamberlynn, mimeo (University of Michigan: Institute of Policy Studies, 1975).

21 There are, of course, other explanations for this particular phenomenon such as the one given by Frances Piven and Richard Cloward that welfare payments are a tech-nique for "regulating the poor," or interdependent utility functions, i.e., other individ-uals have utility functions that are concerned with the welfare of mothers, *Regulating the Poor: The Functions of Public Welfare* (New York: Random House, 1971).

22 In order to use an essential static model to explain the response of the political system to a dynamic situation (inflation), we will assume that concentrated interests have not completely exhausted the benefits of concentration and still have marginal influence which is greater than that of the diffuse interests.

There have been several papers written on the relationship of the political process to aggregate inflation and other macro-economics variables. For example, see Robert Gordon, "The Politics of Inflation," National Bureau of Economic Research Confer-ence on Economic Analysis of Political Behavior, 1975; Bruno Frey, "A Politico-Economic System: A Simulation Model," *Kyklos* 28 (1974): 227–254; and Gerald Kramer, "Short Run Fluctuation in U.S. Voting Behavior, 1896–1964," *American Political Science Review* 65 (March 1971): 131–143.

23 Sometimes there may be concentrated interests who will fight inflation (for example, the purchasers of intermediate goods). However, these are relatively weak in medical care and construction. Everyone would be for the public good (or against the public bad) if the gainers could bribe the losers; however, the high cost of bargaining across issues effectively prevents this theoretical possibility from taking place.

24 It may be in the interest of the politician to act as an entrepreneur in discovering public goods and offering policies that promote public goods. However, we doubt that it is complete—that all public goods are captured by politicians. For more information concerning entrepreneurialism, see Norman Froehlich, Joe Oppenheimer and Oran Young, *Political Leadership and Collective Goods* (Princeton, N.J.: Princeton Uni-versity Press, 1971).

25 Of course, some providers might benefit from a decrease in expenditures and clearly some customers would benefit from increased health expenditures; but we *believe* that intergroup conflict and variation is greater than the intragroup variation.

26 Odin Anderson, *Health Care: Can There Be Equity? The United States, Sweden and England* (New York: John Wiley and Sons, 1975); R.D. Fraser, "Overview: Canadian National Health Insurance," paper presented at the Conference of Canadian Health Economists, Queens University, Ontario. September 1974; and Theodore Marmor et al., "Canadian National Health Insurance: Policy Implications for the United States," *Policy Sciences* (December 1975). Also, in different form, see Spyros Andrepoulos, ed., *National Health Insurance* (New York: John Wiley and Sons, 1975).

27 U.S., Department of Health, Education, and Welfare, *Expenditures for Personal Health Services: National Trends and Variations—1953–1970,* by Ronald Andersen et al., U.S. Department HEW Publication No. (HRA) 74-3105 (Washington, D.C.: Bureau of Health Services Research and Evaluation, 1973) and U.S., Department of Health, Education, and Welfare, *Health Service Use: National Trends and Variations—1953–1971,* by Ronald Andersen et al., U.S. Department HEW Publication No. (HSM) 73-3004 (Washington, D.C.: National Center for Health Services Research and Development, 1972).

28 Robert Stevens and Rosemary Stevens, *Welfare Medicine in America: A Case Study of Medicaid* (New York: The Free Press, 1974).

29 Karen Davis, "The Impact of Inflation and Unemployment on Health Care of Low Income People," in Zubkoff, *Health.*

30 Stevens and Stevens, *Welfare Medicine in America.*

31 Social Security Administration, *Background Information on Medical Expenditures, Prices and Costs* (Washington, D.C.: Office of Research and Statistics, September 1974).

32 Of course, there are models of hospital regulation which could have desirable effects on inflation. If unnecessary beds were excluded from cost reimbursement as one of our referees suggests is possible, both price and expenditure growth *could* be moderated.

33 L. Lewin, Ann Somers and Herman Somers, "Issues in the Structure and Administration of State Health Cost Regulation."

34 Milton Friedman, "Leonard Woodcock's Free Lunch," *Newsweek,* 21 April 1975.

35 Rudolph Klein, ed., *Social Policy and Public Expenditure 1975: Inflation and Priorities* (London: Centre for Studies in Social Policy, 1975), p. 83.

36 U.S. Department of Health, Education, and Welfare, *Health Service Use: National Trends and Variations—1953–1971;* R. D. Fraser, "Overview: Canadian National Health Insurance"; and Marmor et al., "Canadian National Health Insurance."

37 Andreopoulos, ed: *National Health Insurance* (especially chapters by R. G. Evans, M. LeClair, and T. R. Marmor).

38 Lester Lave, "The Effect of Inflation on Providers," in Zubkoff, *Health.*

39 Robert G. Evans, "Beyond the Medical Marketplace: Expenditure, Utilization, and Pricing of Insured Health Care in Canada," in Andreopoulos, *National Health Insurance.*

40 For a discussion of how the controls worked, see Paul Ginsburg, "The Economic Stabilization Program," in Zubkoff, *Health.*

41 Robert R. Alford, *Health Care Politics: Ideological and Interest Group Barriers to Reform* (Chicago: University of Chicago Press, 1974).

42 The question of the precise comparative advantage of these respective markets has not been systematically studied.

4. Representing consumer interests: the case of American health planning

JAMES A. MORONE, THEODORE R. MARMOR

I. Introduction

The National Health Planning and Resources Development Act of 1974 authorized a national network of local health planning institutions. The statute, Public
Law 93–641, called for more than two hundred planning bodies—health systems
agencies (HSAs)—which consumers were to dominate. The law required a
consumer majority on each HSA governing board. These consumers were to be
"broadly representative of the social, economic, linguistic and racial populations
of the area."[1] Consumer majorities, the program's framers assumed, would be
powerful forces in shaping local health plans and thus in directing American
medicine toward the wants, concerns, and interests of consumers.

The institutionalization of consumer participation accompanied an ambitious
conception of health planning itself. The new program was to produce "scientific
planning with teeth," cut medical care costs, improve access to medical care, and
assure its high quality. The HSA plans would select local health priorities and
identify proposals that satisfied community goals for medical care. Their way of
working was envisaged as follows: hospitals or nursing homes intent on expanding would submit to the HSA detailed proposals taking into account the official

This chapter is taken from *Ethics*, 91:431–450, 1981. Copyright ©1981 by the University
of Chicago. Reprinted by permission.

Other versions have been published as "Representing Consumer Interests: Imbalanced
Markets, Health Planning, and the HSAs," *Milbank Memorial Fund Quarterly/Health and
Society*, 58(1):125–165, 1980, and in T.R. Marmor and J.B. Christianson, eds., *Health
Care Policy: A Political Economy Approach* (Beverly Hills, Calif.: Sage, 1982), Chap. 8.

Our thinking, particularly at the outset, was greatly helped by the writings and comments of Charles Anderson. Our friend Rudolf Klein's *Politics of Consumer Representation*, written with Janet Lewis (London: Centre for Social Policy, 1976), which focused
on Britain, first directed our concern to thinking about issues of consumer participation
and representation in an American context. We want to thank as well colleagues at the
Institution for Social and Policy Studies, Yale University, and the Center for Health
Administration Studies, University of Chicago, for their helpful criticism, most particularly Charles E. Lindblom and Brian Barry. The written comments of Adina Schwartz,
Owen Fiss, Peter Steinfels, Arthur Caplan, Albert Weale, and Eugene Bardach were
particularly useful to us in revising this essay.

HSA plan. The HSA decisions would be serial, one after the other, each expansion measured against the planning vision of the consumer-dominated agency. In theory, each proposal would either advance the pursuit of community health aims or be rejected.

In practice, however, the HSAs' regulatory authority is severely restricted, almost wholly negative in character, and almost certainly insufficient to reshape the local politics of medicine. The HSAs do review institutional proposals for capital expenditures over $150,000, but their role is in fact advisory to the state governments which are legally empowered to issue required certificates of need. The HSAs are also supposed to review the appropriateness of all medical facilities in their area, but they have neither the positive authority to make improvements nor clear sanctions by which to constrain present operations. Overall, HSAs exhibit a curious structure: decentralized planning bodies with consumer majorities, a highly rationalistic planning mission, and limited regulatory authority to deal with the pluralistic financing and delivery features of the American medical arrangements they are to reshape.

This is not a conception of governance likely to generate confidence among the skeptical. But it is precisely what one would have expected in the context of American health politics of the mid-1970s. At that time, there was widespread alarm about rising health expenditures. Whereas in the 1950s Americans spent 5 percent of GNP on medical care, a quarter of a century later expenditures had risen 50 percent, to some 7.5 percent of GNP by 1975. These increases, heightened in the wake of Medicare and Medicaid legislation in 1965, prompted near-panic in the early 1970s. The Economic Stabilization Program (1971–74) retained controls in medical care longer than other goods and services, but by 1974 and the end of price controls, it was clear another spurt of medical inflation was in progress. Prompted by inflationary fears, the Congress that year debated the broader question of national health insurance but was stalemated by the contending proposals of a Republican administration and a Democratic Congress. Watergate deflected congressional attention from forging new coalitions, so committees with newly expanded responsibilities for health confined their actions to reshaping health *planning* institutions amid intense but narrow political scrutiny.

What emerged as the new health planning program, then, was a compound of stalemate, a commitment to scientific planning, and a faith in democratic participation. That latter faith was central, as the law's words make plain. If consumers dominated and were broadly representative, how could health planning fail to reflect consumer interests? A microcosm of the community would act on the community's behalf. Making sure the HSA board is a microcosm was the rationale for the original insistence that racial, economic, social, geographic, and linguistic categories of constituencies be explicitly represented.

Whatever the intentions of the health planning legislation, the structure of HSAs promised operational problems. What the framers never considered were the implications of the jury model of representation that the microcosm idea expressed. They had no ready answers about how diverse consumer interests in health were to be either articulated or balanced. They presumed that the *representativeness* of HSA governing bodies was the crucial feature of their legitimacy. They failed to link the board's functional task—making choices about health resources—to the representational requirements. Set against the jury notion is what one might call the instrumental view of representation. How well, one asks in this connection, do given institutional practices express the interests of constituencies? What means do constituents have to hold their representatives to account? How well do representative institutions settle the policy problems they were designed to confront? Such questions are precisely what the descriptive model of representation—the model of the jury—neglects. The central HSA dilemma is that it employs a jury model of representativeness to assure the representation of consumer interests. As we will argue, the result is conceptual confusion and practical disappointment.

The next section briefly discusses the terms of the law with regard to consumer representation and the legal cases that have practically illustrated the program's conceptual difficulties. The core of the paper sketches the competing notions of representation—and the associated ideas of participation and accountability. We think of this part as a philosophical map that analysts of consumer involvement in public policymaking should want to consider. In the particular case of health planning, we go on to discuss the kind of unbalanced political arena that promoters of policy change confront. Thus, when we turn at the close to prescriptions for improving the representation of consumer interests, it is in the light of practical constraints as well as philosophical considerations. The epilogue suggests what problems would remain with health planning even if the difficulties of its provisions for consumer representation were adequately worked out.

II. Conceptual muddles, consumer representation, and HSAs

The health planning law was plain enough about consumer majorities on HSAs. Indeed, the statute required no less than 51 and no more than 60 percent of every board to be broadly representative of consumers. But the law and its regulations were silent on the details of implementing this microcosmic conception of representation. How representatives were to be chosen, for instance, was ignored. Which demographic groups should dominate under the broad headings of social, linguistic, and economic representation was not addressed. The clearest representational requirement was that metropolitan and nonmetropolitan representatives precisely mirror their proportions in the population at large.

What was explicitly addressed was the openness in which HSAs should conduct their business. Thus, there was a substitution of participatory conditions for clarity about consumer representation. Agencies, for example, were required to hold public meetings, with agendas widely available beforehand and the minutes available afterward. There were to be opportunities for public comment on almost every phase of HSA activity. All of these provisions—central to the acceptability of a legitimate substitute for representative government—failed to make the crucial connections between consumer interests and consumer representation.

Disputes over consumer roles in health planning reached the courts almost immediately and there exposed the conceptual difficulties of health planning's model of representation. Several suits claimed inadequate means for selecting consumer representatives. But a New York court ruled, in *Aldamuy* v. *Pirro*, that there were no criteria by which it could choose between two competing minority representatives even if one had been selected by election.[2] As long as the requisite *number* of a particular minority were board members, the law's representation requirements were satisfied. A district court in Texas determined that requisite number by referring to the census tract.[3]

In *Rakestraw* v. *Califano* and other cases, various social groups sued, demanding seats on the local board; the law and its regulations incorporated no principles for differentiating those with valid objections from those with merely frivolous ones.[4] Across the nation, HSAs scrambled to find poor, even uneducated consumers in a legally mandated but conceptually misguided effort to mirror the demographic characteristics of their area. And after selection, the problems of effective consumer representation continued to bedevil the HSA boards. The technical details of health planning bewildered inexperienced board members. Many had no idea whom they spoke for and, in places, were unwilling to attend meetings. There were reports, particularly in the South, of HSA meetings attended only by provider representatives.[5]

III. Representation's conceptual puzzles

Establishing representative institutions requires fundamental choices. Decisions must be made about the selection of representatives, what those representatives should be like, and the expectations that should govern their behavior. Whom to represent—the constituencies—is a central puzzle where geographic representation is abandoned. In addition, the organizational structures within which representatives operate must be specified. Do these structures enhance or impede effective representation? Is the tendency toward political imbalance redressed?

The character of consumer involvement in HSAs is contingent on the answers to these general questions. Indeed, many of the difficulties that plague the health planning act follow from a failure to consider most of them.

We consider these questions in this section through discussion of three topics: the distinction between participation and representation, several conceptions of representation, and their implications for democratic accountability.

A. Participation

Self-government can mean direct citizen participation in public decisions. But the conditions which make such participation feasible are largely absent in modern industrial societies. As a consequence, political representation often replaces direct participation as an operational expression of the principle that "every man has the right to have a say in what happens to him."[6] The rhetoric of the 1974 planning law emphasized consumer representation. The law itself, by contrast, concentrated on guidelines for direct public participation. Direct participation provisions tend to reinforce the political dominance of medical providers over consumers. Hospital administrators, state medical association officials, and other employed medical personnel are far more likely to pay the costs of participating in HSA meetings. The general public is not likely to do so.

Furthermore, the difficulties of fostering direct consumer participation are aggravated by the nature of most health issues. Health concerns, through important, are intermittent for most people.[7] They are not as clearly or regularly salient as the condition of housing or children's schools—situations that citizens confront daily. Consequently, it is far more difficult to establish public participation in HSAs than in renters' associations or school districts.[8]

The point is not that participation is objectionable in health planning. Rather, we argue that, without being tied to accountability and the representation of consumer health interests, the provisions for participation are at best marginally useful to consumers. They are more likely to be utilized by aroused provider institutions.

B. Descriptive representation

Descriptive representation—the type of representation required in PL 93-641—emphasizes the characteristics of representatives. Where constituencies cannot be present themselves for public choice, the descriptive model calls for a representative "body which [is] an exact portrait, in miniature, of the people at large." The argument is straightforward. Since all the people cannot be present to make decisions, representative bodies ought to be miniature versions—microcosms—of the public they represent.

The similarity of composition is expected to result in similarity of outcomes; the assembly will "think, feel, reason and [therefore] act" as the public would have.[9] A number of difficulties make this formulation problematic. First, "the public" is a broad category. What aspect of it ought to be reflected in a representative body? John Stuart Mill argued that opinions should be represented; Bentham and James Mill emphasized subjective interests; Sterne, a more ambiguous "opinions, aspirations and wishes"; Burke, broad fixed interest. Swabey suggested that citizens were equivalent units, that if all had roughly equal political opportunities, representatives would be a proper random selection and, consequently, descriptively representative. Whichever may be the case, a failure to specify precisely what characteristics are represented renders microcosm theories unworkable.

Even when the relevant criteria for selecting representatives are properly specified, mirroring an entire nation is impossible. Mill's "every shade of opinion," for example, cannot be reconstructed in the assembly hall on one issue, much less on every issue. One cannot construct a microcosm of a million consumers no matter which sixteen, seventeen, or eighteen consumers represent them on the HSA governing board. Competing opinions or interest can, of course, be represented. But the chief aim of microcosmic representation is mirroring the full spectrum of constituencies. Pitkin notes that the language in which these theories are presented indicates the difficulty of actually implementing them. The theorists constantly resort to metaphor: the assembly as map, mirror, portrait. They are all difficult to express in more practical terms.

Mirroring the community may be as undesirable a criterion for selecting decision makers as it is an infeasible one. The merriment that followed Senator Hruska's proposal that the mediocre deserved representation on the U.S. Supreme Court suggests a common understanding of the limits of simplistic views of descriptive representation.[10]

In addition, if representatives are asked merely to reflect the populace, they have no standards regarding their actions as representatives. Descriptive representation prescribes who representatives should be, not what they should do.[11] Opinion polls measure public views more accurately than does descriptive representation.

Though exacting microcosm theories are not realistic, descriptive standards are relevant to the operation of modern legislatures. Legislators are commonly criticized for not mirroring their constituents' views or interests. In fact, John Adams's formulation might be recast as one guideline to selecting representatives— the public votes, essentially, for candidates who appear to "think, feel, reason and act" as its members do. But this broad conception of descriptive representation is sharply different from the utopian endeavor of forming a microcosm of the population in the HSA.

One contemporary version of the microcosm theory is what Greenstone and Peterson term "socially descriptive representation."[12] Rather than mirroring opinions or interests, this conception proposes mirroring of the social and demographic characteristics of a community's population. This amends Adams's syllogism: if people (*a*) share demographic characteristics, (*b*) they will "think, feel [and] reason" like one another, and (*c*) consequently, act like one another. Shared demographic characteristics, in this view, ensure like policy sentiments.

The problems with mirror theories, enumerated above, are all relevant to this version. Demographically mirroring a populace in an assembly is as unlikely as mirroring its opinions. Obviously, not all social characteristics can or ought to be represented. The problem of discriminating among them is particularly vexing. Common sense rebels against representing left-handers or redheads. What of Lithuanians? Italians? Jews? The uneducated? Mirror views provide few guidelines for selecting which social characteristics merit representation.

Even when the characteristics to be mirrored are specified, as regulations to PL 93-641 eventually did, problems remain. All individual members of a social group will not, in fact, "think, feel [and] reason" alike. And all will not represent their fellows with equal efficacy. Yet, by itself, mirror representation does not distinguish among members of a population group—one low-income representative is, for example, interchangeable with any other. As long as the requisite number of a population group is seated, the society is represented—mirrored—in the appropriate aspect. Such actors are not so much representatives as instances of population groups.

Socially descriptive representation is pernicious because it makes recourse to constituencies unnecessary. Attention to means of selection and accountability is reduced by emphasizing broad representativeness. Skin color or income, for example, mark a representative acceptable or unacceptable, regardless of what the constituency thinks. The result is that any member of the group is as qualified a representative as any other. It is a situation that invites tokenism. If the health planning law's only requirement is that a fixed percentage of a board be drawn from a specific group, there is nothing to recommend a black elected by fellow blacks or selected by the NAACP, or a woman elected by women or selected by NOW, over blacks and women drafted onto a board because they will not "rock the boat."

Aldamuy v. *Pirro*, cited earlier, illustrates the application of the theory of mirror representation. The court found no criteria in either the law or the regulations by which to appraise the representativeness of the HSA board except for descriptive characteristics. Since both the representatives of the board and their challengers satisfied the criterion of minority status, there was no way to choose between them. It was not possible to select one as any better or more representative than another.

It has been suggested that socially descriptive representation might be effective if representatives were tied to their constituencies by some mechanism of oversight. That stipulation, however, changes the theory of socially descriptive representation. Selected agents are then representatives not because they share a group's features but because they are acceptable to that group. As it has been interpreted in several of the cited court cases, PL 93-641 includes no such view. It requires only that the composition of the board be a statistical microcosm of the area's racial, social, linguistic, and income distribution. Still, for all its inadequacies, there is a kernel of truth in theories of socially descriptive representation. Obviously, social characteristics are sometimes related to interests, and, as the following section argues, interests are precisely what ought to be represented. Thus, religious affiliations bespeak clear interests in Northern Ireland, race affects interests in America, and poverty relates to interests everywhere.

C. Substantive representation

The key issue in substantive representation is not what representatives look like but whom they look after, whose interests they pursue. Put simply, substantive representation means acting in the interests of constituencies. Doing so involves both properly apprehending those interests and effectively pursuing them.

The classic problem of ascertaining interests is immediately apparent. Are interests objective facts that intelligent leaders can best discern? Or are they more like subjective preferences that must be conveyed to representatives? The latter require a delegatory view where representatives follow constituent wishes. A more objective view of interests supports a trustee role, representatives acting in the constituency's best interest regardless of constituent desires.

In practice, substantive representation involves neither of these extremes. Representatives are neither unabashed messengers nor unfettered guardians, for interests are not completely objective or merely subjective. Various principles of representation are defensible within these broad limits—substantive representation is a general category rather than a particular principle. What we wish to stress is the change from the descriptive conception to a substantive one structured around the pursuit of consumer interests.

The nature of interests is easily caricatured in health politics. Health policy is often technical and complex. The guardian role is most often assumed not by the consumer representatives but by health professionals, accountable to professional norms rather than consumers' desires. The claim that they know the consumer's best interest is accurate, but only within the confines of the physician's office. For the issues that HSAs confront—such as the distribution of limited resources among competing, needy claimants—trusteeship on the basis of medical knowledge is inappropriate.

In practical politics, representatives regularly consider claims for which the interests of specified constituencies are no guide. Bringing the wants of various groups to the bargaining arenas of politics is insufficient; the consideration of ideal-regarding interests—for which there may be no organized constituency—is no less important in policy areas like the distribution and costs of medical care. Our emphasis on constituency interest—in contrast to socially descriptive representativeness—should not be taken as indifference to the questions for which the representation of different interests is insufficient. The intellectual failings of descriptive representation, in short, are one subject; the proper design of institutions for resolving politically charged issues of medical care is another and one beyond our capacities here. But, for that design, attention to the representation of substantive interests is a crucial requisite.

The effectiveness of representatives is crucial to substantive representation. An eloquent speaker or a skillful political operator can be said to provide better substantive representation than another with an equal understanding of constituent interests but without the same skills. And representatives in influential positions—chairs of congressional committees, officers of HSA boards—may well be more effective than less well placed representatives. The reverse, representatives in positions of little influence, can provide only minimal substantive representation. A largely submerged issue for HSAs pertains to precisely this point. If HSAs are powerless and inconsequential bodies, the furor over representation is misplaced—consumer interests are substantively represented within the HSAs but not in matters of important health policy.

The drafters of the health planning act confused representativeness with substantive representation, mistakenly believing that socially descriptive representation would lead to effective representation of interests. They presumed that a local agency with a jury-like board would adequately represent the interests of consumers and legitimate their regulatory interventions in the medical care market. Although jury-like bodies serve a representative and legitimating function in some governmental contexts—notably determinations of guilt in criminal trials—their capacity for substantive representation of interests in circumstances requiring problem solving and complex conflict resolution is limited.

D. Accountability

Jurors have no constituencies to answer to. Substantive representation introduces constituencies and the necessity of means of making their representatives accountable. That link is the crux of accountability.

Put simply, accountability means "having to answer to." One is accountable to agents who control scarce resources one desires. In the classic electoral example, officials are accountable to voters whose votes are desired. Health officials may be accountable to legislatures that control funds, pressure groups that can extend or withdraw support, or even medical care providers who can choose whether or not to cooperate with health planning officials.

The crucial element in each case is that accountability stems from some resource valued by the accountable actor. Accountability is not merely an ideal, like honesty, that public actors ought to strive to achieve. Rather, the disposition of valued, scarce resources is manipulable by the relevant constituency.

We term the means by which actors are held accountable "mechanisms of accountability." These mechanisms can vary enormously in character and in the extent of control they impose. Voters occasionally exert some control with a yes or no decision, whereas work supervisors regularly monitor their subordinates' work, enforcing compliance with specific demands.

There is often, to be sure, a give-and-take process in which actors try to maximize their freedom of action and minimize accountability. And those indifferent to the scarce resources in question, such as officials with no desire to be reelected, are not, strictly speaking, accountable. But this illustrates the central point in speaking of accountability. One must be able to point to specific scarce resources, particular mechanisms holding representatives to account.

Many of the HSA requirements expected to enhance accountability to the public are, in fact, necessary but not sufficient conditions for constraining HSA representatives. The emphasis on public participation and openness both legitimates HSAs and eases the task of reviewing HSA performance, as the following HSA requirements illustrate: a public record of court proceedings;[13] open meetings, with notice of meetings published in two newspapers and an address given where a proposed agenda may be obtained;[14] and an opportunity to comment, either in writing or in public meeting, about designation,[15] or health system plans,[16] or annual implementation plans.[17]

Yet these requirements facilitate public accounting, not direct accountability. Since requirements for public participation and disclosure incorporate no formal mechanisms forcing boards to answer to consumers, there is little direct public accountability. Well-defined mechanisms of accountability are central to a strong conception of accountability. Propositions which substitute relationships described as "winning over" or "working with" the community for an identifiable mechanism are much weaker, conflating one common language usage of accounting for action with a stronger view of accountability to a constituency.[18]

Suggesting that HSAs would be ineffective without public support reflects an equally weak conception of accountability to consumers. The "say" of the citizenry is not expressed by "inhospitality" or "lack of trust" or "written protests" but by an authoritative decision institutionalized as a mechanism of accountability.

Accountability can be to more than one constituency. As health planning is now structured, the Department of Health and Human Services (HHS), state government, local government, consumers, providers and numerous other groups can all attempt to hold the HSA accountable. These competing claims introduce significant tensions. One especially problematic tension lies between accountability to local communities and to national government. Since the rules of HSA operations are decided locally, the potential for local accountability is present. Yet insofar as the law takes up the issue explicitly, it presses accountability to HHS.[19]

The department is responsible for reviewing the plans, structure, and operation of every agency at least once every twelve months.[20] Renewal of designation is annually at stake. This is accountability in every important sense. But it can be traced to the public only by the long theoretical strand leading through the presidency. From this perspective, HSA boards are no more accountable to the public than any other federal executive agency, certainly a far cry from the rhetoric that accompanied PL 93-641's enactment. As the law now stands, public accountability (either directly to constituents or indirectly through states and localities) is not prohibited or rendered impossible. But neither is accountability to the public institutionalized or even significantly facilitated.

The success of instituting accountability relates in large measure to the formal means of selecting representatives. But PL 93-641 and its regulations say little about selection. In the *Rakestraw* case, HHS was sued not only regarding the composition but also the selection of HSA boards. The plaintiffs demanded not the mere specification of formal selection procedures but a means that guaranteed accountability to the public. They were even willing to waive socially descriptive representation in favor of accountability through explicit selection provisions.

E. Who is to be represented: a prescription

Only one representational category is precisely delineated in the planning act— the public in nonmetropolitan areas must be represented on the board in proportion to their population. Otherwise, the National Health Planning and Resources Development Act cuts representation loose from geography; representatives stand for social groups rather than precincts, and difficult choices are avoided by entitling all groups to representation. However, the liberalism which provides the theoretical foundation of the act incorporates a vision of shifting, crosscutting interests that makes it impossible to name functional categories that enfranchise everyone equally. No matter what the representational categories, some groups will gain, others lose.

Considerable HSA litigation followed from insufficiently specified representational categories. It can be halted by changing the sweeping grant of representation that flows from the microcosm view to an enumeration of the interests to be represented. Rather than boards that are broadly representative of the population, we would suggest boards that represent specified interests in that population. The specification of interests that we urge must be made on the national level, either in amendments to the act or—as is more likely—in its implementing regulations. Decisions at the national level are crucial since Congress sought to bypass the local political process in the establishment of HSAs.[21]

The next obvious question is, which consumer health interests should be represented on the HSA board? There are groups that, while part of the population and therefore potentially included on a board constituted on the microcosm principle, do not have distinctive health care interests. For example, it is not clear that those with little formal education have the distinguishable health needs that characterize the low-income or aged populations.

Interests with claims to be heard vary by health issue. Regarding access, there are different problems for rural and uban populations, or for the chronically, as opposed to the intermittently, ill. The infirm could claim representation for each of their diseases whenever the issue of new facilities arises. So could every ethnic group regarding specific genetic diseases that disproportionately or exclusively afflict its members. The list of health interests is theoretically very long. However, Congress (or its delegate) must make these difficult choices and specify the various health interests that merit representation on HSA boards.[22]

Selecting the interests to be represented requires an assessment of the purpose of consumer involvement. Presumably, it is to facilitate the articulation and satisfaction of health needs now underrepresented in American communities. As an illustration of interest selection furthering this purpose, we suggest certain representational categories for the HSAs. Although there is no inherent symmetry or formal relationship between any two categories, there is a plausible, a priori justification for representation of the following interests:

a) Payers.—The most pressing issue in health politics is rising costs. The interests with the clearest stake in controlling them are the aggregated health care payers—unions, large employers, insurance companies. In traditional markets, consumers are payers, but the dominance of direct or third-party health payers has necessitated the distinction between payer and patient. Excluding the former is likely to result in biased boards, for payers have a clearly articulated financial interest that conflicts directly with that of most health care providers.

b) The poor.—Reducing health services to control expenditures threatens groups that now receive insufficient care, most obviously the poor. Their interests—more and better care—conflict with those of the payers. Providing board positions for advocates of the poor may activate group interests that are difficult to organize and thus often overlooked.

c) Racial minorities.—Many racial minorities have the same difficulty receiving adequate medical care as the poor because of poverty or discrimination or both.

d) The elderly.—The old rely on health services more than any other age group. Despite a clear interest in medical care, their concerns about access, quality, and cost are easily overlooked in local politics.

e) Women.—Women require a different mix of health care services from men. They too have clear health care interests that are not represented because of their near-exclusion from local political processes.

f) Catchment areas.—Most health planning issues are, at bottom, issues of geography—where to introduce a new service or shut down an old hospital. With the exception of the criteria for metropolitan and rural representation the planning act attempts to replace areal with functional representation. But the two are not incompatible. Indeed, the empirical evidence suggests that geographic categories are emerging on many boards as counties, towns, and neighborhoods win representatives. To carry the process further, each HSA area could be broken into large catchment areas corresponding to the distribution of hospitals and health services. Representatives could be drawn from the various areas in approximate proportion to the population.

g) Special interests.—There should also be a miscellaneous category for interests that form a significant segment of the HSA's population—for example migrant workers, black-lung victims, or other persons exposed to special occupational hazards. These interests would be specified by the secretary of HHS, either on the recommendation of the state or by appeal of the special interest. However, it is crucial that this be recognized as a residual category, filled by discretion of the secretary, not as a sweeping grant of representation to interests that count themselves a significant segment of some population.

Numerous objections can be raised to this specification of health interests that deserve representation on HSA boards.[23] People representing these interests may not value health in the same way as those having the same objective characteristics— whether they be related to sex, income, or minority status. They may also be members of a wide variety of groups, each with partially conflicting interests. This leads to two distinct problems: first, the temptation to multiply the number of interest groups represented until the board becomes unmanageable; and second, the tendency for representatives to neglect to speak for those interests which might be shared.

Admittedly, the notion of consumer interests in health is crude. And while we can state that some provider interests work against the interests of all consumers, we cannot unambiguously specify consumer interests because of their diversity. But this diversity of consumer interests is itself the strongest argument for interest-based representation as a necessary, if not sufficient, condition for substantive representation of consumers. Without the quasi-corporatist amalgamations that interest representation can engender, consumer interests will simply not be pursued.

Naming specific representational categories will resolve some political and legal confusion. However, it suggests a deeper dilemma. As the categories we propose illustrate, the public is not neatly divisible into broad, roughly equivalent functional categories. How can the HSA claim legitimacy to act as a public body when it does not equally enfranchise the entire population?

Following Charles Anderson, we suggest two criteria for assessing the legitimacy of such quasi-corporatist boards in a liberal setting.[24] First, the criteria for representation must be embedded in the board's function. Who is seated depends on what the body is expected to accomplish. Policy goals guide the selection of representational categories and constituencies. Interests are granted representation because it is reasonable to include them given the nature and goals of the program. Within this rubric, particular attention might be paid to interests that past politics have subordinated despite the importance of health programs to them.

More important, however, legitimacy does not flow from elaborate representational schemes. The HSAs are administrative agencies established by Congress. Their legitimacy to act as public bodies lies in that legislative mandate. Functional representation schemes may stave off provider dominance, promote sensitivity to previously overlooked interests, or engender some accountability to local groups; but such achievements make HSAs no more or less legitimate than other congressional initiatives. Ultimately, geographic majoritarianism is supplemented, not supplanted.

Of course, designation of interests deserving representation is only one part of the resolution of representational difficulties in HSAs. Another part relates to the mechanisms that will guarantee substantive and accountable representation. The treatment of such policies follows our discussion of political imbalance and health issues.

IV. Imbalanced political arenas

The puzzles of representation are exacerbated in circumstances that stimulate representation without explicitly structuring it—where there are no elections, no clearly defined channels of influence, or only vague conceptions of constituency. The politics of regulatory agencies or regional authorities provides examples of these circumstances. Though representatives of groups commonly press their interests within such contexts, there are no systematic canvasses of relevant interests such as are provided by geographically based elections. It is unclear who legitimately merits representation or how representation should be organized and operated.[25]

Interest-group theorists address the problems of representation in precisely such political settings. In their view, unrepresented interests that are harmed coalesce and seek redress through the political system. Despite the absence of electoral mechanisms of representation, the theorists' conception of representation is central to their view of legitimate governance; every interest that is strongly felt can organize a group to speak for it. And, at their most sanguine, group theorists suggest that "all legitimate groups can make themselves heard at some crucial stage in the decision-making process."[26] Politics itself, in this view, is characterized by legions of groups bargaining at every level of government about policies that affect them. Government is viewed as the bargaining broker, policy choices as the consequences of mutual adjustment among the bargaining groups.

The group model is now partially in eclipse among political scientists.[27] One criticism is relevant here: groups that organize themselves for political action form a highly biased sample of affected interests.[28] Furthermore, that bias is predictable and recurs on almost every level of the political process. We refer to it as a tendency toward imbalanced political arenas, the unequal representation of equally legitimate but differently affected interests.

Imbalance is present in part because organizing for political action is difficult and costly. Even if considerable benefits are at stake, potential beneficiaries may choose not to pursue them. If collective goods are involved (i.e., if they are shared among members of a group regardless of the costs any one member paid to attain them), potential beneficiaries often let other members of the collectivity pay the costs and simply enjoy the benefits—the classic free-rider problem.

Free riders aside, the probability of political action generally varies with the material incentives. If either the benefits or costs of political action are concentrated, political action is more likely. A tax or a tariff on tea, for example, clearly and significantly affects the tea industry. To tea consumers, the tax is of marginal importance, a few dollars a year perhaps. The tea producers, with their livelihood at stake, are more likely to organize for political action, though even they are most likely to act if expected benefits outweigh costs. "The clearer the material incentives of the organization's members, the more prompt, focused and vigorous the action."[29]

The most common stimulant to group organization is threat to occupational status, as observers of American politics from de Tocqueville to David Truman have argued. If the group model overstated the facility and extent of group organization, some of its proponents isolated the most significant factor: narrow, concentrated producer interests are more likely to pay the costs of political action than broad, diffuse consumer interests.

Not only do concentrated interests have a larger incentive to engage in political action; they also act with two notable advantages. First, they typically have ongoing organizations with staff and other resources available. This dramatically lowers the marginal cost of political action. Second, most organizations have an expertise that rivals or exceeds that of any other political interest, even government agencies. Their superior grasp, and sometimes monopoly, of relevant information translates into political influence. The more technical an area, the more powerful the advantage, but it is almost always present to some extent.

In sum, two phenomena work to unbalance political arenas: unequal interests and disproportionate resources. The two are interrelated—groups with more at stake will invest more to secure an outcome. However, the distinction warrants emphasis for it has important policy implications, Attempts to stimulate countervailing powers by making resources available to subordinate groups will fail if they do not account for differing incentives in their employment. For example, even a resource such as equal access to policymakers (now the goal of considerable political effort) is meaningless if the incentives to utilize it over time are grossly unequal. The reverse case—equal interests, unequal resources—is too obvious to require comment. But that clarity should not obscure the fact that the dilemma of imbalance is deeper than the obvious inequality of group resources suggests.

Naturally, diffuse consumer interests are not always somnolent. There are purposive as well as material incentives to political action. A revolt against a sales tax might necessitate cuts in programs that benefit specific groups—diffuse payers defeating concentrated beneficiaries. Tea drinkers may be swept into political action, even to the point of dumping tea into Boston Harbor. Both are examples of diffuse interests uniting for political action. Such coalitions tend to have a grass-roots style of organization. Since sustained, long-term political action requires careful organization, they tend to be temporary. With the end of political deliberation, the group disbands or sets out in search of new issues. Concentrated interests, however, carry on, motivated by the same material incentives that first prompted political action.

The advantages of organized groups increase after a policy's inception. Such groups can be expected to pursue the policy through the stages of implementation and administration. Administrative politics are far less visible than legislative ones. They are not bounded by discrete decisions, and they are cluttered with technical detail rather than the emotive symbols likely to arouse diffuse constituencies. The policy focus of program administration is dispersed—temporally, conceptually, even geographically. Concentrated groups are much more likely to sustain a commitment to participate.

Administrative processes may even grow biased to the point that other affected parties are shut out from deliberations that concern them. Important decisions are made in agencies and bureaus that define, qualify, or even subvert original legislative intent. For example, Congress included a consumer participation provision in the Hill-Burton Act, but the implementing agency never wrote the regulations for it. When consumers overcame the imbalance of interests and sued for participation, they were denied standing. Since the regulations had never been written, consumer representatives had no entry into the policymaking process.[30]

The major question for HSAs is how to overcome these tendencies and balance the politics of health or even promote consumer control. The law's emphasis on participation, its naive conception of representation, and the political economy of health all point to a continuation of imbalanced health planning arenas. The HSAs were created to exert control over health providers, yet the major issue concerning their governing boards is how to avoid provider domination.

V. Representing consumer interests: overcoming the political obstacles

The task is overcoming political imbalance rather than just getting consumers on health planning boards. This section suggests how more effective representation of and accountability to local health interests might be established.

The HSA staffs could help consumers achieve political parity. Staffs have considerable expertise in issues of medical care and health. Occupying full-time positions in health planning, they have a concentrated interest in the industry. If they ally with providers or fail to take consumers seriously, they will surely undermine consumer representatives who cannot match the combined expertise of providers and staff. The support of the staff is essential to an active consumer role on HSA boards. The problem is systematically harnessing the market-balancing potential of the staff to consumer interests.

The most direct approach is to restructure the HSAs so that part of the professional staff is placed under consumer control—to be selected and accountable to the consumers. The tasks of these staff members could be specified in any number of ways, but the critical function would be providing professional (i.e., expert, full-time) support to the consumer effort.

Another potential for balancing the health planning market lies in organizations that already exist within the consumer population.[31] The very existence of these groups attests to a commitment to enhance the life circumstances of some part of the population. Furthermore, they have already paid the costs of organizing. We can expect them to devote attention to issues in a relatively sustained manner; and they can often overcome low expertise by redeploying their staffs. Representatives from these groups will have clearly defined constituencies, experience in organizational politics, and resources at their disposal. These attributes will help them both in identifying group interests and in pursuing them, regardless of their other characteristics. Even minorities suing for representation in Texas, for example, were willing to accept whites representing blacks if the NAACP selected them. It is telling that much of the litigation challenging HSA boards comes from organizations formed to further the rights or general circumstances of disadvantaged groups within the consumer population.

The empirical evidence that exists supports our contention. The poverty boards of the 1960s (particularly the War on Poverty's Community Action Projects) tended to be most capable when their members were selected by organizations. Impressionistic evidence from some HSAs in which organizations have been involved in selection suggests similar experiences.

Ideally, then, the imbalanced political features of health planning will be tempered by two mechanisms—one internal to the HSA (staff assigned to the consumer representatives), the other external (selection of representatives by groups). We expect the former to facilitate organization and expertise among the consumer representatives, the latter to improve substantive representation and heighten their accountability.

Various reform groups have called for election of consumer representatives in a model roughly based on the selection of school boards. The surface plausibility of the proposal should not be permitted to obscure its difficulties. One problem with direct election of representatives to HSA boards stems from the failure of most Americans to consider themselves part of an ongoing health care community. They typically seek care sporadically and do not conceive of health care in terms of local systems. Both factors distinguish health planning from education or housing issues, where specific elections may be more effective.

Evidence from other programs supports the view that elections are problematic; less than 3 percent of the eligible population voted for local poverty boards in Philadelphia, less than 1 percent in Los Angeles. Those who did vote were moved to do so by personal, not policy, considerations. Overwhelmingly, they voted for neighbors and personal acquaintances. The policy formulated by these representatives was, predictably, particularistic. It helped their friends, not the community or the interests they ostensibly represented. Representatives generated little community interest or support. They tended to be ineffective advocates.

The evidence from HSAs that have held elections is strikingly similar—low turnout at the polls and high turnover among representatives. Representatives are uncertain of their task and their constituency. Furthermore, direct elections have facilitated the takeover of entire boards by single organizations. In northeastern Illinois, for example, abortion foes captured the HSA, linking every health concern to their own preoccupation; in Illinois, Arkansas, and Massachusetts, provider institutions chartered buses and flooded the polling places with hospital workers who voted for docile consumer representatives.[32]

Elections are appealing to reformers because they permit the public to choose health planning representatives directly; theoretically, the representatives can be held accountable with relative ease. In practice, the predictable electoral apathy of diffuse interests undermines direct elections as the mechanism of accountability to consumer constituencies.

VI. Health policy and the HSAs

The National Health Planning and Resources Development Act's vision of representation is impossibly flawed, but not irretrievably so. We have suggested one plan for achieving reasonably effective consumer representation and balancing provider dominance. But representing consumers, overcoming imbalance, even discerning the public interest in HSAs will not alter the American health system in any profound fashion. The HSA mandate—limiting costs, expanding access, and improving the quality of health—reaches far beyond the agencies' capabilities. Measured by these standards, the act's program is trivial—more symbol and rhetoric than significant potential.

Because the HSAs' planning functions are largely isolated from the process of health resource allocation, planning becomes too often a smoke screen, an empty symbol, or simply wheel spinning. The agencies' difficulties of limited authority are compounded by the uncertain relationship between HSAs and the rest of government. In their reliance on "scientific planning," HSAs are yet another manifestation of the effort to find objective solutions to political choices. But scientific planning cannot relieve the tensions between national demands and local desires or between representing community interests and programmatic efficiency.[33]

Despite these problems, the health planning law does have significance, and that significance lies in its stimulation of a broad range of consumer interests.

Viewed as an effort to organize communities into caring about their own health systems, it is the largest program of its kind. And one that could influence health politics long after its particular institutional manifestation—HSA planning boards —has been forgotten.

Notes

1 PL 93–641 § 1512(b)(3)(c)(iii)(2).
2 Aldamuy et al. v. Pirro et al., C.A. No. 76 CV-204 (N.D.N.Y., April 7, 1977).
3 Texas Association of Community Organizations for Reform Now (ACORN) et al. v. Texas Area V Health Systems Agency et al., C.A. No. S-76–102-CA (E.D. Texas, Sherman Div., March 1, 1977).
4 Rakestraw et al. v. Califano et al., C.A. No. C77–635A (N.D.Ga., Atlanta Div., filed April 22, 1977); The Louisiana Association of Community Organizations for Reform Now (ACORN) et al. v. New Orleans Area/Bayou Rivers Health Systems Agency et al., C.A. No. 17–361 (E.D. La., filed March 15, 1977); Amos et al. v. Central California Health Systems Agency et al., C.A. No. 76–174 (E.D. Calif., filed Sept. 10, 1976).
5 See Wayne Clark, "Placebo or Cure? State and Local Health Planning Agencies in the South," photocopied (Atlanta: Southern Governmental Monitoring Project, Southern Regional Council, 1977), for examples of such reports.
6 H.F. Pitkin, *The Concept of Representation* (Berkeley and Los Angeles: University of California Press, 1967), p. 3.
7 This is not so for certain groups—e.g., the parents of children with special diseases— as our colleague Owen Fiss points out.
8 T.R. Marmor, "Consumer Representation: Beneath the Consensus, Many Difficulties," *Trustee* 30 (1977): 37–40.
9 John Adams, cited in Pitkin, *Concept of Representation*, p. 60.
10 For notable formulations of this common idea, see Edmund Burke, "The English Constitutional System," in *Representation*, ed. H.F. Pitkin (New York: Atherton Press, 1969); or Alexander Hamilton et al., *Federalist Papers*, no. 10, by James Madison (New York: Modern Library, Inc., 1937).
11 Judged by the model of a jury, such standards are unnecessary; representativeness is the condition for legitimacy. We want to thank Owen Fiss for stressing this competing model of representation.
12 J.D. Greenstone and P.E. Peterson, *Race and Authority in Urban Politics: Consumer Participation and the War on Poverty* (Chicago: University of Chicago Press, 1973), chap. 6. We have profited immensely from this analysis.
13 41 Federal Register 12812 (March 26, 1976), § 122.114.
14 Ibid., §§ 122.104(b)(I)(viii) and 122.109(e)(3).
15 Ibid., §§ 122.104(a)(8) and 122.104(b)(7).
16 Ibid., § 122.107(c)(2).
17 Ibid., § 122.107(c)(3).
18 We are grateful to our colleague Douglas Yates for pointing out this distinction.
19 There are indications that precisely this tension is asserting itself as HHS, e.g., drafts guidelines and local communities protest that they do not apply in their specific situations.
20 PL 93–641 § 1515(c)(1).
21 Allowing local politics to define constituencies is fraught with trouble. Note the cycle: Congress, claiming that many interests were shut out of local politics, established

entirely new governmental structures for health planning and mandated that they be "broadly representative." That requirement is itself so broad that it is unclear what interests qualify: the decision is left to the local political process which Congress sought to bypass in the first place. The vagaries of congressional consistency aside, local selection of the interests to be represented will not break the cycle of litigation. Interests that are shunned will sue, arguing that the local process which excluded them does not conform to the federal mandate to broadly represent.

22 As Owen Fiss has pointed out to us, the impossibility of mirroring a community's demography is equally true for specifying its health interests. But treating the selection of interests as a political choice need not reach the impossibility test of mirroring all interests.

23 We have profited particularly from Albert Weale's incisive comments on the topic of interests.

24 Charles Anderson, "Political Design and the Representation of Interests," *Comparative Political Studies* 10 (1977): 127–52.

25 The problem is less nettlesome in legislatures. On a practical level, lobbying legislatures appears only marginally effective: analysts have generally found that politicians are most likely to follow their own opinions or apparent consituency desires. More important, there is at least a formal representation of every voting citizen. Of course, this does not minimize the complexities of electoral representation. But elective systems do afford a systematic canvas of community sentiment, however vague a guide it may be to policy formulation.

26 Robert Dahl, *A Preface to Democratic Theory* (Chicago: University of Chicago Press, 1964), p. 137.

27 See Andrew McFarland, "Recent Social Movements and Theories of Power in America," microfilmed (paper delivered at the American Political Science Association Convention, Washington, D.C., August 1979).

28 Recall the epigram, "The flaw in the pluralist heaven is that the heavenly chorus sings with a strong upper class accent. Probably about 90 percent of the people cannot get into the pressure system," by E.E. Schattschneider, *The Semisovereign People* (Hinsdale, Ill.: Dryden Press, 1960), p. 34.

29 James Q. Wilson, *Political Organizations* (New York: Basic Books, 1973), p. 318; [chapter 3 in this volume].

30 Rand Rosenblatt, "Health Care Reform and Administrative Law, a Structural Approach," *Yale Law Journal* (1978): 243–336.

31 P.C. Schmitter, "An Inventory of Analytical Pluralist Propositions" (monograph, University of Chicago, Department of Political Science, Autumn 1975).

32 See Mark Kleiman, "What's in It for Us: A Consumer Analysis of the 1979 Health Planning Amendments," *Health Law Project Library Bulletin* 4 (1979): 329–36; and Barry Checkoway, "Citizens on Local Health Planning Boards: What Are the Obstacles?" *Journal of the Community Development Society* 10 (1979): 101–16.

33 For a fuller discussion of these issues, see the version of this paper published in *Health and Society* 58 (1980): 125–65.

5. American health planning and the lessons of comparative policy analysis

THEODORE R. MARMOR, AMY BRIDGES

Introduction

Our interest is in the implications for the United States of comparative health planning processes and effects. Our materials are case studies of eighteen countries presented at the Pan American Health Organization/World Health Organization Health Planning Conference held in Copenhagen, Denmark, May 31–June 4, 1977—studies of nations as diverse as Honduras and West Germany, Pakistan and Finland. These twin features—comparative lessons as the object, and diverse systems as the subject of scrutiny—deserve some preliminary comment before proceeding to the central question of what the United States can learn from abroad about how to improve its health planning efforts.

Cross-national policy studies permit a variety of different types of learning: (1) they advance the limits of what is possible and teach us different ways of regarding familiar problems; (2) they allow us to weigh more carefully the determinants of policy, distinguishing what is culturally specific from what is generic, thus highlighting the difference between the more or less manipulable features of given policies; (3) they provide information for evaluating new policy options, and (4) they help identify the ways the institutional structure of policy implementation shapes the politics of administration.

These topics of learning raise quite different questions, focus one's attention differentially, and call upon one of two basic research designs. One is termed the "different systems" design; its principle is to increase the variation across national systems and to seek generalizations that hold over a wide range of examples. Useful for identifying new options as well, such a research strategy increases the complexity and the validity of posited relationships. The second design— usually referred to as the "similar systems" approach—tries to control for system variation by grouping broadly similar sociopolitical systems. Most useful for

From the *Journal of Health Politics, Policy and Law*, 5 (3): 419–430, 1980. Copyright © 1980 by the Department of Health Administration, Duke University. Reprinted with permission.

predicting the effects of given policies, this design has the vice of its virtue: it restricts the range of options to be studied. Our discussion of lessons for American planning will draw from both these approaches.

Our study of health planning processes in eighteen countries[1] is an effort to draw policy-relevant lessons for the United States. There is a common impetus to health planning in the United States and other industrial countries: the concern to curb rapidly escalating costs. With other advanced countries, the United States shares a set of goals for reshaping the delivery of medical care. We can anticipate our argument by saying that what is striking, given these shared features, is the peculiarity of our medical care planning arrangements. For example, although many countries have tried to integrate regional or local governmental authorities with health planning institutions, Health Systems Agencies (HSAs) stand out as independent of elected state and municipal governments; and while elsewhere elected officials are seen as advocates of the general interest, HSAs attempt to provide for representation of various publics. Since there is reason to think our arrangements for medical care planning may not be effective, we may profit by looking at our foreign counterparts.

That examination is not for the purpose of discovering which country is "best" at health care planning; rather, it initially surveys the whole set of countries for which information was gathered in order to identify the range of approaches to medical care planning. Following this is a presentation of planning processes that are common across diverse systems. The discussion then turns to a set of countries similar to the United States in order to explore the policy objectives we share with them, and to identify arrangements that may be of value to us.[2]

Two preliminary discussions are in order before turning to the foregoing topics. First, we outline some explanations for the current form of United States medical care planning institutions. Second, we provide some clarification of the concept of planning.

HSAs as planning institutions

P.L. 93-641 states its purpose of facilitating "the development of recommendations for a national health planning policy" and augmenting "area-wide and state planning for services, manpower, and facilities." The institutions P.L. 93-641 created, Health Service Agencies (HSAs), reflect the American political experience of the 1960s and 1970s in two respects. First, like the Community Action and the early Model Cities programs, HSAs operate independently of, rather than through, local government. The rationale for the earlier programs was that direct federal intervention was necessary to counter the racially exclusive politics of local government, that federal money sent directly to minority (or poor) communities would enable them to organize and, as a result, be included in local political coalitions.[3] In the case of HSAs the rationale is less clear, and the strategy may be equally problematic. American experience with other regional arms of federal institutions (state Agencies on Aging, for example[4]) demonstrates that, if they are to be effective, these agencies need to make alliances with state and local government officials. In addition, the European cases as well as some third world cases fail to support the sharp separation of planning from decision making. As the author of a Bolivian case study wrote: "One realization was that the achievement of planning goals had to be the responsibility of the politician."[5]

The concern for consumer representation on HSAs also reflects the experience of the 1960s. One source of this concern is the public interest advocacy movement, whose legacy is suspicion of professional autonomy, a distrust of leaving the governance of health institutions to those who have traditionally dominated them.[6] The other source is the poverty programs, particularly community action programs and neighborhood health centers, in which participation by the poor was given much formal significance. This history means that the future of health representation is likely to carry over some of the goals of the poverty movement. As a result, representation in HSAs has been geared to the presence of representatives of particular groups, rather than the interest of the public. Also, the legal mandate for such representation has resulted in a mass of litigation by those who feel their interest remains unrepresented.[7]

A number of distinctive features of the health industry make it difficult to reconcile participatory goals and the governance of health institutions. One is that most persons use hospitals sporadically, quite unlike the way they use schools or apartments. This makes it difficult to identify health communities from which to recruit constituents. It also means that medical care may be more problematic as a potential rallying element for constituency pressures and communities may be harder to mobilize politically than, for example, on issues of rental housing or the provision of daily urban services. In an era of constrained resources and consequent service cutbacks, however, community mobilization around health issues is already increasing. Whether HSAs have the power or the will to respond to popular pressures—even when the required quota of community representatives is present—remains for the moment an open question.

If the way of institutionalizing the concern for community representation in health care planning is peculiar to the United States, the concern itself is not. How representatives of community or public interests are best selected and involved in the planning process is a question to which comparative analysis gives a variety of possible answers, as we will see below.

HSAs represent a step away from our historically noninterventionist policies with respect to the delivery of medical care. The absence of major governmental intervention in the medical care sector, however, leaves American planning institutions in an anomalous position compared with their counterparts in similar systems. Elsewhere, the separate planning programs that have grown up emerged long after the expansion of public financing of medical care. In Scotland, Germany, and Finland,[8] for example, concerns about the impact of health expenditures on the social policy budget preceded the establishment of new planning institutions. In Canada—a recent addition to the set of advanced countries with national health insurance programs—interest in cost containment and local planning have gone hand in hand. At the very least, then, those governments have greater control over the resources for which they are attempting to plan.

Where public financing is still contentious, as in Israel and Japan, efforts to create planning institutions have proven very controversial, and have been resisted vociferously by health pressure groups. The situation in the United States is similar, insofar as planning activities and resource allocation through provider reimbursement remain widely separate here. The experiences of other countries cast doubt on the viability of such an arrangement, however it was determined.

Thinking about planning

Our discussion of health planning in other countries should be preceded by some clarification as to the structures and processes which are being examined. Three major distinctions must be made; the first regards planning itself. On one hand, there is the activity of making plans; on the other, there are decisions about the allocation of resources which express planning assumptions about what is sought and how to achieve it. There is no necessary institutional connection between the two activities; consequently, the processes and structures of health planning are ambiguously defined. How nations, in fact, plan for health—that is, make allocation decisions about future states—is not exhaustively illuminated (indeed, is sometimes not seriously touched) by studies of how *official* health planning bodies operate. Put another way, we have two subjects: the processes leading to effective choice about future states of health care affairs, and the behavior of health planning organizations.[9]

Further, one ought to distinguish between planning for health and planning for medical care services. The factors affecting health are far broader than medical care services, as P.L. 93-641 recognized. What it is that we or others plan for must be identified before trying to extract lessons from cross-national experiences. Many of the serious planning efforts undertaken by other countries have only concerned medical care services.

A third important distinction is between planning for decisions and planning for targets. Structured thinking about the distribution of health status, the susceptibility of problems to current technology, and the costs of alternative courses of remedial action are tasks which characterize informed decision making. Whether goal-setting is useful depends on the connection between choosing goals and the capacity to implement resource decisions to reach them. Where the connection is loose, target planning varies between empty exercise and smoke screens for inaction. As a consequence, our emphasis is on planning as political process, rather than on its technical or rationalistic aspects.

Planning and authoritative decisions

In an era of fiscal strain, it is not surprising that the Ministry of Finance (or its equivalent) figures most prominently, across the national systems we examined, in the role of authoritative decision maker: health planning and decisions about the use of resources go hand in hand.

The integration of planning and decisions about resources commonly takes two forms. First, at the national level, representatives of the Ministry of Finance participate in planning organizations. This is the case in Colombia, Bolivia, Ecuador, Finland, Israel, Sweden, Germany, and Great Britain. In Sweden, for example, "the treasury has had the main influence over the five year planning and budgeting" and annual revision of five year plans "is...closely connected with the yearly budgeting process."[10]

Second, planning and decisions about resources are passed on to regional and local authorities when the national government supplies guidelines and budget ceilings for them. With known resources, regional and local levels of government may make choices and plans. This is the arrangement in Scotland and, with some differences, Finland. In Scotland major resource allocations are made at the center: the Scottish Ministry of Health sets the budget limits and allocations within broad categories. The role of local area planners is to work out the details of that allocation, to consult with affected parties, to gain compliance with allocations, and to make and execute plans for detailed implementation. One cannot help but note the seriousness of the consultative and adjustive role of area planners; at the same time, the limits on their choices are clearly set.

The Finnish case marks a variant of the model of fused plan-making and resource allocation. Local health boards are the dominant management and plan-making units in that system. They administer primary care and some inpatient and long-term care services. Using guidelines provided by the central government, local boards in Finland, as in Scotland, make plans as instruments for maintaining control of the distribution of overall health resources in a local area. In addition, local boards in Finland, county councils in Sweden, and *land* governments in Germany have taxing powers to secure resources for medical care; their role in planning—but also the possibility for slippage from national objectives— is consequently greater.[11]

Where planning and resource control are not unified institutionally, it is the latter that is decisive. Two examples are offered here. In Japan, requests for funding are made by administrators of categorical health programs; choices between programs, and the relative emphasis given to each, are made when the Ministry of Finance allocates each its budget. In Germany, after painstaking efforts to make long- and related short-term hospital building plans, alarm about costs at the national level provoked a "stop to construction" order, which made those plans inoperative, and will probably cause some deterioration in the general planning process as well.

Planning conducted in isolation from decision making authority, then, is likely to be ineffective. And, since the key to the effective exercise of authority is control of resources, planners (or, for that matter, governments) without such control will be unable to meet their objectives.

Planning and bargaining

Health planning potentially affects a variety of interests: hospitals, insurers,[12] medical care professionals, consumers, political authorities (local, regional, and national agencies, as well as elected officials), and political parties. Most of these have their own aims, prerogatives, and autonomy to protect and goals to be realized; with varying degrees of ability and varying amounts of resources, they will organize to secure those ends. We will review some of these needs and goals, and then turn to their relation to the planning process.

Hospitals have a stake in expansion, access to patients, and prestige. They resist efforts at coordination (which tends to reduce the range of services any single hospital can provide) and at service provision in primary care institutions like clinics. Insurers have an interest in shifting costs from their members to government, while maintaining the appearance of facilitating the provision of service. These goals make insurers likely to resist attempts to rationalize insurance by nationalizing its administration.

Professionals have interests in retaining discretion about appropriate levels of care, making choices about where to practice, and in maintaining or increasing their income. Consumers want access to a broad range of services, and often express desires for continuity of care and opposition to impersonality, bureaucratism, or discrimination in the delivery of services.

Finally, political authorities typically attempt to pursue goals of coordination, improved access and, sometimes, improved health status. Particular political authorities may have special goals of cost control or self-aggrandizement; regional and local authorities may compete with national authorities over resources and discretion. Since many of the goals of nongovernmental groups may be embraced by the demand for more services while planners and governmental authorities generally want coordination and cost control; planning not only affects providers and consumers, it threatens them.

We can examine the role of consumers to show the variety of institutional settings in which bargaining takes place. At one extreme is Yugoslavia, where local health planning is the result of authoritative negotiations between representatives of providers and representatives of consumers. With funding arrangements comparable to those of other nations we have discussed (guidelines and a portion of resources come from the national level of government, additional resources and decisions are adjusted to needs determined at the local level), Yugoslavia simply grants political authority to consumers whose money is being spent, and to professionals who are to provide services. Their negotiations resolve, on an annual basis, familiar issues of capital-intensive medicine versus primary care, wage levels, and—from the consumer point of view—the opportunity cost of increasing medical care spending rather than using resources for other social services.

A more common arrangement, found in France, Germany, Sweden, and Finland, is one in which the interests of consumers are incorporated into medical care planning, not by the presence of "consumer representatives" but by elected officials. Claims that this leads to public representation are probably best grounded when the elected officials are local (as in the Swedish county councils) and medical care planning is a major part of their responsibility. It is interesting, in this respect, that German federal policy requires that sickness funds, hospitals, and governmental agencies all be "heard" in the planning process at the state level; in one state, private health insurance interests, doctors' organizations, private charitable providers and denominational organizations were legally incorporated into the consultative process, while consumers' representatives were not. This is the opposite extreme from the Yugoslav or British cases where consumers are not formally involved in planning. As a result, Germany represents (with some reservation, expressed below) a case of provider captivity more than anything else.

Finally, in Great Britain the large scale development of consumer councils explicitly tries to identify separate advocates of patient interest. Specifically designed to balance fiscal accountability to the central government with responsiveness to consumer views at the local level, community health councils have not revolutionized the National Health Service; nor have they been empty exercises.[13]

The absence of a formal role for consumers does not always disable them from exerting pressure. In Japan, the lack of national planning structures is balanced by local health planning efforts that are largely the result of popular mobilization and political activities. In the United States, groups that have felt unrepresented have gone to the courts; communities that have felt adversely affected by hospital closing decisions have protested. These activities illustrate a more general point: where the institutional role provided for participation is unsatisfactory or nonexistent, consumers or others will mobilize their resources to exert pressures outside the planning process. Most often, these pressures will be exercised to block implementation of cutbacks.

In Germany, national plans have been blocked at the state level by provider groups acting through the Christian Democratic Union (CDU).[14] In 1972, attempts by the national ministry to revise the 1965 Federal Tariff Structure were defeated when legislation was blocked by states acting on behalf of physician groups. The 1965 tariff structure, intended to control prices in a fee-for-service system, was ineffective because negotiations at the state level between physicians and individual sickness funds continued. A similar process occurred in France, where the need for regional variation, incorporated in the national law, worked in practice to make national price guidelines meaningless. At a minimum, more participatory structures might have served to forge consensus on policies.

Planning and the delivery of medical care

Across the advanced market societies, concerns about the medical care system, goals for reshaping it, and administrative and political arrangements for implementing these goals are converging. The most pressing concern, cost, is related to a critique of the uncoordinated expansion of capital intensive hospital-centered medical care. At the same time, it is felt that the provision of primary care is insufficient, as is an emphasis on preventive medicine, and attention to the environment. Finally, in the United States and Europe, there are perceived geographical inequities in access to and supply of medical care, particularly primary care.

The response has been encouragement of regional coordination, incentives to group practice and the expansion of clinics—independent of hospitals—to provide primary care, and a redistribution of resources through the national government to overcome regional inequities. The institutional form for these policies has already been sketched: in Scotland, England and Wales, France, Germany, Sweden and Finland, regional and local planning and administration are conducted by authorities whose boundaries are coterminous with the boundaries of political subunits (states, provinces, municipalities or districts). Incentives to group practice and the provision of primary care, and disincentives to hospital expansion have been established. Increased coordination among institutional providers means attention to the division of labor between them, and an effort to establish a "hierarchy," with different institutions providing primary, secondary, and tertiary care.

It is worth emphasizing that the goals of HSAs and, in some respects, their structure are not altogether dissimilar to those of planning agencies in other countries. P.L. 93–641 lists among its goals the development of medical group practices, multi-institutional coordination of services to prevent duplication and, along with that, a clearer division of labor among medical institutions, or "hierarchification." While HSAs' boundaries have not been as consistently coterminous with political boundaries as have those of their European counterparts (and HSA ties to state and local governments are more tenuous), they represent a comparable emphasis on alleviating regional inequalities and promoting coordination within regions.

Two subsets from the similar nations are particularly relevant to projecting the likelihood of HSA success at reaching these goals: first, the nations that share a federal structure and, second, those where, as in the United States, medical care continues to be dominated by private providers.

Our sample of cases is not suited to drawing generalizations about the effects of federalism on planning processes. Indeed, where one is using the most similar systems approach, the countries should share a broad array of factors likely to determine policy formulation and consequences. Whether measured by levels of economic development, types of political regime, or modes of medical care financing, our eighteen cases vary, literally, all over the map. Restricting the set to advanced industrial nations with liberal democratic regimes, the cases shrink from fourteen to at most four: Scotland, Finland, Germany, and, arguably, Japan.

For purposes of comparative federalism, that leaves a single case, Germany. Ideally, we would want to study Australia and Canada along with Germany, but the materials were not available for that purpose. Therefore, we are restricted to speculation about federalism. Where sub-national states have traditionally overseen medical matters, there is an obvious block to uniform implementation of national policy. Where states can raise funds to supplement central subsidies for medical ones, variation is entailed. But what is striking about the planning discussion among the advanced industrial states is not federalism *per se*, but decentralization: the division of labor between national and sub-national units of government. From that standpoint, federalism is but one version of the centralization being recommended, with its attendant problems.

What makes the United States most anomalous is the rationalistic case of its planning mission and the pluralistic features of the health finance structure its planners confront. Cost containment undeniably motivated the expansion of authority for the new HSAs (as compared with the earlier Comprehensive Health Planning Agencies). However, the separation of the HSA structure for planning and the financing of most medical care by other third parties are, comparatively, still striking. The experience of other countries casts doubt on the effectiveness of such an arrangement, whatever its particular set of American determinants.

Planning to reshape the delivery of medical care requires intervention, or the creation of incentives and disincentives, to change the behavior and organization of providers. As the authors of the Swedish report pointed out, most prior efforts at increasing access to medical care, and the quality of medical care, took the form of reducing financial barriers through insurance and promoting the growth of the medical care sector. The current effort is, by contrast, directed at the supply side of the medical service relationship. In countries like the United States, Germany, France, the Netherlands and Israel, where the provision of medical care is dominated by the private sector, government controls a smaller proportion of medical care resources and faces stronger opposition to its attempted interventions.

We can see the difficulties of lack of control over resources in our own experience with hospital reimbursement. In the absence of unified cost-accounting procedures, and short of continuous auditing, it is almost impossible for government to insure that its monies are used only for the purposes it approves.[15] Experiences elsewhere have been similar. In France and the Netherlands, for example, national plans for regionalization were ineffective because insurance funds, operating independently of regional authorities, provided financial incentives to providers.[16] Like the United States, Germany and France attempted to restrict facilities construction by denying government monies to proposed facilities not in accord with government plans. In France, this sanction was found to be insufficient, and such construction, even without government funds, is illegal.

Similar difficulties exist in the case of individual providers. It is very difficult for governments to provide incentives great enough to move doctors to underserved areas. One response, common to the United States and some European countries, is to increase the supply of physician substitutes, whose opportunities in the private sector have traditionally been restricted.

These issues, and the broader question of the political nature of planning, will become more pressing in the United States as National Health Insurance proposals resurface on the legislative agenda. If government is not simply to pump resources into the medical care sector, which it can ill afford to do (and, some would argue, if government spending is to have an impact on health status as well as on individual pocketbooks), then the design of our planning institutions must enable them to mediate the competing political claims that will inevitably arise. Finally, their authority must be equal to the task of implementing the policies that result from that political process.

Notes

1 Our review is based on case studies prepared for a conference sponsored by the Pan American Health Organization/World Health Organization, held in Copenhagen, Denmark, May 31–June 4, 1977. Included among them are studies of: Bolivia, Brazil, Colombia, Ecuador, Finland, Honduras, Israel, Japan, Mexico, Pakistan, Philippines, Scotland, Sweden, Thailand, West Germany and Yugoslavia. Also useful was Jean Blanpain et al., *International Approaches to Health Resources Development for National Health Programs* (Louvain, Belgium: Institute for European Health Services Research, 1977), a study of England and Wales, the Netherlands, France, Sweden, and the Federal Republic of Germany.
2 This approach to comparative policy analysis has already been discussed in chapter 2 of this volume.
3 F.F. Piven, "The Urban Crisis, Who Got What, and Why," in *The Politics of Turmoil: Essays on Poverty, Race and the Urban Crisis*, eds.: F.F. Piven and R.A. Cloward (New York: Vintage, 1975).

4 T. R. Marmor and E. A. Kutza, *Analysis of Federal Regulations Related to Aging: Legislative Barriers to Coordination Under Title III*. Report submitted to the United States Department of Health, Education, and Welfare, The Administration on Aging under Grant No. DHEW (SRS) 90-A-364-01, October 1975.

5 See the Bolivian case cited in footnote 1 (above), p. 18.

6 J. Metsch and J. Veney, "Consumer Participation and Social Accountability," *Medical Care* 14 (April 1976): 283–93.

7 See chapter 4.

8 Blanpain et al., p. 14.

9 Similar distinctions are found in O. Gish, "Alternative Approaches to Health Planning," *Les Carnets de l'Enfance*, No. 33, January–March 1976 (Geneva: UNICEF, 1976).

10 See the Bolivian case cited in footnote 1 (above), pp. 19, 28.

11 Contrast our own difficulties arriving at an appropriate division of labor between nations and states. For a discussion, see B.C.Vladeck, "The Design of Failure: Health Policy and the Structure of Federalism," *Journal of Health Politics, Policy and Law* 4 (Fall, 1979): 522–35.

12 Other interests, of course, also work through parties. It is interesting that Israel's Labor Party, and Germany's Social Democratic Party, because of their historical recruitment of membership through sickness funds (workers' insurance associations), have opposed state provision of health insurance–a striking contrast to the role of labor parties in England, Sweden or Finland in securing national health insurance and government health services.

13 See, for a fuller report, R. Klein and J. Lewis, *The Politics of Consumer Representation* (London: Centre for Studies in Social Policy, 1976).

14 The Scottish case shows the way the allocation of decision making tasks has directed the attention of pressure groups. It is true that traditions in Great Britain of explicit consultation facilitate this process, but the clarity of responsibility reinforces the effects of the tradition. However, there is a further lesson to be drawn. The work of these consultative bodies is difficult. Gaining consensus is a demanding process, time-consuming, sometimes angering, always a drain on resources. What the Scottish case shows is that morale is an important variable. It will become a serious problem if the roles of local planning actors are ambiguous, their mission overstated, and their impact greatly diluted. Local HSAs should take this to heart. The grandiosity of their plans will not be matched by their political capacity or scope of authority. Too much of what happens in local health markets falls outside their jurisdiction: the terms of reimbursement, the closing down of facilities, the positive choice of places to expand, and the like. The Scottish authorities pay considerable attention to the problem; we would do well to copy their example.

15 J. Feder and B. Spitz, "The Politics of Hospital Payment," *Journal of Health Politics, Policy and Law* 4 (Fall, 1979): 435–63.

16 Blanpain et al., p. 14.

6. Doctors, politics and pay disputes: "pressure group politics" revisited

THEODORE R. MARMOR, DAVID THOMAS

Studies of medical politics usually emphasize one of the following types of inquiries: (*a*) analyzing the internal politics of medical organizations, as with Oliver Garceau's classic study of the American Medical Association;[1] (*b*) describing and explaining the roles individual physicians play in the political life of the community as voters, officials, or citizen participants in civic life;[2] or, (*c*) assessing the impact of medical groups and organizations on public policy, particularly health policy.[3] Harry Eckstein's widely known study of the British Medical Association is primarily a study of the third type, a discussion of the *channels of influence*, the *tactics*, and the *effectiveness* of the BMA in shaping public policy to its ends.

This paper comprises an essay review of the Eckstein work and a research report on medical payment disputes which the authors conducted in England, Sweden, and the United States, 1965–8. The research report tentatively suggests ways to correct the difficulties we identify in the Eckstein research, particularly problems that arise from Eckstein's failure to use comparative data to test his hypotheses explaining the influence of the BMA on health policy. Our larger concern, of which this study is a part, is an investigation of the outcomes of conflicts over the methods by which doctors ought to be paid in western industrial countries. England, Sweden, and the United States provide the primary comparative data, but we fortunately have extensive secondary evidence on other countries from the recently published work by William Glaser, *Paying the Doctor*. The first section discusses the Eckstein book; the second presents our preferred research alternative.

1. Eckstein examined

In pursuing the comparative politics of medical remuneration we turned naturally to Eckstein's pioneering study; for our purposes that work proved to be both

From the *British Journal of Political Science*, 2:421–442, 1972. Copyright © 1972 by Cambridge University Press.

An earlier version of the concluding section, "The Politics of Paying Physicians: US, UK, Sweden," was published in the *International Journal of Health Services*, 1:71–78, 1971.

unclear and incorrect. We here will concentrate on only one part of the Eckstein analysis: his attempt to theorize about the effectiveness of the BMA in influencing public policies that affect the interests of English physicians. Eckstein is concerned about other matters as well, in describing and accounting for the form, intensity, and scope of the BMA's pressure group politics, and in purportedly broader generalizations about groups of which this is a case. We shall comment on the latter issue as well but the former questions will be considered here only insofar as they pertain to the issue of BMA effectiveness. Our objections to Eckstein's work are both methodological and substantive.

Eckstein is interested both in why, in general, pressure groups are effective and why, in particular, the BMA appears to have been extremely successful in influencing the nature and scope of governmental health policies. He uses two case studies of past medical conflicts to 'illustrate' his general theory. He states, quite emphatically and correctly, that 'case studies never "prove" anything; their purpose is to illustrate generalizations which are established otherwise, or to direct attention towards such generalizations.'[4] But there is more to the relation of case studies and generalizations than that. This paper first considers the general theory of effectiveness offered in the opening section of *Pressure Group Politics*, and then assesses the account of BMA effectiveness by considering both Eckstein's own illustrations and evidence beyond his study on the general practitioner crisis, 1965–6.

Eckstein, despite his broad interest in pressure group influence, is not clear about what it would mean for a pressure group to be 'effective' at all. Rather, he catalogues the 'factors' which are determinants of whether such a group warrants such a description. It is uncertain whether Eckstein considers the satisfaction of group goals as the criterion of effectiveness, or whether the ability to triumph over the conflicting goals of other actors is the chief standard. This conceptual vagueness about effectiveness is a considerable handicap in evaluating Eckstein's work, though one could assess his theory for these two of the possible meanings of effectiveness: satisfaction of goals, and satisfaction of goals over opposition from the government or other groups. Despite this conceptual difficulty, Eckstein is convinced he is presenting a hypothesis about the effectiveness of all pressure groups, a set of general statements connecting various features of the political environment with the policy outcomes that measure the effectiveness of the pressure group.

What is the character of this theory? This question should be examined before looking at the case study application. 'Factors determining the effectiveness of pressure groups,' we are told, 'may be classified under three headings: (*a*) attributes of the pressure groups themselves; (*b*) attributes of the activities of government; (*c*) attributes of the governmental decision-making structure.'[5] Now it is not clear what kind of statement this is intended to be. Eckstein likely intends it to be a hypothesis.[6] Language such as 'factors determining the effectiveness' would seem to so indicate. Such language conjures up the prevailing hypothetical-deductive model of scientific explanation, which Eckstein surely accepts. Yet on its canons this is scarcely a hypothesis at all. Is it falsifiable? What would it mean to say that the 'attributes of the pressure groups themselves' plus the other two 'factors' did not affect the effectiveness of a given pressure group? These factors encompass virtually the range of plausible causal possibilities, but they are not marshalled in a significant; determinate relation.

In fact, this is a pre-theoretical rather than a theoretical formulation.[7] It is a very general set of categories in terms of which data may be set and hypotheses cast. The categories may or may not be useful; that can be decided only by using them determinately. To this end we need, for instance, an assertion about a specifiable relationship between the structure of government and the activities of pressure groups that in principle is falsifiable; that is, for which one could imagine contrary evidence.

The attributes of the pressure group itself constitute Eckstein's first class of factors. Rich or poor, large or small, centralized or decentralized—such group features may be important; but to list them is not to make a hypothesis about pressure group effectiveness. Eckstein states, 'certain characteristics of groups are likely to determine decisively their effectiveness under almost any pattern of policies or structure of government (popular government, of course): for example, physical resources, size, organization, cohesiveness, and political skills.'[8] One can imagine hypotheses which employ some of these features as independent variables and make testable claims about their relationship to dependent variables like 'effectiveness.' But, stated in this way, Eckstein's formulation does not constitute a hypothesis at all; it is only a catalogue of possibly relevant phenomena. The same criticism applies to the two other classes of 'factors' determining pressure group effectiveness, but it is redundant to repeat the above analysis for them.

Eckstein does indeed make a number of very specific observations under these headings, but in their *ad hoc* character they do no more than marginally increase the plausible utility of the categories. The movement in *Pressure Group Politics* from the very general to the very concrete neglects the vital need for mediating, determinate connectives. In a later work, Eckstein complains about those social scientists who 'save' their hypotheses by redefining them in the face of unexpected factual findings.[9] One might say that Eckstein himself has not so much saved his hypotheses in the BMA study as innoculated them against the test of proof or disproof.[10] In short, no body of data could be appropriately manipulated to prove or disprove Eckstein's claims at this general level.

Thus far, we have discussed one of the major difficulties in Eckstein's study: the lack of a usable theory of pressure group effectiveness. We will how turn to the relationship between hypothesis and evidence in the case studies Eckstein presents. Discussion will focus on the implicit hypotheses which Ecksein actually employs instead of the above 'theory.' We will then show how the failure to use comparative data accounts for those problems in Eckstein's case studies which are not attributable to the general scheme.

Two chapters, each containing a detailed and fascinating history of a prolonged negotiation between the BMA and the Ministry of Health, are devoted to illustrating Eckstein's general comments about the effectiveness of the BMA. The general characterization of BMA-Ministry relations is that they are 'intimate' ('on the whole, strikingly close and friendly')[11] and that this feature of intimacy is causally important. The BMA, while not always getting its way, exerts a large influence on medical policy, and this indisputable finding is accounted for in large part by what Eckstein describes as the continuing, close relations between the pressured and the pressurers.

What has this intimacy of relations to do with particular failures and successes of the BMA? The bitter, intense dispute over remuneration in 1950–1 is offered as an illustration of a BMA 'failure.' Now here Eckstein is either stipulating a highly idiosyncratic meaning of failure or using the word incorrectly. For, measured by the demands the BMA made for payment, the Danckwerts award was an extraordinary success, giving the doctors more than their negotiators had demanded, though the basis of the grant was the same: the Spens Report and the government's original promise of large raises over prewar incomes and changes in the scheme of distribution.[12] How can this success be considered a failure? Only by positing a goal which the process of bargaining frustrated: the goal, in this instance, of keeping negotiations over remuneration a matter of BMA-Ministry bilateral relations without the use of arbitration. The pay dispute negotiations were terminated and Mr. Justice Danckwerts arbitrated; the BMA was not opposed in principle to arbitration, making the Eckstein characterization of the case all the more problematical. The lesson that our interviewees in the Ministry of Health learned was that it is extraordinarily expensive to have medical payment disputes arbitrated, the significance of which lesson was again to be evident in the Review Body award of 1966.

This case study of 'failure' might have been more relevant to the issue of BMA effectiveness if Eckstein had heeded the logical requirements of testing a hypothesis. This problem is particularly evident in the Eckstein discussion of the remuneration issue. If influence—or effectiveness—is defined as the capacity to get opposed others to do one's bidding, the analyst must be clear about the conflict of goals and the degree to which a given outcome can be attributed to the activities of the influencer. Otherwise, influence and satisfaction become synonymous. Prescribing for political scientists, of course, is considerably easier than performing these tasks. It nonetheless remains the case that an illustration of effectiveness will not emerge from an empirical study that neglects those logical requirements.

It is important here to explicate the relationship between attributions of influence and explanations of policy outcomes. The latter is a necessary requirement for the former. Unless one can account for why it was that an event or set of events did or did not take place, it is impossible to attribute 'influence' at all. But beyond the causal account one must also have evidence about the intentions of the actors whose effectiveness or influence is being assessed. Because policy outcomes are involved in assessments of pressure group influence, one must therefore be clear about how one accounts for a policy outcome.

The first requirement is that one not look exclusively at final decisions. Decisions are about matters of dispute or uncertainty, and the timing and breadth of considerations is a crucial element in the range of possible outcomes. Pressure groups may be thought to be engaged in influencing the policy-making process at three different stages:

(*a*) the timing of disputes over relevant issues;
(*b*) the range of matters at issue;
(*c*) the decisions about those disputed matters.

Pressure group influence can be evaluated at any of these stages. Eckstein's view is that the intimate relations between the BMA and the Ministry best account for BMA successes, although he does not explicitly outline a scheme of the policy-making process. In any event, one cannot assess a pressure group's influence over public policy without accounting for outcomes at each of these three stages in the policy-making process. Having said that, and having shown that Eckstein's general formulation is untestable and his specific account of a BMA failure paradoxical, we will turn to the main hypothesis implicit in Eckstein's account of BMA activities.

In his introductory remarks, Eckstein pays equal attention to the attributes of the pressure group, the policy area, and the relevant decision-making structure as 'determinants' of influence. In practice, however, he places special stress on the latter in explaining why the BMA does or does not get its way. Two features of the decision-making structure are, in Eckstein's view, crucial for the outcome: whether the dispute is carried out in *public view*, with other departments, large blocs of doctors, and the mass media anxious about and interested in the result; and whether BMA-Ministry negotiations are carried out in a *co-operative or disputatious manner*.[13] When BMA-Ministry negotiations are subject to 'external pressures,' both sets of officials lose their 'normal freedom of accommodation,' a situation particularly the case in, as Eckstein puts it, that 'touchiest of all areas of policy: remuneration.'[14]

'Remuneration has remained the chief area of tension between the Ministry and the Association,' he reaffirms.[15] What has this to do with the achievements of the BMA? We are told that the same 'four basic factors which account for the BMA's failures also account for its achievements.'[16] This is a logical absurdity (*X*s account for both *Y* and non-*Y*); one cannot explain a variable by a constant. Eckstein in practice does choose factors which operate selectively to promote success or failure. The degree to which negotiations are private and restricted to the BMA and the Ministry constitutes a resource for the BMA. The less constrained the Ministry is by the Treasury and various external publics, the more likely the BMA is to get its way. This is a testable hypothesis. In accounting for why the BMA got the Ministry to change its policy on redundant registrars in the early 1950s (his 'successful negotiation' example), Eckstein specifically emphasizes the importance of the unpublicized private atmosphere of negotiations. The issue was 'treated as a matter between the Ministry and the profession, even by the Treasury, for which the financial stakes were picayune...Under these circumstances, the *powers* of the profession *were at their maximum*, those of the Ministry at their minimum, and the final result...just what might have been expected [a BMA victory].'[17] How useful is this hypothesis in explaining policy decisions in the area of remuneration?

For the case Eckstein cites as a failure, his hypothesis does not hold. As he himself states, '*Clearly, the BMA had the better of the argument in the end.* Not only did it obtain the increase in pay it had demanded for three years—indeed, slightly more than it had demanded—but it had forced the Government to adhere to the Spens proposal, it had obtained arbitration, and it had gained the abolition of the much disliked basic salary.'[18] So, 'in the end,' Eckstein concludes of the remuneration fight of 1950–1, the doctors 'got what they wanted,' and qualifications about their failure to keep negotiations 'closed' do not change that signal measure of success.

On Eckstein's own evidence it was precisely this remuneration dispute that least conformed to the model of closed, intimate negotiations. According to Eckstein, 'disputes over general practitioner remuneration which cannot be resolved by easy accommodation among the principal parties seem to be inherent in the National Health Service.'[19] BMA members cannot be controlled by their leadership on remuneration issues and it is the one issue 'on which the Ministry's freedom of action is sure to be restricted by powerful extra-departmental pressures.'[20] With this characterization we agree. We disagree that the negotiations were a failure and therefore that intimacy of negotiation was a key differentiating explanatory factor.

2. The doctors' pay crisis in Britain 1965–6

This section of the paper presents a research report on the doctors' pay crisis in Britain (1965–6) as well as a commentary on both when and why the BMA is successful in getting its way on the methods and amount of its remuneration. We want to know—through the use of remuneration disputes in England—why it is that Eckstein's local, national explanation of BMA influence is faulty (the 'closest imaginable relationship' between the BMA and the Ministry). And we want to suggest, through the use of comparative data in the next section, a more promising account of the unquestionable success doctors in Western Europe and America have in controlling the form and amount of their remuneration by the state.

Neither internal nor external evidence supports Eckstein's view that bargaining structures determine much of the British Medical Association's effectiveness. The internal evidence—remuneration disputes over time within England—already has suggested that intimacy of negotiations is not a crucial factor in accounting for BMA success on pay. External evidence is another check on this causal scheme. We have taken three countries for study—Great Britain, Sweden, and the US—and analyzed three policy decisions about how doctors are to be paid by the state: (*a*) the changes in methods of remuneration following the general practitioner crisis (1965–6) in Great Britain, (*b*) the fee-for-service policy of the National Health Insurance Act in Sweden (1955), and (*c*) the Medicare 'reasonable charge policy' in the US. Two features of this type of comparative study should be made clear at the outset. First, the countries differ markedly in the setting and atmosphere of negotiations about medical remuneration.[21] Second, the policy decisions in each case are strikingly similar, when measured by the intentions of the medical organizations. That is to say, methods known to be preferred by the respective medical organizations were, broadly speaking, what the government policy became in each of the three episodes. Here we have a common burden on a political system—the requirement of settling methods of remunerating physicians in public programs—and three different decision-making structures which cope with this burden. The existence of a common outcome suggests that the causal factor lies in the first of Eckstein's three categories—the nature of the pressure group and the resources which doctors, as opposed to other producer groups in the society, share. The question of why it is that doctors in different national settings prefer different methods is a separate issue in the history and sociology of professions, which some sociologists have explored, particularly Mark Field and Talcott Parsons. For present purposes, it is enough to know that knowledge of their preferences is the single best predictor of policy decisions in this area.

The politics of medical remuneration methods involves three separate areas of argument, not all of which are equally at issue in remuneration disputes in the three countries. Method may refer to the *unit* of payment: whether by person, by item of service, by time, etc. The *source* of payment may be the method feature at issue, either in the sense of whether the patient should transfer funds to the doctor and be reimbursed by the public program, or whether the doctor should be paid by the state directly or by agencies mediating between the profession and the government. Finally, the *bases of differentiating doctors* for payment may be the issue; the dispute may involve whether age, training, setting of work, etc. should count in the amounts paid physicians. The political influence of medical organizations in remuneration policy may be understood as the ability of physician groups to raise issues, suppress issues, delimit alternatives, and produce desirable policy outcomes in these three types of conflict.

What does the British case of 1965–6 tell one about the influence of the BMA, when influence is understood in the terms suggested above? The very creation of a dispute was the work of the BMA, its answer to the Review Body's decision in 1965 to give doctors a net 10 per cent increase and to leave the methods of remuneration substantially unchanged.[22] No changes in unit, source, or bases of differentiation were made in the fifth report of the Review Body on Doctors' and Dentists' Remuneration. Interviews with government actors suggest the conclusion that hesitancy about changing the methods of remuneration grew out of the unwillingness to pay the doctors in ways they themselves had not suggested. The response to the Fifth Review Body Report was unexpectedly heated; the BMA asked for signed but undated letters of resignation from the National Health Service, and demanded that a complete review of methods and amount of remuneration take place. Approximately 16,500 of Britain's 22,000 general practitioners sent in these letters by 17 March 1965,[23] and the stage was set for raising a wide variety of issues about method and amount of state payment to general practitioners.

How did the BMA fare in delimiting the range of issues considered and getting its way on those which were at issue? On the question of the unit of payment, the BMA was able to get consideration of all three of the typical possibilities: capitation, item-of-service, and salary. The outcome was, first, the continuation of capitation and, second, the expression of the Ministry's willingness to pay doctors in health centres by salary (subject to later negotiation). Finally, the government rejected the BMA demand that item-of-service payment be permitted. The latter result superficially suggests a BMA defeat. But it should be added that no widespread enthusiasm for item-of-service payment was evident in the profession, except among the numerically insignificant Fellowship for Freedom in Medicine. In the course of BMA-Ministry negotiations on units of payment during the summer of 1965 it became clear that item-of-service recommended itself to the BMA only insofar as it involved lifting any ceiling on the income of doctors who used it. When the Ministry cited the case of dentists to suggest it would be unwilling to let amounts of remuneration expand without control, the BMA leadership quickly gave up. BMA leaders then asked the Ministry to write up its argument so that they could explain how unappealing the necessary control would be, and how irrelevant this means was to their general aim to reduce workloads, an aim unlikely to be satisfied if doctors' pay varied largely with respect to the incidence of their consultations. In this case, the issue of payment amount was dominant, both in the sense of the global increases attributable to this unit of payment, and in the sense of the uneven distribution of income which item-of-service payment would entail if it were not limited by an income ceiling.[24]

The source of payment was not raised as an issue during the course of negotiations, except for occasional laments that patients had no financial incentives to avoid excessive medical consultations. The profession was not interested in patients actually paying physicians. In England, payment by the patient was not so much an issue of remunerating doctors as controlling the distribution of medical services. The decisive argument raised against patient payment was that such pecuniary arrangements always present a dilemma. If costly enough to dissuade hypochondriacs, payment would also dissuade those who really needed medical attention. If inexpensive enough to avoid that latter problem, direct payment would not prevent nasty or casual consumers from pestering doctors. From a comparative standpoint, the striking fact is that source of payment was not a controversial matter. Doctors raise this issue in both the US and the Swedish context; in both cases the patient is involved in the actual transfer of money to doctors, a practice at the insistence of the medical organizations, and done against the original intentions of the government health reformers. In Great Britain, the source of payment is not a political issue in that there is no conflict over what source ought to be used.

But, if there is consensus on the source of payment, there is disagreement between the BMA and the Ministry on what sorts of doctors ought to be differentially regarded. This disagreement arises on all three of the most common ways of discriminating one general practitioner from another: the nature of his output (health measure, quality), the nature of his practice setting (shoddy, underdoctored group), and the characteristics of the doctor himself (age, training, etc.). Since the Royal Commission (1957–60) there have been persistent attempts to reward something called superior general practitioners. Both the Ministry and the Review Body have encouraged this form of differentiation, using tactics from persuasion to ear-marked funds, as in 1966. The recent outcome, a rejection of ear-marked merit awards to general practitioners (by a BMA vote of 16,000 to 4,000), illustrates the capacity of the BMA and its membership to shape public policy. But note that merit awards represent a small expected expenditure, and as such fall under the conditions whereby the government is not constrained financially from conceding medical wishes on the methods of their payment.[25]

The use of merit awards is but one of the controversial ways by which physicians may by differentiated for payment purposes. Another attribute of the physician that the BMA has made relevant to general practitioner remuneration is age. Seniority payments have never been a Ministry of Health preference, and because such payments would have financial implications for a very large proportion of the participating physicians, they are worrisome from a budgetary standpoint. The fate of seniority payments during 1965–6 is an excellent illustration of the limited ability of the government to resist medical preferences on methods when the profession is acknowledged to be angry, militant, and prepared to create difficulties for the continuation of normal health services. The precise timing of the demand for seniority payments is difficult to establish, but it is absolutely clear that the BMA took the initiative in pressing for this type of differentiation during negotiations with Minister of Health, Robinson, in the summer of 1965. The Ministry, on the other hand, was anxious that differentiation by type of doctor should reflect differences in quality. Either subjective judgments of physicians or objective measures of training (to become better doctors presumably) were the preferred methods. In the end, the subjective judgment approach (merit awards) was rejected by a vote of the profession and the training criterion was incorporated into seniority payments. After a short delay, seniority payments would only be paid to physicians who took a prescribed number of refresher courses. Here was a case in which the Ministry was able to add a quality consideration to a method of remuneration which only very indirectly measured ability (through experience) and was unable to get more direct measures of quality practice.

The same pattern is evident in the other methods of payment which the Ministry and the BMA agreed upon during the summer and fall of 1965.[26] Either the BMA was able to satisfy its charter demands fully, or the government, while agreeing in principle, placed constraints on the amount or scope of special payments. The BMA demanded full reimbursement for practice expenses, but the Ministry was unable to recommend this to the Review Body, arguing for some proportion below 100 per cent to avoid the necessity of direct supervision of the expenditures and reimbursement. The BMA insistence on special payment for work outside the hours of a normal working day met with substantial but not unlimited success. The government reluctantly agreed to pay physicians both for being responsible for patient cases between 8.00 pm and 8.00 am and for actually going out on home visits between midnight and 7.00 am. The BMA had requested actual payment for any night call during the whole period outside the normal working day.

The evident pattern is that of the government intermittently qualifying or slightly adjusting the requests that the BMA makes on method. These requests may well be those which the government at an earlier date has suggested. But the timing of their serious consideration is determined by the BMA. In short, the BMA exercises both positive and negative influence, determining what is done through suggestion and veto. Typically, the government manages to get its way only when a preferred method of payment is known to be favored by only a small proportion of the physicians, as was the case in item-for-service remuneration. Only a small proportion favored salary, but the Ministry itself approved of this unit, and the lack of sharp disagreement produced the expected outcome. Until the profession had given up its crusade against salary, the Ministry avoided serious suggestion of it.

As with the old issue of salary, the use of a pool in establishing a desirable average physician income was sacrosanct until the profession itself recommended its abolition. As early as 1960, discussions took place within the Treasury and the Ministry of Health on the anomalies of the pool. But the government refrained from suggesting to the Royal Commission that the pool be either done away with or substantially changed. Instead, discussion took place with BMA leaders on whether the pool would be changed so that practice expenses could be reimbursed more directly. These discussions proceeded in the early 1960s, and there was substantial agreement by 1965 that this change should take place. When the profession took the view, after the crisis over the Fifth Report, that the pool should be abolished, the government acceded to their wishes. Here was another illustration of the veto and initiating power of the professional organization. Since 1948 they had been able to foreclose the suggestion of doing away with the pool. In 1965, they were able to go beyond the limited Ministry suggestion of extracting practice expenses from the pool payments.

It is idle to provide further illustrations of BMA influence during the 1965–6 period. What should be clear is the basis for their successes. None of the variables mentioned by Eckstein changed between 1964 and 1966, except the constituency resources of the BMA. The style of negotiations leading up to the 1965 crisis was the same, regular consultations at the top floor of the Ministry of Health that took place in the summer of 1965. The Review Body was the authoritative decision-maker on the amount of payment both in 1965 and 1966. What had changed was the mobilization of professional opinion. The threat to strike had intervened. The Ministry at no time was worried about the resignation of 17,000 doctors, and the BMA was never confident that more than a third of that number would actually go out of the NHS.[27] But the fear was that substantial sections of the country would be faced with a crisis of medical supply, that a government with only a bare majority would face a crisis of confidence. Even after the election of 1966 the government was not willing to face such a NHS catastrophe, although it is clear that some members of the Cabinet were willing to consider a rejection of the Review Body recommendations on amount, and hence the negotiated methods that had preceded the determination of amount. But these pressures were, it appears, rejected almost as soon as they were brought forward.

The 1965–6 crisis represents an almost unbroken string of BMA victories. These victories support the hypothesis that doctors get their way on methods of payment when two conditions are satisfied: when intense and widespread doctors' preferences are known by the actors in the decision-making process, and when large additional public funding is not entailed. We would offer this hypothesis as one covering all medical-political systems in the democratic and developed world except Israel, where the relative oversupply of physicians reduces the threat of a breakdown in the public provision of medical care. In fact, large Exchequer contributions were also conceded in the 1965–6 crisis, but the victory on amount is *analytically and temporally distinct* from the policy changes on method. The granting of a 35 per cent payment increase in a time of general wage squeeze can only be interpreted as an extraordinary concession to medical demands. This is doubly evident when one considers that the profession was given a 10 per cent increase just a year earlier, and no criteria used to establish the 10 per cent figure had changed to promote an upward revision; rather, pressure had arisen for lower payments to all government employees.

The comparative study of the US and Swedish cases offers support for both the positive hypothesis and the rejection of the Eckstein emphasis on the 'style' of bargaining in explaining medical policy decisions. In the United States, any method other than item-of-service payment was foreclosed by what might be termed *tacit* bargaining. The medical profession did not in fact take part in the detailed drafting of the Medicare law, and only consultation took place at the administrative stage in 1966–7. But the outcome was precisely what the AMA would have demanded had they been asked, and these implicit preferences were recognized by all the legislative and administrative actors concerned: a clear case of anticipated reaction. Interviews show that, although many of the executive officials would have preferred other methods (a limited fee schedule), they were unwilling to precipitate an open dispute with the profession. And they recognized that members of the profession were not simply income maximizers (at least in the short run) when they insisted that patients be permitted to be the source of payment under the Medicare program. A reimbursement plan (direct billing option) involved the possibility that some patients would not pay their doctors, while billing the insurance companies (assignment option) would have insured 100 per cent payment, but up to the reasonable charge standard. The AMA contended that patient payment would keep the doctor further removed from the state. It also meant that some of the aged would be faced with either borrowing the money to pay the physician directly or signing promissory notes to the physician. In either case, the doctor was trading off income certainty for a preferred source of payment and risking money losses for the gain of distance from the federal government program. However odd such insistence may appear by international comparison, this demand illustrates the goals of status and independence which doctors seek to maximize in payment method disputes. What they prefer for these ends varies with the cultural definition of status and independence. But that they seek non-income ends and are successful in securing them against the insistence of the state holds for all three of the countries studied.[28]

The Swedish case testifies as well to the influence of medical organizations on payment policy. Without going into detail, it is apparent that the Swedish experience parallels that of England and the United States. The Swedish medical profession, a small and disciplined group, has obligingly accepted both a national health insurance scheme and expansion of its numbers, but has retained most of what it values in high status and remuneration. The SL has been successful in its attempts to retain a mixed system of employment and compensation methods. Options are kept open by retaining a sector of private practice not rigidly bound to a fee schedule. Thus, doctors, in both the private and public sector, are able to retain an important bargaining lever, a lever that has been used by the SL to resist government sponsored schemes to increase ambulatory medical care in the hospital polyclinics.[29]

The very fact of similar successes by medical organizations in very dissimilar political settings is evidence against the local explanation of Eckstein and support for the hypothesis we have put forward. Decisive support would come from a comparison of effectiveness of those pressure groups which can withhold vital services (through limited substitutability or supply) and those, like teachers, who share national styles and methods of bargaining, but do not have the resources of a producer group like physicians.

It should be clear that the most promising tests of pressure group theory are not single country studies, but those which use the comparative data that, at a theoretical level, are the only type of data that could confirm hypotheses like those Eckstein has put forward. When one reviewer commented that the Eckstein book is an 'excellent example of how to conduct a case study if it is to have analytic value,'[30] he was surely unclear about the logical requirements of a study of pressure group effectiveness. What Eckstein provides is a conceptual introduction which is little more than the substitution of words like 'all' and 'every' for singular adjectives referring to the British case. He provides a case illustration of the use of a would-be universalistic theory which proceeds to individual cases without the intervention of comparative data and determinate hypotheses. As such, it is a book with a crippling methodological flaw. And, since it is widely read as a description of medical politics, its assumptions and conclusion are legitimate objects of analysis for those interested in explaining public health policy decisions in Western Europe and America.

3. The determinants of government payment methods for physicians: Britain, Sweden and USA

This section sets forth more formally our findings about medical remuneration disputes in the above three countries and assesses the implications of these findings for scholarly analyses of health politics and of future policy decisions about how doctors ought to and will be paid.

The method of paying physicians in government programs is an important political issue in every society in which there are substantial public programs of personal medical care services. The issue of method is important, first, because there are substantial conflicts over the appropriate ways of paying physicians, conflicts both between the state and medical organizations and within the medical organizations. Second, it is important because the preferences for particular payment methods are intensely held, particularly by physicians. Hence disagreement over how to pay doctors usually becomes not only a public issue, but a strikingly bitter type of issue. Finally, decisions about payment methods are important because they have significant financial implications for both the governments and physicians involved. Western industrial nations typically spend more than 5 per cent of the gross national product on medical care services.[31] Health is thus a substantial industry within these nations; it is an industry with expensive component services, and the costs of those services are almost certainly going to continue to rise rapidly in the foreseeable future. As a result controversies over medical payment methods are likely to continue to be deeply divisive and important. Increasing prices and their fiscal impact on public programs ensure that much.

The problem

This discussion focuses upon controversies concerning methods of pay and does not concentrate on disputes over the amount of income doctors should receive from the state. Both issues are important, and the decision to exclude the question of total payments in no way reflects the judgment that the latter topic is unimportant. The chief reason for excluding the amounts of payment as the object of investigation is that public decisions on methods of pay, while obviously affecting total expenditures, are not always about the amounts of pay that doctors receive. That is to say, governments make explicit decisions about the total income of physicians in some societies, or the total income physicians can expect to receive from the state. But this is not the case in all western industrial societies with substantial medical care programs. In some societies, notably the United States, decisions are in fact made about methods of pay (e.g., Medicare, 1965) and no explicit recognition is given to the likely implications of such methods for the total income physicians will enjoy. The latter issue becomes important if use of payment methods generates unexpectedly high program costs, as for example took place in the United States after 1966.[32] Hence, if one is interested in illustrating the workings of various political systems by taking into account the way they cope with a common burden, the common burden most easily discussed in the medical remuneration area is the public methods of paying doctors, not the amounts paid.

All governments must make decisions about how doctors are to be paid, whether those decisions are negative ones to exclude alternatives or positive ones to select among logical possibilities one method rather than another. By method of payment we mean the unit of payment (by person, by item-of-service, by salary units), the source of payment (patient, intermediary, government), and the bases of differentiating doctors for payment purposes (by type of practice, type of doctor, or type of result).[33]

Public medical care programs must answer, even through tacit acceptance, the question of which unit, which source, and which basis of differentiation are to be used in state payment of doctors. One way of framing the issue for comparative politics is to say: there are a finite number of logically possible units, sources, and bases of differentiation to be chosen among by governments; among these options governments must and do choose; hence the outcome of the decision process can be seen as the way by which a given political system copes with a burden common to a large class of political systems. Such studies offer the bases for estimating both the determinants of payment method decisions and, through comparative analysis, the constraints on what is not possible for western industrial countries to do in this controversial area of public policy.

Central issues

The central research interest was in the following hypothesis: 'Whatever the political and medical structure of a western industrial country, physician preferences determine the governmental methods of payment.' This outcome takes place except when the preferences stated express views known by both doctors and government bargainers to represent only a minority of physicians within the relevant physician group. A striking example was the demand for item-of-service payments made in the course of the general practitioners' crisis in England in 1965.[34] The British government knew that this demand did not represent a widely held physician preference; so did the BMA. In the end, the BMA, to deal with its militant members, asked the government privately to set forth in writing the reasons why such a unit of payment could not be granted.[35]

As producers of a crucial service in industrial countries, and a service for which governments can seldom provide short-run substitutes, physicians have the overwhelming political resources to influence decisions regarding payment methods quite apart from the form of bargaining their organizations employ. The hypothesis thus links directly the economic and political attributes of physicians to public policy outcomes, and asserts that intervening bargaining variables are not central to explaining public policy decisions in this area. This hypothesis challenges the assumption that bargaining conditions are key factors in medical policy outcomes, an assumption set forth explicitly in Eckstein's *Pressure Group Politics*.[36]

The evidence gathered in the testing of this hypothesis is of two sorts. First, we have investigated the pattern of payment method decisions since World War II in three western industrial countries—Sweden, Great Britain, and the United States. Data from these countries include broad patterns of medical payment methods over time in the postwar period, reported in the secondary literature, and our own analysis of three extraordinarily controversial instances of payment method decisions in each of the three societies: the Medicare payment method decisions in the United States in 1965, the payment policy changes following the general practitioner strike crisis in Great Britain in 1965–6, and the payment methods introduced at the outset of the Swedish national health insurance program in 1955. The second major type of data collected was secondary analysis of payment methods used in other industrial countries, notably the Netherlands, West Germany, France, Switzerland, Spain, Italy, Canada, Greece, Poland, the Soviet Union and Israel.[37] We have considered our hypothesis in the light of both the secondary evidence and our fuller data on Swedish, English, and American decision patterns. We have analyzed the decisions on the basis of a model of payment method decisions, and tried to estimate the conditions under which the premises of the model are true—and hence the conclusion (our hypothesis) entailed. The model may be described as follows.

The model of explanation

Premise 1. Doctors in western industrial countries prefer payment methods in public programs with which they were familiar before the onset of the public program in question.

Premise 2. Doctors are presumed[38] to be willing to strike over government efforts to change these familiar payment methods or to prevent changes which the overwhelming majority of the profession is thought to want and has expressed the desire for in programs outside the public sector.

Premise 3. Western industrial states will never risk a medical strike because of the high political costs associated with the interruption of personal health services, irrespective of government views on the merits of physician demands concerning payment methods.

Premise 4. Such governments, while often disagreeing with physicians and their organizations about desirable methods of payment, prefer gaining medical concessions on the amount of expenditures in exchange for concessions on methods of payment.

Premise 5. The failure to satisfy widely understood medical preferences on payment methods is presumed in western industrial countries to be a sufficient condition for a physicians' strike.

Premise 6. In general, government medical officials prefer a salary method of payment.

Conclusions. Hence, whatever the political and medical structure of the western industrial country, medical preferences determine the methods of payment used in public medical care programs (subject to the constraint cited above). World-wide, the methods for paying physicians are extraordinarily diverse. What they share, however, is a remarkably close resemblance to what physicians were used to before the programs began.[39]

The application of this model to the three national settings we have investigated highlights our disagreement with two prominent types of political science analysis:

(*a*) Individual country studies cannot logically test the explanatory power of hypotheses which emphasize distinctive features of the individual political systems. On the basis of our model, the relevant structural attributes are the central elements in an explanation of payment method decisions by western industrial governments. If factors common to these countries account for common patterns of decision making, it is impossible to find this out by studying decisions of individual nations. In addition, there is no way of testing the superfluity or centrality of one or another attribute of a political system in explaining the pattern of decisions within a nation in the absence of comparison.

(*b*) Studies which focus on political culture as a causal variable are called into question by our model, or more precisely, by the data used in testing our model. Political culture may well be an important variable in the explanation of some public policies, but our findings suggest that the economic power of physicians is an overriding political resource which washes away the effects of both the bargaining styles employed by physician organizations and the attributes of the political culture such as mass and elite conceptions of the nature and legitimacy of physician demands.

The explication of the model

We now turn to an explication of both the premises and the conclusions of the model. First, in the most general terms, the argument is simply that doctors get their way on the methods of their pay. This generalization has very wide scope: the Western European industrial countries, North America, and the countries of the British Commonwealth at comparable levels of industrialization. The reason for this can be deduced from an analysis of the economic producer position of physicians (what it is they can produce, withhold, and whether or not their services are substitutable in the short run) and the ranking of goals on the part of bargaining antagonists, represented abstractly in the model as doctors and governments (see Fig. 1). Generally put, we argue that the political resources of physicians in western industrial countries are so overwhelming that institutional differences among the countries are rendered unimportant in accounting for public policies regulating the payment of physicians.

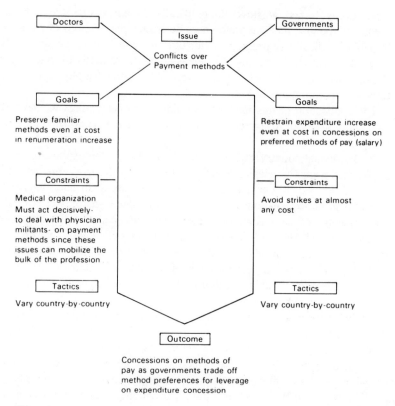

Figure 1

These comments on the geographic and economic limits of the application of the model should be extended to discussions of the limits of the model related to timing. The conditions under which the hypothesis is most likely to be true are twofold: (1) the initiation of a public medical care program in which the political costs of noncompliance by doctors are at their highest, given the expectations aroused by the statutory enactment of such a program and the increased likelihood that opposing doctors could be mobilized in preventing the initiation of such a program; and (2) circumstances in which mass physician protest is expressed, thus making salient again the possibility of a medical strike, a possibility that always exists on payment disputes, but neither is nor is perceived to be equally probable under all circumstances. A premise of the model is that a strike threat is a credible possibility. We argue that such a strike threat is always credible when traditional medical demands are violated or initiatives blocked, but that this constraint on government behavior is most evident at the time of mass protest or the initiation of a new public program.

Under what conditions are the other premises of the model true? Since the conclusion of the model follows logically from the premises, the description of the conditions under which the premises are true permits predicting the outcome we have described. Our factual premises concerning the preferences of physicians and governments do not arise from either polling data concerning mass publics or structured interviews with a random sample of involved bureaucrats in the countries studied. Rather this distribution of preferences is inferred from secondary country studies[40] and interviews with key officials in England, Sweden, and the United States. We take confidence in these findings because only preferences widely understood are relevant to the model we have used. Typically, medical organizations and their government counterparts articulate the issues that shape medical care disputes. Our presumption about preferences is not restricted to these subgroups, but extends to widely held presumptions concerning the preferences of governments and doctors. Secondly, the description of preferences concerning methods of pay applies not to all features of the transmission of income from states to doctors, but rather to the three above-mentioned types of method issues. That is to say, preferences are relevant if and only if they deal with the unit, source, or basis of differentiation in the payment of doctors. Disputes about which unit to use, whether in England, for example, to pay general practitioners by salary or by capitation in the 1940s, exemplify the type of payment issue for which the model is relevant. Disputes about whether or not physicians paid by salary ought to be compensated every week or every two weeks are not relevant to the model. In short, mechanisms used in the administration of the type of unit, source, and basis of differentiation are not subject to the constraints to which the selection of the unit, source, or differentiation basis themselves are subject. We should add that why it is that doctors prefer the method they are used to is an issue in the sociology of the profession separable from the question of whether or not their preferences predict public policy results. It is worth adding, perhaps, that fee-for-service preferences have a logical relationship to market ideologies and may well be more extensive in societies where the social distance between physicians and patients is less marked, and where the imposition of market relationships is part of the subordination of patient by doctor, and doctor by patient. Likewise, the source of payment may well be more at issue in market-oriented societies because of the obligations generally entailed by the transfer of cash from consumers to producers (patients to doctors). Finally, differentiation of doctors for payment purposes may well reflect the degree to which there is wide acceptance of formal training accomplishment as an accurate indicator of medical ability, beliefs more typical in societies with marked class differences and aristocratic legacies.

The proposition that doctors prefer concessions on methods over concessions on amounts when they are forced to choose and are thought willing to strike over method disputes is true for all the cases investigated. But the political costs of an interruption of medical care services are reduced in societies like the USSR, where the supply of physicians has been expanded enormously through the revolutionary takeover of the medical profession. Israel is another exception. There the *per capita* supply of doctors is comparatively high, and hence the bargaining position of governments is comparatively stronger. By stronger, we mean that the government has a larger pool of physicians to call upon for emergency purposes. The ability of medical organizations to cripple health programs is thus diminished; the political costs of strike efforts are, as a result, lower for the state.

The third type of limit on the political costs of medical strikes is the degree to which politically relevant consumer groups take medical care to be a vital public service, one whose interruption counts as an extraordinary failure of the government in power. Non-modern societies, with major population groups outside the market economy, are what we have in mind. Public medical programs in such societies usually focus on environmental health problems (sanitation, epidemic control, and so forth) and the relevant elite groups are usually not dependent upon the public health service for their personal health care. This means that the interruption of public medical care programs is a burden for those sectors of the population least powerful politically and less likely than urban, middle class groups to consider the restriction of public health services decisive grounds for militant political protest.

Finally, we ought to make clear that in describing bargaining agents as governments and physicians we are well aware of the lack of descriptive realism. We have made use of simplifying abstractions for purposes of clarifying the main line of argument. We have specified the model in such terms while recognizing that qualifications could be made throughout. We are saying, however, that the bargaining process can be represented as if the relevant agents were in a dyadic relationship (doctors and government), and the test of the model is not the realism of the premises, but whether the model accurately predicts public policies governing medical pay methods.

Research procedures

Our research design specified the analysis of instances of medical payment conflict in three dissimilar institutional settings. Our purpose was to vary the political setting so as to test for the impact of what we took to be the comparable economic power of physicians in the three societies studied. Our second strategy was to use secondary information on the patterns of medical payment policy for a wider range of countries. Here our aim was to provide secondary confirmation (or disconfirmation) of the scope of the hypothesis we applied to the British, Swedish, and American experiences. Finally, our concern was to give case analyses of the initiation of issues, the limitation of what became at issue, and the

Table 1. *Present payment methods*

	Type of public medical system	Specialists		General practitioners	
		Unit of payment*	Source†	Unit of payment	Source
France	Insurance	Fee	Reimbursement	Fee	Reimbursement
Germany (Fed. Rep.)	Insurance	Fee	Direct	Fee	Direct
Great Britain	Health Service	Salary‡	Direct	Capitation	Direct
Israel	Insurance	Salary‡	Direct	Salary‡	Direct
Netherlands	Insurance	Salary, Fee, Case	Direct	Capitation	Direct
Sweden	Insurance	Salary, Fee	Reimbursement	Fee	Reimbursement
Switzerland	Insurance	Fee	Direct, Reimbursement	Fee	Direct, Reimbursement
USSR	Health Service	Salary‡	Direct	Salary‡	Direct
USA	Insurance	Fee	Direct, Reimbursement	Fee	Direct, Reimbursement
Canada	Insurance	Fee	Reimbursement	Fee	Direct Reimbursement

* Method of payment: salary, capitation, fee for service, case payments.
† Source of physician remuneration: direct government payment or patient payment and government reimbursement.
‡ In these cases changes have been made in public programs to introduce salaries instead of fees.
Source: adapted from Glaser, *Paying the Doctor*, p. 24.

policy outcomes in the three settings. Our design involved detailed analysis for three national arenas of medical payment policy and more summary evidence from the rest of the western industrial countries.

Research findings

The most important research finding was that the conclusion of the model accurately described public policy outcomes in the three countries studied. This was the case not only for the three instances studied in depth, but also for medical care payment conflicts over time in these countries. Moreover, the secondary evidence supported the extension of the hypothesis to the larger class of western industrial nations. (See Table 1.)

The major implications of these findings, first, is that national explanations of public policy in this controversial area are invalid, that explanations must use structural and economic variables rather than political and cultural ones in accounting for why it is that doctors get their way on how they ought to be paid. Second, there are methodological implications, the primary one being that cross-national research is essential for the adequate explanation of public policy outcomes. Finally, the policy implications are extraordinarily important.

Policy implications

First, the most important thing for governments to understand is both the nature of medical power and the limits on that medical power. We conclude that certain features of payment method controversies are, in fact, not negotiable however much these disputes are raised in the course of medical–government confrontations. That is the negative case we want to claim, the limits on what governments are able to do. Why governments are not able to control medical payment methods is accounted for in terms of the different priorities and economic power of the bargaining antagonists.

Knowing what governments cannot do, and what outcomes will take place, is of obvious importance to government officials involved in controversial negotiations. In health policy, such knowledge may permit concentrating on alternative means to the goals which traditional government payment preferences express. There are two alternatives to continually disputing the choice of payment methods. One is to concede the choice of method to physicians and concentrate on administrative technique to make undesirable methods less so. The other is to seek alternative ways to accomplish the goals which payment methods were to serve: reward of quality education, limits on excessive services, and so on. The application of this perspective in individual cases is best left out of this article. We want to suggest here only the direction such applications should take, based on our findings.

Notes

1 Oliver Garceau, *The Political Life of the American Medical Association* (Cambridge, Mass.: Harvard University Press, 1941).
2 See, for example, William Glaser, 'Doctors and Politics,' *American Journal of Sociology*, LXVI (1960), 230–45.
3 A number of books exemplify or include this type of investigation: James Gordon Burrow, *AMA: Voice of American Medicine* (Baltimore: Johns Hopkins Press, 1963); Robin F. Badgley and Samuel Wolfe, *Doctors' Strike: Medical Care and Conflict in Saskatchewan* (New York: Atherton Press, 1967); Rosemary Stevens, *American Medicine and the Public Interest* (New Haven: Yale University Press, 1971); William Glaser, *Paying the Doctor* (Baltimore: Johns Hopkins Press, 1970).
4 Harry Eckstein, *Pressure Group Politics: The Case of the British Medical Association* (London: Allen & Unwin, 1960), p. 15.
5 Eckstein, *Pressure Group Politics*, pp. 33–4.
6 In the Preface he refers to 'the hypotheses in Chapter 1' (Eckstein, *Pressure Group Politics*, p. 7) of which this presumably is one.
7 As Eckstein perhaps suspects by once referring to his own 'theoretical framework' in half quotes. Eckstein, *Pressure Group Politics*, p. 7.

8 Eckstein, *Pressure Group Politics*, p. 34.

9 Harry Eckstein, *Internal War* (New York: The Free Press of Glencoe, 1964), pp. 5–6.

10 'To sum up the argument in very general terms, pressure group politics in its various aspects is a function of three main variables: the pattern of policy, the structure of decision-making both in government and voluntary associations, and the attitudes— broadly speaking, the "political culture"—of the society concerned. Each affects the form, the intensity and scope, and the effectiveness of pressure group politics, although in each case the significance of the variables differs—structure, for example, being especially important in determining the form of pressure group politics, policy especially important in determining its scope and intensity . . . I will sketch broadly, in light of these major variables, the conditions under which the Association acts as a pressure group.' Eckstein, *Pressure Group Politics*, p. 38.

11 Eckstein, *Pressure Group Politics*, p. 88.

12 The Spens Report recommended that general practitioners as a group should receive raises and specified the net amounts to be earned by various proportions of them (in 1939 values): three-fourths were to earn at least £1,000 net a year, one-half over £1,300, one fourth over £1,600, and about 10 percent over £2,000. Mr. Justice Danckwerts' decision of March 1952 applied a betterment factor of 100 percent for 1952 and of 85 percent for 1948, and used a percentage of 38.7 per cent for practice expenses, both higher than the BMA's original claims. In addition, maximum lists were reduced from 4,000 to 3,500 patients; a special 'loadings payment' of ten shillings per patient would be paid for patients in the range 501 to 1,500 on doctors' lists; and the 'basic salary' was abolished and replaced by an 'initial practice allowance' of £600, £450, and £200 payable only in the first, second, and third years of practice. Eckstein, *Pressure Group Politics*, pp. 127, 148.

13 Eckstein, *Pressure Group Politics*, pp. 84–91.

14 Eckstein, *Pressure Group Politics*, p. 89.

15 Eckstein, *Pressure Group Politics*, p. 95. That this particular issue on which we focus is not idiosyncratically chosen is acknowledged by Eckstein when he refers to 'the most important trade-union activity of the Association, pressure for greater remuneration'. Eckstein, *Pressure Group Politics*, p. 96.

16 Eckstein, *Pressure Group Politics*, p. 109.

17 Eckstein, *Pressure Group Politics*, p. 125 (our italics).

18 Eckstein, *Pressure Group Politics*, p. 148 (our italics).

19 Eckstein, *Pressure Group Politics*, p. 126.

20 Eckstein, *Pressure Group Politics*, p. 126.

21 Highly structured and regular in Great Britain and Sweden; diffuse and irregular in the United States, where consultation may take place in congressional hearings or through *ad hoc* meetings with executive officials responsible for public medical care programs.

22 Interview with Sir Donald Fraser, formerly Permanent Secretary of the Ministry of Health (April 1967).

23 David Mechanic and Ronald Faich, 'Doctors in Revolt: The Crisis in the British Nationalized Health Service', *Medical Care*, VIII (1970), p. 444.

24 Interviews with both BMA and governmental officials in 1967 provided the basis for this account. These officials understandably prefer to remain anonymous. See Mechanic and Faich, 'Doctors in Revolt,' for a similar interpretation.

25 For information on this episode, see Mechanic and Faich, 'Doctors in Revolt.'

26 For documentation of these decisions, see Mechanic and Faich, 'Doctors in Revolt.'

27 Interviews with BMA Secretary and National Health Service officials, Spring 1967.

28 See Glaser, *Paying the Doctor*, and Section 3 of this paper.
29 David J. Thomas, *Postwar Swedish Medical Politics*, unpublished research report for US Public Health Service, 1968.
30 Ralph M. Goldman, Review of Harry Eckstein, *Pressure Group Politics, American Political Science Review*, LX (1961), 141.
31 B. Abel-Smith, 'Health Expenditure in Seven Countries,' *The Times Review of Industry and Technology*, March 1963, p. vi.
32 Department of Health, Education and Welfare, *A Report to the President on Medical Care Prices* (Government Printing Office, February 1967), and a report published by the Ways and Means Committee, July 1971, for evidence of interest in physician incomes and the impact of public programs on those incomes. See also L. H. Horowitz, 'Medical care price changes during the first year of Medicare,' Research and Statistics Note No. 18, pp. 3–4 (Social Security Administration, 31 October 1967); E. T. Chase, 'The Doctors' Bonanza,' *The New Republic*, XV (1967), 15–16.
33 Theodore R. Marmor, 'Why Medicare helped raise doctors' fees,' *Trans-action*, September 1968.
34 British Medical Association, *A Charter for the Family Doctor Service* (London: British Medical Association, 1965), p. 1.
35 Confidential interviews with British Medical Association officers and Ministry of Health officials, Spring 1967.
36 Eckstein asserts that negotiations with the British Medical Association are typically 'intimate,' that the issues are 'treated as a matter between the Ministry and the profession. . .the powers of the profession [are] at their maximum, those of the Ministry at their minimum' (8, p. 125). The two case studies Eckstein presents to illustrate this generalization provide ambiguous support. More important, varying the bargaining tactics and atmosphere across the three countries does not coincide with differences in medical influence on the salient question of payment methods.
37 B. Abel-Smith, 'Paying the Family Doctor,' *Medical Care*, I (1963), 27–35; B. Abel-Smith, 'The major pattern of financing and organization of medical services that have emerged in other countries,' *Medicare Care*, III (1965), 33–40; Glaser, *Paying the Doctor*; J. A. Schnur and R. D. Hollenberg, "The Saskatchewan medical care crisis in retrospect,' *Medical Care*, IV (1966), 111–19; Badgley and Wolfe, *Doctors' Strike*.
38 The actors whose views are referred to here are government officials responsible for payment decisions concerning doctors. References to the government are broader, meaning the whole range of actors involved in the fiscal decisions of a modern industrial state.
39 Marmor, 'Why Medicare helped raise doctors' fees,' p. 25; Abel-Smith, 'Paying the Family Doctor,' p. 27.
40 Abel-Smith, 'Paying the Family Doctor,' p. 27; 'The major pattern of financing and organization,' p. 36; Glaser, *Paying the Doctor*, p. 26.

7. The health programs of the Kennedy-Johnson years: an overview

THEODORE R. MARMOR with JAMES A. MORONE

This chapter addresses its topic from both philosophical and political perspectives. The first section analyzes the concept of a right to health in the context of other, competing, principles for the distribution of medical care. The second section places the major health financing initiatives of the Kennedy-Johnson years—Medicare and Medicaid—in an historical perspective. It outlines the political forces which dominated the vitriolic debate over government's involvement in financing personal medical care services and notes their effect on several generations of health insurance proposals. The concluding section appraises the medical policy initiatives of the Kennedy-Johnson Administrations in the light of the dispute over the government's proper role in guaranteeing the "right to health."

The right to health and medical care

In its most egalitarian expression, the right to medical care means the equal access of all citizens to equivalent medical services.[1] In this formulation the distribution of services should vary solely with the degree of sickness. Other socioeconomic factors—wealth, race, geographical location, etc.—ought not to prevent the same response to similar medical conditions. Treating similarly ill persons similarly does not mean that all illnesses will be treated. Rather, the egalitarian criterion requires that rationing of access be made by category of ailment, not by the social class of the ill.

There are two features of this formulation that require immediate clarification. First, the guarantee addresses medical services, not health. The stipulation that equally ill persons be equally treated does not entail that action be taken such that various socioeconomic groups have equal chances of avoiding illness. Insuring equal access requires far more intervention than guaranteeing that once ill, citizens will be treated equally. Almost all of the 20th century debate over the "right to *health*" in fact has addressed issues concerning not health *per se* but the

Reprinted from David C. Warner, ed., *Toward New Human Rights: The Social Policies of the Kennedy and Johnson Administrations* (Austin: Lyndon B. Johnson School of Public Affairs, University of Texas at Austin, 1977), pp. 157–182. Reprinted by permission of the publisher. The authors express appreciation to Jenny Brorsen and Lynn Carter for their assistance in research and editing.

distribution of access to *medical care*.[2] Secondly, note that the right asserted is associated with citizenship, not merit, contribution, or any other indicator of deservingness. At its simplest, the egalitarian medical care argument asserts the injustice of permitting access to so fundamental a service to depend on anything but the "need" for it.

Like many egalitarian arguments, the right to equal care is open to the criticism of failing to distinguish among individuals on the basis of their *merit*. Some persons deserve better treatment than others, according to this view, though the basis of individual desert varies with meritarian philosophers. Even if the basis of merit were agreed to—a daunting task itself—there are strong arguments against distributing medical care on merit grounds. Gene Outka has argued that the equalities of medical need and of merit require different responses; those called for by need and those earned by effort.[3] Ill health—cancer, heart disease, and stroke to name only the most frightening—strikes some in all groups regardless of merit; the substantial differences in the probabilities of some being sicker—the poor for instance—does not invalidate the proposition that persons unequal in merit will find themselves equally in need of care. If merit is largely irrelevant in the origins of illness, it is wrong to apply that criterion in the distribution of the corresponding good. The relevant criterion would be medical condition.

There are two familiar responses to this criticism of the merit principle of distributing medical care. One, recalling the old fable about the industrious ants and the lazy grasshoppers, holds that the prudent, who with foresight and discipline prepare for the possibility of illness, deserve superior treatment. Unlike the fable's inevitable winter, however, the worst crises of health tend to be unpredictable. Second, the capacity to cope with the unpredictable costs has as much to do with wealth as foresight and discipline.

A more profound objection to the egalitarian position arises when the premise of illness' unpredictability is questioned. The assumption that health crises are random, that the patient bears no blame for his condition, is in some cases simply false. Many reckless drivers are maimed in auto wrecks, many lungs corroded by nicotine and livers by excess alcohol. If patients are sometimes partially responsible for their medical "needs,"[4] then questions of desert are not so irrelevant. Egalitarians concede such patient responsibility. But they argue that employing this knowledge in the allocation of medical care is excruciatingly difficult. Outka has outlined a series of emergency cases which bring out how perplexing the issue of access to medical treatment is. The cases illustrate how people

suffer in varying ratios the effects of their natural and undeserved vulnerabilities, the irresponsibility and brutality of others, and their own desires and weaknesses:
(1) A person with a heart attack who is seriously overweight; (2) a football hero who has suffered a concussion; (3) a man with lung cancer who has smoked cigarettes for 40 years; (4) a 60-year-old man who has always taken excellent care of himself and is suddenly stricken by leukemia; (5) a three-year-old girl who has swallowed poison left out care-

lessly by her parents; (6) a 14-year-old boy who has been beaten without provocation by a gang and suffers brain damage and recurrent attacks of uncontrollable terror; (7) a college student who has slashed his wrists (and not for the first time) from a psychological need for attention; (8) a woman raised in the ghetto who is found unconscious due to an overdose of heroin.[5]

Thus even when the merit criterion is relevant to the distribution of medical services, it may for all practical purposes be impossible to apply.

A more precise meritocratic view of medical care can be extracted from the free market tradition in economic theory. If one accepts the view that workers earn their marginal product and that marginal product measures social contribution, then the distribution of goods purchasable by earned income reflects the social contribution of citizens. Free market theorists regard medical care like any other valued item; individuals purchase either care or insurance out of earnings in whatever amounts they choose, given their income levels. The free market claim is that government programs to redistribute medical care distort individual choices. Different people, it is argued, want varying amounts and types of medical care—beyond some minimum—and will treat medical services differently. One might prefer the most expensive surgery available despite the fact that the more routine procedure is 98 percent as effective; his neighbor might forego the advantage to have more disposable income for other purposes. By failing to distinguish care according to willingness to pay, the argument goes, there is no measure of the marginal benefit of a given treatment to a given person.[6] Ultimately, free market theorists expect to maximize both freedom of choice and efficiency through the interplay of a medical market left to itself; they argue that government should finance no more than some minimum health care to the genuinely (and demonstrably) needy.

There is, of course, some merit in this critique of government intervention in the medical care market. Yet there is an enormous gap between the rhetoric of freedom of choice and the realities of purchasing medical care. The important fact about critical medical care—at birth, near death—is not what one would prefer but what doctors choose and patients can afford. Most analysts do not consider medical care a typical market good. In important cases, consumers (patients) have urgent needs and little information on which to base their choices. Physicians make many of the significant decisions; indeed, their professional discretion is fundamentally based on the knowledge gap between the patient and the provider.

Furthermore, it can be argued that, since medical care is so fundamental a need, it is more appropriately viewed as a prerequisite rather than a consequence of societal contribution. What someone can afford—even if it truly measures societal contribution—should be considered irrelevant. This suggestion returns us to something like the completely egalitarian "right of all citizens to equivalent medical services."

Clearly, the right to medical care is entangled in a number of vexing theoretical problems. The issue of equal treatment reaches to the most controversial questions about the role of the state in promoting equality. The argument over whether access to medical care should be a need- or merit-based claim proves particularly vexing when questions are raised about the extent to which illness is randomly distributed as opposed to patient-caused. The right to a minimum amount of health care—a physician's obligation under the Hippocratic oath— raises far less controversial issues than the equal right to equal treatment. And finally, the structuring of individual options by a government pursuing an ideal of equal access provokes the whole range of free-market arguments against the expansion of the role of the modern state. Some of these theoretical issues were crucial to the battle over government-financed medical insurance; others remained implicit through most of the debate.

Background to the health policies of the Kennedy-Johnson years

To appraise the health initiatives of the Kennedy and Johnson years, it is necessary to understand them in historical perspective. First, we will trace the legacy of government health insurance proposals, from the sweeping plans of Harry Truman to the far more modest ones of the late fifties; then we will consider the style and tone of the political forces which combined to produce the policy outcomes of those years.

Throughout the government health insurance debates, reformers espousing the right to medical care sought to overturn the prevailing view that, above some relatively meagre minimum, one deserved the medical care one could afford. They asserted that it was government's duty to reduce financial barriers between illness and care and proposed some form of national health insurance as the means to do so. For 60 years, national health insurance was the most deeply divisive issue in which the right to medical care played a part; at the same time, other government actions which affected the distribution of care—local support of hospitals, public health measures, research support particularly after World War II, and later financial support to the medical training centers—never produced the broad political and philosophical cleavages which the various demands for national health insurance provoked.

From national health insurance to Medicare

As noted previously, American demands for government involvement in health insurance date back to the first decade of this century. But it was not until the Great Depression, in an atmosphere of general concern for economic insecurity, that a sustained interest in government health insurance reappeared. The evolution of what became the 1965 Medicare and Medicaid programs reaches back to this New Deal period. To understand the form government health insurance took in the 1960s and to understand the two preceding decades of controversy one must begin here.[7]

The source of renewed interest in government health insurance was President Roosevelt's Advisory Committee on Economic Security, created in 1934 to draft a social security bill providing a minimum income for the aged, the unemployed, the blind, and the widowed and their children. The result was the Social Security Act of 1935 which, in addition to proposing insurance protection against the loss of workers' income, broached the subject of a government health insurance program.

Roosevelt's fear that the controversial issue of government health insurance would jeopardize the Social Security bill kept him from sponsoring the health insurance plan.[8] For many of his advisors, however, the discussions of this issue in the mid-thirties marked the beginning of an active interest in the subject. The divorce of compulsory health insurance from the original Social Security bill had alerted critics within the medical world to the possibility of attempts to get a "foot in the door for socialized medicine." On the other hand, passage of the Social Security Act freed social insurance activists to address the question of how unequally medical care was distributed in post-Depression America. From 1939 on, their activities were reflected in the annual introduction of bills proposing compulsory health insurance for the entire population. An unaccomplished task of the New Deal, government health insurance became one of the most prominent aspirations of Harry Truman's Fair Deal.

Although compulsory health insurance was originally raised in conjunction with Social Security income protection, New Deal-Fair Deal advocates viewed health insurance primarily as a remedy for the unequal distribution of medical services. The proponents of the Murray-Wagner-Dingell bills took for granted the egalitarian argument noted before, the view that financial means should not determine the quality and quantity of medical care a citizen received. "Access to the means of attainment and preservation of health," Truman's Commission on the Health Needs of the Nation flatly stated, "is a basic human right." The health insurance problem in this view was the degree to which the use of health services varied with income, and not simply with illness. In contrast, for those who considered minimum accessibility to health services a standard of adequacy, the provision of charity medicine in doctors' offices and general hospitals represented a solution, and the problem was to fill in where present charity care was unavailable.

The Truman solution to the problem of unequal access to health services was to remove the financial barriers to care through government action. A radical redistribution of income was, in theory, an alternative solution, but not one which the Truman Administration felt moved to advocate. Rather, as he made clear in his State of the Union message in 1948, Truman's goal was "to enact a comprehensive insurance system which would remove the money barrier between illness and therapy...[and thus] protect all our people equally...against ill health." But on the issue of comprehensive health insurance for all Americans there were simply too few legislative supporters for enactment of Truman's plan and his demands were repeatedly frustrated. Truman responded to stalemate with vitriolic criticism of the American Medical Association (AMA) as the public's worst enemy in the effort to redistribute medical care more equitably. But the fact was that Truman could not command majorities for any of his major domestic proposals—lambasting the AMA was one way of coping with this executive-legislative impasse.

The persistent failure of Truman's health proposals had made the need for a new strategy evident; a plan was developed which limited health insurance to the beneficiaries of the Old Age and Survivors Insurance program. It was hoped that a broader program could be incrementally built on this foundation—precisely what conservatives feared. The American public's apparent acceptance of Social Security programs made the content of the new strategy appear politically feasible. Thus the stage was set in early 1951 for what came to be called "Medicare" proposals. Millions of dollars spent on propaganda, the activation of a broad cleavage in American politics, the framing of choice in health insurance between socialism and "the voluntary way," the bitter, personally vindictive battle between Truman's supporters and the AMA-led opposition—these comprised the legacy of the fight over general health insurance and provided the setting for the emergence of Medicare as an issue. What had begun in the 1930s as a movement to redistribute medical services for the entire population was now a proposal to help defray some of the hospital costs of some of the elderly. Still, the fight was just as bitter, the specific arguments—on either side—very much the same.

The appeal of focusing on the aged

The selection of the aged as the problem group is comprehensible in the context of American politics, however distinctive it appears in comparative perspective. No other industrial country in the world has begun its government health insurance program with the aged. The typical pattern has been the initial coverage of low-income workers, with subsequent extensions to dependents and then to higher income groups. Insuring low-income workers, however, involves use of means tests, and the cardinal assumption of Social Security advocates in America has been that the stigma of such tests must be avoided. Seeking to avoid both general insurance and humiliating means tests, the Federal Security Agency strategists had to find a socioeconomic group whose average member could be presumed to be in need. The aged passed this test easily; everyone intuitively knew the aged were worst off. Wilbur Cohen was later to say that the subsequent massing of statistical data to prove the aged were sicker, poorer, and less insured than other adult groups was like using a steamroller to crush an ant of opposition.

Everyone also knew that the aged—like children and the disabled—commanded public sympathy. They were one of the few population groupings about whom the moralistic arguments of self-help did not apply. One could not say the old should take care of their financial-medical problems by earning and saving more money. The Social Security system makes unemployment (except for limited part-time work) a condition for the receipt of pensions, and a fixed retirement age is widely accepted as desirable public policy. In addition, the post-war growth in private health insurance was uneven, with lower proportions of the aged covered, and the extent of their insurance protection more limited than that enjoyed by the working population. Only the most contorted reasoning could blame the aged for this condition by attributing their insurance status to improvidence. Retirement forces many workers to give up work-related group insurance. The aged could not easily shift to individual policies because they comprised a high-risk group which insurance companies were reluctant to cover except at relatively expensive premium rates. The alternative of private insurance seemed in the 1950s incapable of coping with the stubborn fact that the aged were subject to inadequate private coverage at a time when their medical requirements were greatest and their financial resources were lowest. Under these circumstances many of the aged fell back upon their children for financial assistance, thus giving Medicare's emphasis upon the aged additional political appeal. The strategists expected support from families burdened by the requirement, moral or legal, to assume the medical debts of their aged relatives.

The same strategy of seeking broad public agreement was evident in the benefits and financial arrangements chosen. The 1951 selection of hospitalization benefits reflected the search for a "problem" less disputable than the one to which the Truman plans had been addressed. General health insurance was a means for solving the problem of the unequal distribution of medical care services; its aim was to make health care more equally accessible by removing financial barriers to utilizing those services, an aim broadly similar to that of the British National Health Service. A program of hospital insurance identifies the aged's problem not as the inaccessibility of health services, but the *financial consequences of using those services*. The provision of 60 days of free hospital care only indirectly encourages preventive health measures and cannot allay financial problems of the long-term chronically ill. The hospital benefit was designed, however, not so much to cope with all the health problems of the elderly as to reduce their most onerous financial difficulties. This shift in emphasis left gaping inadequacies. But, in the context of the early 1950s, reformers accepted the political realities which made broader conceptions of the aged's health problems unsusceptible to governmental solution.

The differences between making health services more accessible and coping with the financial consequences of hospital utilization were continually revealed in the next 15 years. The statistical profiles of the aged—first provided by the Truman health commission of 1952—uniformly supported the popular conception of aged Americans as sicker, poorer, and less insured than their countrymen. Health surveys reported that persons 65 and over were twice as likely as those under 65 to be chronically ill, and were hospitalized twice as long. In 1957–58, the average medical expenses per aged person were $177, more than twice the $86 average reported for persons under 65. As age increases, income decreases, producing an inverse relationship between medical expenses and personal income. While slightly more than half the persons over 65 had some type of health insurance in 1962, only 38 percent of the aged no longer working had any insurance at all. Moreover, the less healthy the aged considered themselves, the less likely they were to have insurance; 37 percent of those in "poor health" as opposed to 67 percent who evaluated their health as "good" had health insurance. Of those insured aged, a survey of hospital patients reported, only one-fourteenth of their total costs of illness were met through insurance. There could be no question that the aged faced serious problems coping with health expenses, though it was easy to point out that averages conceal the variation in illness and expenditures *among* the aged.

For those who saw Medicare as prevention against financial catastrophe, the vital question was which bills were the largest for any spell of serious illness. The ready answer was hospital care. Not only was the price of hospital care doubling in the decade 1951–61, but the aged found themselves in hospital beds far more often than younger Americans. One in six aged persons entered a hospital in a given year, and they stayed in hospitals twice as long as those under 65, facing an average daily charge per patient bed of $35 by 1961. Hospitalization insurance was, according to this information, a necessity which the aged had to have to avoid financial catastrophe. But what the advocates did not point out was that financial catastrophe could easily overtake 60 days of hospital insurance. Such a catastrophe is defined by the gap between medical bills and available resources. Medicare's protection against the high unit costs of hospital care drew attention away from the financial costs of unusually extensive utilization of health services, whether high or low in average prices.

The concentration on the burdens of the aged was a ploy for sympathy. The disavowal of aims to change fundamentally the American medical system was a stop to AMA fears, and the exclusion of physician services benefits was a response to past AMA hysteria. The focus on the financial burdens of receiving hospital care took as given the existing structure of the private medical care world, and stressed the issue of spreading the costs of using available services within that world. The organization of health care, with its inefficiencies and resistance to cost reduction, was a fundamental but politically sensitive problem which consensus-minded reformers wanted to avoid in 1951 when they opted for

60 days of hospitalization insurance for the aged under Social Security as a promising "small" beginning.

The legitimacy of Social Security: earned rights

The use of Social Security funding was an obvious effort to tap the widespread legitimacy which OASI programs enjoyed among all classes of Americans. But it was a tactic with an equally obvious defect. Proof that the aged were the most needy was based on calculation for *all* persons over 65. Yet Social Security financing would in 1952 have restricted Medicare benefits to 7 million pensioners out of the 12.5 million persons over 65. This would have meant not insuring 5.5 million aged whose medical and financial circumstances had been used to establish the "need" for a Medicare program in the first place. Nonetheless, Social Security financing offered so many other advantages that its advocates were prepared to live with this gap between the problem posed and the remedy offered.

The notion that Social Security recipients pay for their benefits is one traditional American response to the charge that government assistance programs are "give-aways" which undermine the willingness of individuals to save and take care of their own problems. Medicare advocates thought they had to squash that charge if they were both to gain mass public support and to shield the aged from the indignity of a means test. The contributory requirement of Social Security— the limitation of benefits to those having paid Social Security taxes—gives the system a resemblance to private insurance. Thus Social Security members would appear to have paid for hospital insurance. In fact, Social Security beneficiaries are entitled to pensions exceeding those which, in a strict actuarial sense, they have "earned" through contributions. But this is a point generally lost in the avalanche of words about how contributions, as a former Commissioner of Social Security, Robert Ball, once remarked, "give American workers the *feeling* they have earned their benefits."[9] The notion that contributions confer rights analogous to those which premiums entail within private insurance was one which deeply permeated the advocacy of Medicare.

The public legitimacy surrounding the Social Security program made it an ideal mechanism for avoiding the stigma attached to most public welfare programs. The distinction between public assistance for the poor and Social Security rights for contributors is, in fact, less clear in law than might be expected. Rights are prescriptions specified in law, and welfare legislation—for any class of persons—confers rights in this sense. But those who insist on the distinction between public assistance and Social Security focus less on the legal basis of rights than on the different ways in which these programs are viewed and administered. Social Security manuals insist on treating beneficiaries as "claimants," and stress that the government "owes" claimants their benefits. The stereotype of welfare is comprised of legacies from charity and the notorious Poor Laws, a combination of unappealing associations connected with intrusive investigation of need, invasion of privacy, and loss of citizenship rights. The unfavorable stereotype of welfare programs thus supports the contention that Social Security funds are the proper financing instrument for providing benefits while safeguarding self-respect.

Pressure groups and medicine: the lobbying of millions

Serious congressional interest in special health insurance programs for the aged developed in 1958, six years after the initial Medicare proposal. From 1958 to 1965, congressional committees held annual hearings which became a battle-ground for hundreds of pressure groups. The same intemperate debate of the Truman years (and often the same debaters) reappeared. The acrimonious discussion of the problems, prospects, and desires of the aged illustrated a lesson of the Truman period: the federal government's role in the financing of personal health services is one of the small class of public issues which can be counted on to activate deep, emotional, and bitter cleavages between what political commentators call "liberal" and "conservative" pressure groups.

For all the important differences in scope and content between the Truman general health program and the Medicare proposals, the lineup of proponents and opponents was strikingly similar. Among the supporters, organized labor was the most powerful single source of pressure. Organizations of the aged were the result more than cause of these heightened Medicare demands. The AMA sparked the opposition and framed its objections in such a way that disparate groups only tenuously involved with medical care or the aged could rally around the AMA. A small sample, representing a fraction of all groups involved in the lobbying, illustrates the continuity between the broad economic and ideological divisions of the Truman fight and that over health insurance for the aged:

For:	Against:
AFL-CIO	American Medical Association
American Nurses Association	American Hospital Association
Council of Jewish Federations and Retired Workers	Life Insurance Association of America
American Association of Retired Workers	National Association of Manu-facturers
National Association of Social Workers	National Association of Blue Shield Plans
National Farmers Union	American Farm Bureau Federation
The Socialist Party	The Chamber of Commerce
American Geriatrics Society	The American Legion

Three features of this pressure group alignment merit mention. First, the adversaries who are "liberal" and "conservative" on that issue are similarly aligned on other controversial social policies like federal aid to education and disability insurance. Second, the extreme ideological polarization promoted by these groups has remained markedly stable despite significant changes in the actual objects in dispute, such as the much narrower scope of health insurance proposals since 1952. Proposals for even incremental change in a disputed social policy typically fail to avoid disagreement about "first principles." The polarization of pressure groups on Medicare illustrated the typical structure of conflict over "redistributive"[10] issues in America; the sides, in tone and composition, resembled the contestants in an economic class conflict and framed issues in what some call the terms of "class war." Finally, public dispute continued to be dominated by the AFL-CIO and the AMA. Since the 1940s these two chief adversaries have engaged in what *The New York Times* characterized as a "slugging match," a contest where, as in the fight between public and private power advocates in America,

The sides have little use for one another. They distrust each other's motives; they question each other's integrity; they doubt each other's devotion to the national good.[11]

Both the AFL-CIO and the AMA have the membership, resources, and experience to engage in multi-million dollar lobbying. Their members are sufficiently spread geographically to make congressional electioneering relatively easy to organize.

During the debates of the 1940s and early 1950s, the AMA and its allies in big business and commercial agriculture found it a relatively successful tactic to focus the debate on the evils of collectivism and socialized medicine. The narrowing of health insurance proposals from universal coverage to the aged, however, set new constraints on the anti-Medicare campaigns. In response to the Medicare bills, the aged themselves began to organize into such pressure groups as the Senior Citizens' Councils and the Golden Ring Clubs. Although these groups lacked the financial and membership resources which characterized the better organized lobbies, it was far more difficult for the AMA to engage in open warfare with them than it had been for the doctors to do battle with the powerful AFL-CIO. When critics of governmental Medicare proposals seized on broad ideological objections, they now had also to take into account the possibility of being labeled the enemy of senior citizens. One effect attributable to this set of circumstances was the appearance of a conservative willingness to offer alternatives. In the late 1940s, Republicans and their allies in big business and organized medicine offered nothing but the *status quo* in opposition to the health insurance schemes of that period. By the 1950s, a change of tactics was in order: it was one thing to write off socialism, but the risks of writing off the aged would give the wise politican some second thoughts.

The health and medical programs of the Kennedy-Johnson Administrations

The details of the political struggles that culminated in the 1965 passage of Medicare and Medicaid are not relevant to this essay's focus and have been described elsewhere.[12] But the fact that it was the dominant health preoccupation in the Kennedy and early Johnson Administrations is relevant. Indeed, as President Johnson later said, the overriding "importance" of the struggle over Medicare was the "revolutionary change in our thinking about health care" it "foreshadowed." The meaning of health insurance for the aged, in Johnson's view, was the country's beginning recognition that "good medical care is a right not a privilege."[13]

Appraising the contributions of the medical programs of the Kennedy and Johnson Administrations means beginning with what they regarded as their largest achievements. First, we will review the programmatic expression of the health insurance struggle in Medicare and Medicaid and then turn to the numerous other health initiatives which the budgetary outlays for these programs have dwarfed.

The enactment of Medicare and Medicaid was obviously shaped by the electoral landslide of 1964. The Johnson victory guaranteed the passage of Medicare legislation which congressional stalemate had denied the Kennedy Administration. But the assurance of passage did not mean the absence of surprise in the details of the Medicare statute or the Medicaid program that was unexpectedly tacked on.

The older struggle over health insurance for the aged sharply limited the range of alternatives open to the Johnson Administration, even in the flush of election triumph. That long debate—focused on the aged as the problem group, Social Security versus general revenues as financing mechanisms, and partial versus comprehensive benefits for some or all of the aged—structured the content of the statutory innovations. The character of more than a decade of dispute over health insurance for the elderly explains the programmatic features of the final bill that Representative Wilbur Mills helped engineer, President Johnson took pride in, and the conservative critics in Congress and the AMA inadvertently helped to ensure.

The new law (PL 89-974) was broader than its predecessors in benefit structure, but it did not provide payment for all or even most ordinary expenses for the elderly. It reflected the "insurance" as opposed to "comprehensive prepayment" philosophy of medical care financing. The former assumes that paying substantial portions of large medical bills is sufficient; the problem which Medicare in fact addressed was unbudgetable financial strain (though many of the aged expected more). The prepayment philosophy advocated separation of financing from medical considerations, harkening back to the egalitarian view of the Tru-

Table 1. *Hospital utilization by age* and income** before and after the introduction of Medicare/Medicaid*

	1965–66	1968
Age	*Hospital days per thousand*	
65 and over	2,029	2,993
Under 65	828	787
	(20.5% of all days)	(28.3% of all days)
Income	*Number of persons hospitalized per thousand*	
Under $3,000	107	123
$3,000–4,999	106	107
$5,000–7,999	106	97
$8,000–9,999	96	94
$10,000 or more	89	82

* "Persons Hospitalized," *Health Interview Survey, Series 10, Numbers 50 and 64,* Tables 4, 26, and 28.
** *Ibid.,* Tables D and B.
Source: Joseph P. Newhouse, "Health Care Cost Sharing and Cost Containment," Testimony prepared for the Subcommittee on Public Health and Environment, Committee on Interstate and Foreign Commerce, U.S. House of Representatives, April 1976, p. 26.

man period. On this standard, the fact that Medicare came to finance between 40 and 50 percent of the medical expenses of the aged reflected programmatic inadequacy. Only the complete removal of financial barriers to medical services satisfies the strict standard. Medicare's range of deductibles, exclusions, and coinsurance provisions all reflect the private health insurance benefit models.

Medicare's impact

The impact of Medicare on the elderly is the subject of another chapter in this volume and I will not repeat its findings.[14] But it is worth noting in connection with the "right to health" theme that Medicare's differential impact should have surprised no one familiar with its provisions. The program's emphasis on financing large medical expenses shows in its impact on the aged's increased use of hospitals. As Table 1 indicates, hospital days per aged person rose by nearly 50 percent in Medicare's first three years, while hospital days among the non-aged actually declined. Physician visits do not reflect this marked redistribution across age groups, not surprising in the light of Medicare's deductible and coinsurance provisions for physicians' services (Table 2).

None of this utilization is surprising in the light of Medicare's statutory provisions. But much of Medicare-Medicaid's programmatic implementation was a surprise for the administrators who for years had been anticipating a program

Table 2. *Percentage of persons seeing a physician and physician visits per person per year, by age and income, before and after the introduction of Medicare/Medicaid*

	Percentage seeing a physician		Annual visits per person	
	1963–64	1969	1963–64	1969–71*
Age				
Less than 65	65.9	69.2	4.3	4.4
65 and over	68.3	71.3	6.7	6.4
Income				
Under $3,000	59.5	66.2	4.3	4.8
$3,000–4,999	64.2	66.8	4.5	4.5
$5,000–6,999	67.1	68.2	4.5	3.9
$7,000–9,999	69.8	69.5	4.7	4.1
$10,000–14,999	71.8	71.8	4.8	4.2
$15,000 or more	75.4	74.5	5.8	4.5

* 1969–71 were averaged because the annual figures show some variance. Prepared by Joseph P. Newhouse; see p. 27 in source cited for Table 1.
Source: "Physician Visits" and "Current Estimates," *Health Interview Survey*, Series 10, Numbers 72, 75, and 79. 1969 population weights were used to compute the age figures. Income figures are unadjusted for inflation.

insuring the aged against 60 days of hospitalization expenses. The methods of paying physicians were among the most intractable issues facing the Social Security Administration in the first years of Medicare; for years no one had imagined paying physicians under a Medicare program and no office of HEW had thought out how this burden could best be borne. The Medicaid program of 1965—itself an afterthought addition to the familiar Medicare bill—brought with it serious controversy over exactly who would be designated as medically indigent and how generous the state plans could be.

Perhaps most unexpected was the conflict between assuring the aged access to care and insuring that the facilities they used were not racially discriminatory. In the two decades of debate over government health insurance, almost no one pressed the issue of racially segregated medical services. Yet in the first weeks of Medicare's operations, the question of certifying Southern hospitals took up more time of HEW's top health officials than any other feature of the program. Besides satisfying standards designed to ensure a high quality of care, institutions providing services to Medicare beneficiaries had to offer proof that its services were rendered on a non-discriminatory basis. These requirements frequently posed cruel choices where hospitals unable or unwilling to meet the certification standards were also the only facilities available to the elderly. Civil rights lawyers saw Medicare as a powerful instrument for change, and, though there certainly were and are Southern hospitals not in compliance, a major unanticipated effect of the 1965 legislation was to desegregate the bulk of Southern hospitals.

What Medicare surely did accomplish was practical universalization among the aged of health insurance. That insurance reduced the financial barriers to care for much of the aged population and sharply reduced the fear of pauperization from health expenses among almost all of the aged. But Medicare did not, as President Johnson hoped, mean "good medical care" was a right in the egalitarian sense discussed at the outset of this essay. While the words were the same as Truman's, the health insurance proposals of the Kennedy-Johnson years reflected substantial shrinkage from the ambitions of the Fair Deal. The two sides of the battle used familiar ideological weapons to dispute vastly different programmatic initiatives. That is part of the reason President Johnson wrote of how the country had *begun* to think of medical care as a right with Medicare's passage. While the debate was about broad abstract issues concerning government's responsibility in medical care, the political struggle was conducted at the practical level of securing supporters and defeating opponents. It should come as no surprise that those who measure Medicare's accomplishments by the rhetoric of equal rights to care will be disappointed.

Medicaid

Medicaid, by contrast, was the great program afterthought of 1965. As a scheme for financing the medical care of poor Americans, it was not innovative either programmatically or philosophically. It carried over the tradition of vendor payments for the aged poor, but expanded the minimum eligible population to all of the poor eligible for federal-state public assistance programs. It employed the traditional public welfare mechanisms of federal guidelines and state-county administration. But few anticipated the financial, medical, or political consequences when Medicaid began in 1966. From the outset Medicaid was paradoxical. Unexpectedly expensive, Medicaid has been lampooned for actually accomplishing some of the program's stated purposes, including the provision of health financing to a very substantial portion of the welfare population. As the welfare companion to Medicare, Medicaid was expected to grow slowly. That expectation of slow growth presumed that programs for the poor are unpopular and that, as with Kerr-Mills, the states would restrain both program benefits and eligibility. This approach meant that federal legislators could assume in 1965 that broad language about making medical care available to all the poor by 1975 was safe and HEW regulation writers could presume that federal rules expressing that intent would not be political dynamite. No one fully anticipated the impact of either general medical inflation or the dramatic increases in the welfare rolls.

Medicaid's two announced purposes were to increase the access of poor people to medical care and provide that care in the mainstream of American medicine. The increased use of physician services by the poor is strikingly impressive. In 1964, the year before Medicaid, those whose family income was below the federal poverty line averaged 4.3 visits per year. By 1971, visits for the same group had risen to 5.6, compared to 4.7 and 4.9 for middle- and upper-income family members, respectively. Equally, the poor are hospitalized more frequently.[15] Still, even though Medicaid substantially expanded the poor's access to care, it failed to bring them into the mainstream of providers.

These changes do not establish that the poor have attained meaningful parity of utilization or quality of care. The poor are sicker; equal access to care for the same conditions would mean even higher rates of utilization than now obtained. Moreover, the poor (and rural) are markedly less likely to have a regular source of care than the non-poor (and urban). Children from central cities and rural areas are less likely, according to 1970 data, to see a physician at least once during the year. Perhaps most important, the poor have fewer physician visits in response to days of disability than the rest of the population. Yet the improvement in access associated with the expansion of Medicaid is undeniable.[16]

Whether the care the poor receive equals that of the rest of the population is far more problematic. What is clear is that the poor receive their care in different types of settings and from different sorts of physicians. Medicaid has not markedly improved the access of poor children to private sources of care and has exerted minimal impact on the current pattern of locating and providing care to the poor.[17] The most frequent users of hospital outpatient services are poor children, particularly racial minorities in the central cities. While in 1974 approximately 12 percent of the outpatient visits by the general child population were to hospital-based facilities, the percentage was twice that among poor children in central cities.[18] While the poor use more outpatient departments and general practitioners for their care, the more affluent disproportionately receive specialist care in physician offices. The quality implications of these differences are arguable; the differences in pattern of use are not.

Whatever Medicaid's announced goals, political attention has centered on its costs. Total expenditures have far exceeded official estimates, rising from some $25 million in 1967 to $11 billion in 1974.[19] Similarly, dramatic increases have marked the Medicare program for the elderly, but the political controversy over it has not matched Medicaid's. And part of the reason is that the state-federal financing of welfare programs decentralizes fiscal conflict, while Medicare's Social Security financing centralizes political oversight at great geographic remove from state and local tax disputes.

Other health programs

Despite the political differences between Medicare and Medicaid, they comprise the major programmatic legacy of the Kennedy-Johnson years. In budget terms

Table 3. *Federal health expenditures, 1969 and 1974 (in millions of dollars)*

	1969	1974
Medicare	$6,598*	$9,195*
Medicaid	2,284*	4,405*
Maternal and Child Health Services	209**	580*[a]
OEO Health and Medical Programs	126*	—[a]
(includes neighborhood health centers)		
Alcohol, Drug Abuse, and Mental		
Health Administration	51*	319*
Health Manpower Training	805*	1,240*
Health Related Construction	634*	381*
Health Research	1,475*	1,839*

[a] Funding through HSA when programs transferred; unavailable breakdown for OEO.
Sources: *Russell *et al., Federal Health Spending, 1969–74*. Center for Health Policy Studies, National Planning Association, Washington, D.C., 1974, pp. 3, 55, 56, and 63.
** Department of Health Education and Welfare, *Annual Report, 1969*.

their preeminence is stark, overshadowing all of the other programs, as Table 3 shows, by the end of the Johnson Administration. This budgetary predominance by no means reflected the perspective of the Kennedy-Johnson initiators. They were proud, as President Johnson himself reported, of the widespread efforts to reach problems across all the areas of the health industry. More legislation was, to these minds, better government: Johnson stated "during my administration, 40 national health measures were presented to the Congress and passed by the Congress—more than in all the preceding 175 years of the Republic's history."[20]

Though interpretable as features of a comprehensive health strategy, the initiatives of the Kennedy-Johnson years reflected a diversity of both political origins and programmatic fates. Some prospered, others quickly faded. Some grew, others faced budgetary constraints. All experienced review and criticisms by the Republican Administration of the 1970s. And none have the kind of national salience Medicare began with and Medicaid came to have.

This retrospective sobriety differs sharply of course from the enthusiasm with which the Johnson Administration directed itself to a range of health concerns: medical research; providing care in poor areas; special problems of heart disease, cancer, stroke, and mental illness; and the gap between scientific medical knowledge and the care Americans received. For each problem there was a programmatic response, and, unbeknownst to the reformers, an uncertain future.

The neighborhood health centers initiated in 1965 by the Office of Economic Opportunity were to play a major role in making health care delivery a reality in poor urban neighborhoods. The centers were established in high poverty areas and tailored their services to fit local needs. Their aims were ambitious—to overcome a variety of non-financial barriers to medical care: the lack of medical providers in low-income neighborhoods, inadequate transportation to health care centers, discrimination against the poor, and lack of education. The centers provided comprehensive medical and dental care and some initiated programs to ameliorate inadequate housing, sanitation, sewage, or nutrition. But although intended as companions to Medicaid, they were quickly overshadowed by it.[21] Initial estimates were 25 million individuals served by 1973.[22] Yet, by that time a twentieth of that number—1.3 million people—were registered at 100 centers and annual expenditures were declining. Ultimately, the program was a victim of the budget austerity of the Republican years.

The Maternal and Child Health Programs of the mid-1930s were significantly expanded during the Johnson Administration. Comprehensive care for mothers and infants was introduced at neighborhood centers in an effort to reduce the relatively higher infant mortality rate among the poor; special attention was given to young unwed mothers. In 1965, comprehensive health care was extended to children and youth with a special emphasis on preventive medicine and early treatment. The Crippled Children's Program, which had been included in the original Maternal and Child Care Program of 1935, grew from $62.3 million in 1960 to $152.9 million in 1970. By 1970, 491,000 children were being served. Though enormously helpful for certain groups, the comprehensive children and youth projects have never reached a large proportion of poor Americans and have also experienced budget reductions in the 1970s.

Some ambitious programs have never experienced significant growth. The Early and Periodic Screening, Diagnosis, and Treatment Program (EPSDT), for example, enacted in 1967 was advertised as the first federal policy mandate of comprehensive preventive health services for children. Yet final regulations for the program were not issued until November, 1971, and bureaucratic wrangling, strong professional opposition, and a state disinclination to bear EPSDT's potentially considerable costs have continued to block the successful implementation of this program.

In the area of mental health, there have been both drastic change and subsequent controversies. The Community Mental Health Centers Act of 1963 sought to replace large mental institutions with community mental health services. Subsequent provisions were made for alcohol and drug abuse. By 1974, 626 programs were serving 1.4 million people;[23] the programs were initiated with federal funds and expected to be self-sufficient within 10 years, although special arrangements were made for centers in low-income neighborhoods. Yet, the Nixon and Ford Administrations announced their intention to phase out this legacy of the Kennedy-Johnson years.

Other programs took up the problems of distribution of providers and medical research. The Health Manpower Training Program was instituted in 1965 to increase the number and improve the specialty and geographic distribution of health care providers. Researchers, physicians, nurses, dentists, and paramedics were trained with government funds; $717 million was allocated in 1969, $1.4

billion by 1973. The federal government had actively funded the construction of medical care facilities since World War II; during the 1960s its contribution rose from $195 million (1960) to $4.056 billion (1970).[24] Likewise, the scope of federally funded research (particularly in cancer, heart, and lung diseases; mental health and environmental health) was enormously expanded.

In order to hasten the translation of research breakthroughs into health care practice, the Regional Medical Program Service (RMP) was established. Focusing on the three largest causes of death in America—heart disease, cancer, and stroke—the program attempted to coordinate researchers, medical schools, hospitals, and other health care institutions by disseminating new information about diagnosis and treatment. Finally, in an effort to integrate the burgeoning number of health programs, the Comprehensive Health Planning and Service Act of 1966 (CHP) established health planning agencies in all of the states. By 1972, more than 200 such agencies were in operation.[25]

While of central importance to professionals directly affected, none of these programs dramatically altered the distribution of access to medical care services. In individual communities, a local health center might be the difference between real and financial access to care. Nurse practitioners reached some rural residents where no doctors were available. But nowhere was the commitment to directly provide health services and personnel comparable to the Medicare and Medicaid commitment to pay for it.

Conclusion

The appeal to medical care rights has, as we have seen, been a familiar feature of 20th century American health politics. Though commonly invoked, the concept of a right to care remains philosophically vexing and only loosely related to public policy debate and practice. In the disputes over Medicare, the rhetoric of equal access to care—a legacy of earlier health insurance debates—was evoked in defense of plans that by their nature could not satisfy this standard.

In practice, Medicare and Medicaid highlighted the discrepancy between the language of equal rights and the content of public programs. Medicare—by providing equal insurance benefits—ensured both that medical care would impoverish fewer of the aged and that, through supplementation of its benefits and regional and racial variation in services provided and financed, the aged would not receive equal consideration. Medicaid, by entirely removing financial barriers to care for some of the poor, moved the nation towards greater equalization of access across income classes. But it did not do so equally by state, region, or type of poverty, thus leaving a legacy of uneven improvement, rapid expenditure escalation, and political controversy.

Whatever Medicare and Medicaid did for their beneficiaries, they helped to worsen the inflation problem in medicine.[26] Unwittingly, both programs have contributed to the problems other Americans are having with financial access to care and helped to inflate the costs of any national health insurance plan that might now attempt to make medical care equally accessible financially. Medical inflation constitutes a major current problem for both patients and government. Part of its impact shows up in the reduction of real levels of spending in the health delivery, educational, and research programs of the Kennedy-Johnson years. Medicare and Medicaid reflected an incrementalist approach to extending the "right to medical care." Enormously helpful to some Americans, the very expansion of those programs has made the practical obstacles to national health insurance more formidable than the disputes over the right to care which seemed so central in the middle of the 1960s.

Notes

1 See Gene Outka, "Social Justice and Equal Access to Health Care," *Journal of Religious Ethics*, 2 (1974), pp. 11–32.
2 Blue Cross Association. *Conference in Future Directions of Health Care: The Dimensions of Medicine*. Sponsored by the Blue Cross Association, The Rockefeller Foundation, and the Health Public Policy Program, University of California School of Medicine, December, 1975, p. 4.
3 Outka, *op. cit.*, p. 4.
4 Blue Cross Association, *op. cit.*, pp. 1–3.
5 Outka, *op. cit.*, pp. 16–17.
6 See for example, Robert Sade, "Medical Care as a Right: Refutation," *The New England Journal of Medicine*, 285 (December, 1971).
7 This section draws extensively on T. R. Marmor, *Politics of Medicare* (London: Routledge and Kegan Paul, Ltd., 1970).
8 For an account of this episode, see Daniel Hirschfield, *The Lost Reform: The Campaign for Compulsory Health Insurance in the U.S. from 1932–1943* (Cambridge: Harvard University Press, 1970).
9 Robert M. Ball, "The American Social Security Program," *New England Journal of Medicine*, 170 (January 30, 1964), pp. 232–236.
10 Theodore J. Lowi, "American Business, Public Policy and Political Theory," *World Politics*, 16 (1964).
11 Aaron Wildavsky, *Dixon Yates: A Study in Power Politics* (New Haven: Yale University Press, 1962), pp. 5–6, 304–305.
12 Theodore Marmor, *The Politics of Medicare* (Chicago: Aldine Publishing Co., 1973); Eugene Feingold, *Medicare: Policy and Politics* (San Francisco: Chandler Publishing Co., 1966); Richard Harris, *A Sacred Trust* (Baltimore: Penguin Books, 1969).
13 Lyndon Johnson, *The Vantage Point: Perspectives of the Presidency, 1963–1969*, (New York: Holt, Rinehart, and Winston, 1971), p. 220.
14 Karen Davis, "Health and the Great Society: Successes of the Past Decade and the Road Ahead" in David C. Warner (ed.), *Toward New Human Rights* (Austin: Lyndon B. Johnson School of Public Affairs, University of Texas at Austin, 1977), pp. 183–211.
15 Karen Davis, *National Health Insurance, Benefits, Costs, and Consequences* (Washington, D.C.: The Brookings Institution, 1975), Tables 3–10, p. 43.
16 Lu Ann Aday and Ronald Andersen, *Access to Medical Care* (Ann Arbor, Mich.: Health Administration Press, 1975).

17 See Karen Davis and Roger Reynolds, "The Impact of Medicare and Medicaid on Access to Medical Care" in Richard Rosett (ed.), *The Role of Insurance in the Health Services Sector*. A Universities NBER Conference.

18 See the data prepared by the National Center for Health Statistics for the Child Health Task Force.

19 U.S. Social Security Administration, Compendium of National Health Expenditure Data DHEW (SSA) 73-11903, Table 8, pp. 58, 66.

20 Lyndon Johnson, *op. cit.*, p. 220.

21 See Karen Davis, "A Decade of Policy Developments in Providing Health Care for Low-Income Families" in Robert Haveman (ed.), *A Decade of Federal Anti-Poverty Policy: Failures and Lessons* (Madison: Institute for Research on Poverty, University of Wisconsin, 1977).

22 U.S. Department of Health, Education, and Welfare, Office of the Assistant Secretary for Planning and Evaluation, "Human Investment Program, Delivery and Health Services for the Poor," processed, 1967.

23 U.S. Social Security Administration, *op. cit.*

24 See Alfred Skolnik and Sophie R. Dales, "Social Welfare Expenditures, 1972–73," *Social Security Bulletin*, 37(1)(January, 1974), Table 6, p. 14.

25 Both RMP and CHP legislation expired in 1974 and were replaced by the National Health Planning and Resources Development Act (PL-93-641).

26 This problem is explored much more fully in Michael Zubkoff (ed.), *Health—A Victim or Cause of Inflation* (New York: Prodist, 1976).

III. The politics of national health insurance

8. Welfare medicine: how success can be a failure

THEODORE R. MARMOR

Medical care is a growth industry, in rates of inflation as well as scholarship, in utilization as well as public concern. The inflation rates, public concern, and scholarly attention are all related: rising costs have been chiefly responsible for the shrill claims of a "medical care crisis."

Over the past quarter century, the share of the nation's resources spent on medical care has increased 80%, from 4.6% to 8.3% of GNP in 1975.[1] The increases in the past half decade have been explosive: a 70% rise in total health expenditures and a near doubling of the program costs of Medicare and Medicaid (the two largest governmental health efforts).[2] The trend shows no signs of abating: last year combined public and private health expenditures rose an estimated $14 billion to a total of $118 billion.[3]

The consequent debate on the causes of the cost spiral has posed questions about the impact of such outlays on present and future governmental efforts to finance medical care services. In addition, the economic considerations have prompted reappraisals of the quality, organization, and distribution of America's medical care facilities. Even though most Americans regard their own medical care as satisfactory, there is widespread concern that American medicine is not healthy.[4]

Reflecting that concern, a number of commentators have addressed controversial features of American medicine. Some have critically examined the unequal distribution of access to medical care.[5] Others have reviewed the recent cycles of social concern and governmental response, concentrating on subjects as diverse as the politics of health in New York City and governmental programs for migrant workers.[6] But few have cast their subject against such a broad historical background as Rosemary and Robert Stevens in their recent work, *Welfare Medicine in America*.[7]

Reprinted by permission of The Yale Law Journal Co. and Fred B. Rothman & Co. from *The Yale Law Journal*, 85:1149–1159, 1976. Copyright © 1976 by The Yale Law Journal Co. and Fred B. Rothman & Co.

This chapter is a review essay of *Welfare Medicine in America: A Case Study of Medicaid* by Robert Stevens and Rosemary Stevens (New York: Free Press, 1974). The author wants to thank Norm Groetzinger for his assistance in drafting this review.

Welfare Medicine is primarily a detailed political history of Medicaid since its creation in 1965[8]—a narrative of its origins, enactment, and programmatic instability. In the course of that history, however, the Stevenses touch on a number of the more widely debated aspects of American social policy: the consequences of federal-state matching fund programs for the poor, the relative merits of cash as opposed to in-kind methods of wealth redistribution, the differences between broadly based social insurance programs and selective schemes of public assistance, and the implications of programs such as Medicaid for the current national health insurance debate in the United States. A review of this work is perforce a partial review of America's welfare state and its critics during the past decade. Because the Stevenses chose the historical method, there are significant gaps in *Welfare Medicine*'s discussion. For example, their historical account does not sort out the reasons for Medicaid's unanticipated growth. But the book's most critical omission is the lack of a systematic appraisal of Medicaid's performance. Nor is there much discussion of Medicaid's implications for the future of American medicine. Moreover, even as a history, the work's relatively narrow focus leaves to others the task of portraying fully the recent history of the American welfare state.

I. Medicaid's unanticipated development

From the outset, Medicaid was a paradoxical program. It was enacted as a practically thoughtless addition to the Medicare Act of 1965[9] and was codified as Title XIX of the Social Security Act.[10] A welfare companion to Medicare's social insurance approach, Medicaid was a carryover of the Kerr-Mills program.[11] It continued the latter program's federal-state funding mechanism, and was therefore neither programmatically nor philosophically innovative. As a scheme for financing the medical care of some poor Americans, Medicaid retained the Kerr-Mills tradition of payments to vendors, but expanded the eligible population to include all medically needy beneficiaries of other federal-state public assistance programs.[12] While each state sets maximum income levels for eligibility, the Act required the states to comply with federal administrative guidelines. Once the state program was approved, federal funds became available to match state payments to vendors of medical care. Under the expanded program, vendor payments were available for a variety of services: hospital care for both inpatients and outpatients, certain diagnostic services, nursing home care, and physicians' services.[13]

Medicaid incorporated not only Kerr-Mills's technique of vendor payments but also its supporters' expectation that the states would restrain both the benefits and the number of eligible persons. That expectation of slow growth was reflected in estimates that Medicaid would add only $250 million to the $1.3 billion projected for Kerr-Mills in 1965.[14] Programs for the poor were clearly presumed to be poor programs. This presumption meant that in 1965 federal legislators would confidently write sweeping language about making medical care available to all the poor by 1975; likewise, writers of HEW regulations could assume that federal rules reflecting that language would not be political dynamite. The same presumption enabled policymakers to speak boldly about the comprehensive medical benefits which Medicaid initially would offer to the categorically poor and, within a reasonable period, to all the poor.[15]

Thus, few anticipated the financial, medical, or political consequences when Medicaid began in 1966. The limitations of its predecessor—Kerr-Mills—had not been carefully examined; the inflation in medical care prices which helped justify financial intervention by the government was largely ignored by congressional and HEW program comments; and, most importantly, no one anticipated the dramatic enlargement of the welfare rolls.[16]

When it became apparent that Medicaid was being used far beyond expectation, the adverse reaction was dramatic. Yet, while critics have decried the rise both in the number of eligibles and in the program's expenditures, few have recognized that Medicaid's real outlays have not increased since 1968. In fact, average per capita expenditures, adjusted for inflation, have slightly declined from $167 in 1968 to $162 in 1974.[17]

Welfare Medicine relates the history of political backlash beginning with the drain on state budgets, followed by public outcry, cutbacks on eligibility, recipient frustration, provider resistance, widespread charges of fraud and abuse, and ending with the emergence in the early 1970s of broader governmental efforts to regulate the medical care industry. The primary virtue of the Stevenses' book is that it relates much of this complex history with detail, clarity, and a wealth of rarely accessible sources. The Stevenses provide extensive documentation of Medicaid's political history in New York and California, the evolution of its federal bureaucracy, and the role of the courts in Medicaid's fate. Telling that tale is a difficult historical task; keeping the reader interested, as Stevens and Stevens do, is a substantial scholarly achievement.

II. Appraising Medicaid's performance: the difficulties

While absorbing as administrative and political history, *Welfare Medicine* is less satisfactory as an evaluation of Medicaid. In fairness, the Stevenses do not present their work as essentially an appraisal so much as a history; and they recognize that much remains to be done, including "quantitative studies of selected aspects of the program, and especially its cost and utilization...."[18] Nevertheless, the Stevenses trust that "the historical method" can both relate how the program developed *and* provide an understanding of Medicaid's "strengths" and "weaknesses."[19] Throughout, they do evaluate Medicaid, but because of the historical organization the bases of assessing the program's "strengths" and "weaknesses" are not systematically presented. This problem is in some ways typical of what one may regard as the Fabian school of social policy historians.[20] With a clear notion of what social programs should be like, Fabian historians can treat the gap between standard and fact as evaluation. Telling the tale of a program is, by reference to the ideal program, simultaneously evaluative. But the energy is directed at narrative, not explicit appraisal.

For example, at the time of its enactment Medicaid had two announced purposes: increasing the poor's access to medical care and providing that care in the mainstream of American medicine. In other words, the poor were to receive more medical care and receive it from the same providers utilized by the rest of the population. How well the program satisfied those purposes is only ambivalently treated in *Welfare Medicine*. On the one hand, the Stevenses argue that Medicaid was "phenomenally successful"[21] in the magnitude of its coverage; on the other hand, they seem to believe that Medicaid's root problems, though evidenced by rising costs, inhered in the program's "goals, authority, and administration."[22]

Recent research has demonstrated that Medicaid did substantially expand the poor's access to medical care but failed to bring the poor into the mainstream of providers. The increased use of physician services by the poor since 1965 is impressive. In 1964, families whose incomes were below the federal poverty line averaged 4.3 visits per member to a physician. By 1973, visits for the same group had risen to 5.6, compared to 4.6 and 4.9 for middle and upper income family members, respectively.[23] Furthermore, the poor are now hospitalized more frequently than before Medicaid's implementation.[24] Both these trends make a mockery of any claim that Medicaid has been a complete failure.

Increased access alone does not establish that the poor have attained meaningful parity in utilization or quality of care. The poor suffer from illness more frequently than other segments of the population; thus, equal access to care would mean even higher rates of utilization than now exist. Moreover, the poor (and rural) are markedly less likely to have a regular source of care than the non-poor (and urban).[25] Children from central cities and rural areas are least likely, according to 1970 data, to see a physician at least once during the year. Perhaps most importantly, the poor continue to have fewer physician visits in response to days of disability than the rest of the population.[26] Yet the increased access to *some* medical care associated with the expansion of Medicaid is undeniable.

Whether the quality of care the poor receive equals that of the rest of the population is far more problematic. It is clear, however, that the poor receive their care from different sorts of physicians in different types of settings than do the non-poor. Medicaid has not markedly improved the access of poor children to mainstream private sources of care and has had a minimal impact on the current pattern of locating and providing care to the poor.[27] Poor children, particularly racial minorities in the central cities, are still the most frequent users of hospital outpatient services. In 1974, approximately 4.5% of the regular physician visits by the general child population were to hospital-based facilities; among children in central cities the percentage was twice that.[28] While the poor use more outpatient departments and general practitioners for their care, the more affluent disproportionately receive specialist care in physicians' offices.

While Medicaid has thus moved toward its goals with mixed success, little political attention has been devoted to evaluating those achievements and shortcomings. Instead, as the Stevenses make clear, criticism has focused on Medicaid's costs. Some of that attention is understandable, as total expenditures have far exceeded initial estimates. Yet, while similar dramatic increases have marked the Medicare program for the elderly, the political controversy over it has not matched Medicaid's. Part of the reason is that the federal-state financing of welfare programs decentralizes, and therefore multiplies, fiscal conflict, while financing Medicare through Social Security centralizes political oversight at great geographic remove from state and local tax disputes.

Critics who attribute the increased Medicaid costs to mismanagement fail to perceive the true causes. The predominant reason for the growth in Medicaid's expenditures is the increase in the number of eligibles.[29] The national economic conditions that affect the numerical size of America's welfare population are beyond the control of Medicaid's managers, however competent. A second important factor in Medicaid's expenditure growth over the past decade has been the unmatched inflation in medical care prices.[30] In dealing with increased prices, Medicaid's performance has been mixed, not disastrous as reports of budget overruns would have one believe. But not all cost reduction efforts have been without adverse effect. Many states have reduced costs by restricting eligibility and benefits. The poor in those states have thus borne part of the impact of a medical cost inflation to which Medicaid did not significantly contribute. Some states, most notably California and New York, have paid physicians on a fixed fee schedule lower than Medicaid's "usual and customary" reimbursement schedule. Here again, the impact has been to restrain the growth in Medicaid's program costs at the expense of making poor patients less attractive to mainstream providers of care. The dilemma is clear. Cost control in Medicaid has often conflicted with the goal of expanding access of the poor to mainstream American medicine.

Another misconception underlies the tendency to equate Medicaid's difficulties with the political controversies over Aid to Families with Dependent Children (AFDC). It is politically fashionable to link AFDC growth to the proposition that Medicaid is beyond fiscal control. But Medicaid is significantly affected by the aged's increased use of social welfare programs generally. Nearly 40% of Medicaid expenditures in 1970 were for the elderly. AFDC health outlays for adults and children that year comprised $1.7 billion of the $4.8 billion total, nearly $50 million less than expenditures for the elderly.[31] A realistic appraisal of

Medicaid's growth, therefore, must emphasize the actual distribution of expenditures among recipient groups.

The growth of Medicaid, one must conclude, is paradoxical. Most of the rising costs are explained by the growth of welfare and the general medical cost inflation, not by Medicaid's generosity. To the extent that Medicaid reached more of the poor in the late 1960s, it successfully expanded access. With substantial utilization among both the aged and non-aged, costs had to rise. When costs rose, those who had expected slow expenditure growth were outraged. Substantive program success, ironically, has meant instability in political support and an intense search for scapegoats among the poor and the providers. Unfortunately, in relating the history of the growth of Medicaid expenditures, *Welfare Medicine* fails to sort out and appraise the diverse contributing factors.

III. Medicaid and American medicine

Welfare Medicine is most unabashedly evaluative in examining the interaction of Medicaid with the structure of American medicine. Medicaid's enrichment of providers, the authors assert, occurs because of an "unreconstructed, predominantly private system of medical care delivery."[32] Because they blame the private system for Medicaid's cost difficulties, they conclude that "further extensions of health benefits will have to tackle the structure and function of the health care system."[33]

It is safe to presume that American medical arrangements shaped the fate of Medicaid far more than the program transformed American medicine. As John Holahan has written, "Medicaid has been as much a victim of rising prices as a contributor, and perhaps more so" in view of its financing care for less than 10% of the population.[34] So there is good reason for regarding Medicaid as the expression, not the cause, of American medicine's problems. But are those problems best understood as those of an "unreconstructed, predominantly private system"—problems which would be solved by a reconstructed public system?

It is here that *Welfare Medicine* most strikingly reveals the loyalties of the Stevenses to the British National Health Service model. To decry an "unreconstructed" private American system is to oversimplify the problems which do exist. Our medical care arrangements constitute a mix of public, not-for-profit, and proprietary institutions, of small entrepreneurs and cooperative ventures, all operating amidst a bewildering variety of financing mechanisms. All levels of government combined now finance 40% of all medical care costs;[35] thus, calling the system "private" indicates little more than that facilities are not publicly owned and physicians are not salaried. There are, of course, serious difficulties with the cost, quality, distribution, and organization of American medical care, but they will not yield to public financing alone. The common concern about these topics in the western industrial countries testifies that many of our medical care problems are intractable and not simply the results of an ideological resistance to a larger governmental role in medicine.[36]

The preference for public ownership of facilities and direct control of personnel permeates *Welfare Medicine*. Yet, within the United States, our experience with public schools and public transportation hardly supports the argument that public ownership promotes equity and generosity. Nor is it persuasive to characterize our current cost problems as peculiarly those of a "private" system. It can be argued that fee-for-service remuneration—combined with state failure to monitor the quality of care—leaves the public vulnerable to quackery. It might be that nationalization of medicine within the market economy would address such problems successfully. But it cannot be shown from cross-national research that the cost problems of modern medicine are so closely linked to the nature of the financing and legal control of its facilities and personnel.[37]

Welfare Medicine is also disappointing in its discussion of changes in government regulatory efforts towards medicine. It concentrates on how the states reacted to Medicaid's cost increases but skirts the development of health planning and regulatory bodies. The charges of program overlap, duplication of equipment, and unnecessary surgery are part of the litany of the current public debate over American medical care.[38] The concern for controlling costs, increasing regulation, and expanding financial access through national health insurance partly resulted from the experiences of Medicare and Medicaid, but it was less the impact of these programs on the American poor that prompted reform attention than the threats to private and public budgets from rising medical care expenditures.[39]

IV. Medicaid's place in America's welfare state: the politics of change without choice and choice without change

The overriding concern about costs which has dominated discussion of Medicaid has, in turn, obscured other issues. Of those, possibly the most significant has been the role of Medicaid in the future of America's poverty policy. A programmatic history of Medicaid such as *Welfare Medicine* could not have been expected to address that issue systematically. Nevertheless, the issue is important and merits greater attention.

The focus on costs is understandable: Medicaid's fiscal impact on governmental outlays to the poor has been enormous. It has come to be the largest single program for the poor by the measuring rod of public costs ($9.2 billion in 1973).[40] By contrast, the most controversial welfare program, AFDC, represents a smaller fiscal outlay ($7.8 billion in 1973).[41] Yet the politics of these two types of redistribution—in-kind and in-cash—have been strikingly different. Throughout the late 1960s and early 1970s, the proposal for a guaranteed income to America's poor was continually on the national political agenda. A presidential commission deliberated between 1968 and 1969 on what income maintenance scheme the nation should adopt to replace the allegedly inadequate, inequitable, and fiscally burdensome patchwork of public assistance.[42] During President Nixon's first term, the centerpiece of his domestic strategy was a guaranteed income for families with children—the widely publicized Family Assistance Plan (FAP).[43] Yet, though public choice focused on cash transfers for the poor, policy change did not involve any cash transfer program. Instead, changes were marked by new programs which had not been included in the reform debate.

Within public assistance, the aged, disabled, and blind poor were shifted to a new federal program that emerged in the wake of FAP's flop, the 1974 Supplementary Security Income program.[44] But, even more clearly, the balance of American antipoverty efforts turned without national debate to the categorical noncash schemes of food stamps and Medicaid. Why this happened is a topic *Welfare Medicine* does not address systematically. Where it discusses the struggle over FAP, *Welfare Medicine* regards the debate as having delayed Medicaid reforms.[45] This is no doubt true if only because the debate absorbed the energies of the nation's top federal welfare officials.

Yet there is a more profound relationship between Medicaid's growth and the demise of welfare reform dreams. Just as Medicaid's decentralized financing scheme relegated budget disputes to the state and local levels, the federal welfare reform efforts centralized the dispute over the proper treatment of the poor. The outlays for Medicaid emerged from the dispersed decisions of state political processes; no one chose to spend what Medicaid cost, though governments had to pay for what Medicaid patients used. In contrast, the fight over FAP made explicit the costs of public assistance reform. As recent research on FAP has made clear, the federal politics of redistribution gave liberals and conservatives ample opportunity to weigh the claims of the poor on the nation's resources.[46] Although failing by a close margin in 1972, FAP revealed the powerful opposition of the American public and its politicians to unconditional cash grants to the poor.[47] The Medicaid program, along with food stamps, shows by contrast how rapidly programs for the poor can grow when (a) the benefits are tied to legitimate items of expenditure (food and medical care, not booze) and (b) the costs of relatively generous treatment emerge from decentralized program operations, not national choice.

Welfare Medicine, then, is a fascinating guide to the controversies spawned by Medicaid's unexpected development. Its documentation of Medicaid's fate is inspiringly extensive, and its literary grace is a welcome change from much social policy analysis. But the Stevenses' historical account has left to others the task of fully appraising Medicaid's past. Likewise, *Welfare Medicine* has only an abbreviated discussion of Medicaid's implications for the future of American medicine. Nevertheless, scholars who seek to fill those gaps will owe a substantial debt to the Stevenses for their administrative and political history of the great program afterthought of 1965, Medicaid.

Notes

1 Skolnik & Dales, "Social Welfare Expenditures, 1950–75," 39 *Soc. Security Bull.* 3, 15 (1976).

2 Id.

3 Id.

4 See, e.g., *A Declaration of Interdependence: Developing America's Health Policy* 34–35 (E. Shields ed. 1975); Anderson, Kravits, & Anderson, "The Public's View of the Crisis in Medical Care: An Impetus for Changing Delivery Systems," 24 *Econ. & Bus. Bull.* 44, 45–46, 51 (1971).

5 E.g., Aday, "The Impact of Health Policy on Access to Medical Care," 54 *Health & Soc'y* 215 (1976).

6 R. Alford, *Health Care Politics* (1975); B. Shenkin, *Health Care for Migrant Workers: Policies & Politics* (1974).

7 R. Stevens & R. Stevens, *Welfare Medicine in America: A Case Study of Medicaid* (1974) [hereinafter cited by page number only].

8 As enacted in 1965, Medicaid was but an expansion of existing programs. P. 51. See pp. 1150–51 infra.

9 Pub. L. No. 89–97, tit. I, pt. 2, 79 Stat. 286.

10 42 U.S.C. §§ 1396–1396d (Supp. V 1965–1969) (current version at 42 U.S.C.A. §§ 1396–1396i (West 1974, 1975 Supp. & March 1976 Pamphlet).

11 The Kerr–Mills program increased federal matching grants to states which made payments to welfare recipients under old-age assistance. In addition, it provided new federal funds for the "medically indigent" who were not receiving cash payments and "whose income might be above state eligibility levels for cash assistance." P. 29.

12 Pp. 57–69. See J. Holahan, *Financing Health Care for the Poor* 2–3 (1975). Those programs included Aid to Families with Dependent Children (AFDC), Old Age Assistance (OAA), Aid to the Blind (AB), and Aid to the Permanently and Totally Disabled (APTD). P. 61.

13 Pp. 65–68.

14 J. Holahan, *supra* note 12, at 3, Far outstripping those estimates, by 1967 Medicaid costs exceeded Kerr-Mills expenditures by almost $2 billion. P. 364.

15 This interpretation is drawn from T. Marmor, *The Politics of Medicare* 37, 68 (1973), and from the reviewer's experience in the office of the Undersecretary of HEW during the summer of 1966.

16 Id. at 88, 90.

17 K. Davis, *National Health Insurance: Benefits, Costs, and Consequences* 42 (1975); L. Russell, B. Bourque, & C. Burke, *Federal Health Spending 1969–74*, (1974), p. 64.

18 P. xx.

19 Id.

20 What I have loosely termed Fabianism refers to the mode of social policy analysis often found in the publications of the British Fabian Society but is particularly evident among the Stevenses' former colleagues at the London School of Economics. Examples of such historical writing include B. Abel-Smith, *A History of the Nursing Profession* (1960); B. Abel-Smith, *The Hospital, 1800–1948: A Study in Social Administration in England and Wales* (1964); B. Abel-Smith & R. Stevens, *Lawyers and Courts: A Sociological Study of the English Legal System, 1750–1965* (1967). But the extensive use of historical materials by such authors is not restricted to books of history: their analyses of current issues in social welfare—such as R. Titmuss, *Commitment to Welfare* (1968)—stress the necessity of understanding where we are by how we got there.

21 P. xvi.
22 P. 132.
23 United States Department of Health, Education and Welfare, Public Health Service, *Health United States 1975*, at 289 (1976).
24 Id. at 309.
25 National Center for Health Statistics, Division of Analysis Report, at table C.7 (1974) (on file with *Yale Law Journal*) [hereinafter cited as Report].
26 L. Aday & R. Anderson, *Development of Indices of Access to Medical Care* 42–43 (1975); Aday, *supra* note 5, at 215–16.
27 Report, *supra* note 25, at table C.7.
28 Id.
29 J. Holahan, *supra* note 12, at 27–28, 32.
30 Id. at 27–31.
31 Id. at 10.
32 P. 202.
33 P. 358.
34 J. Holahan, *Supra* note 12, at 31.
35 Office of Management and Budget, *Special Analysis Budget of the United States Government Fiscal Year 1974*, at 170 (1975); Staff of Subcomm. on Health of the House Comm. on Ways and Means, 94th Cong., 2d Sess., *Basic Charts on Health Care* 44–45 (1975).
36 See R. Maxwell, *Health Care—The Growing Dilemma* (1975).
37 The degree of public financing of health does not appear to be the significant factor in lower health expenditures. In Canada, Sweden, and the United States comparable shares of national income are spent on health while the proportion of government spending varies from 40% in the United States to nearly 100% in Canada and Sweden. A stronger case can be made that concentrating financial responsibility and administrative authority at one level of government—and thus diverting political competitors for public health expenditure from other public ministries—produces lower levels of medical care outlays. For a discussion of Great Britain's comparatively ascetic record on this count, see chapter 3 of this volume.
38 P. 357. For a report on one of these complaints, see Subcomm. on Oversight and Investigations of the House Comm. on Interstate and Foreign Commerce, 94th Cong., 2d Sess., *Cost and Quality of Health Care: Unnecessary Surgery* (Comm. Print 1976).
39 For an elaboration of this argument and the polling data on which it is based, see Marmor, "The Politics of National Health Insurance," 3 *Pol'y Analysis* (Winter, 1977; 25–48).
40 Skolnik & Dales, *supra* note 1, at 15.
41 M. Barth, G. Carcagno & J. Palmer, *Toward an Effective Income Support System: Problems, Prospects, and Choices* 15 (1974).
42 For the findings and recommendations of that commission, see *The Report of the President's Commission on Income Maintenance Programs, Poverty Amid Plenty* (1969).
43 For the history of FAP, see Marmor & Rein, "Reforming 'The Welfare Mess': The Fate of the Family Assistance Plan, 1969–72," in *Policy and Politics in America: Six Case Studies* 3 (A. Sindler ed. 1973).
44 42 U.S.C. §§ 1381 (Supp. IV 1974).
45 Pp. 221–26, 327–29.
46 *E.g.*, M. Bowler, *The Nixon Guaranteed Income Proposal: Substance and Process in Policy Change* (1974); V. Burke & V. Burke, *Nixon's Good Deed: Welfare Reform* (1974).
47 See W. Hoffman & T. Marmor, "The Politics of Public Assistance Reform: An Essay Review," 50 *Soc. Serv. Rev.* 11, 15 n.6 (1976).

9. National health insurance: some lessons from the Canadian experience

THEODORE R. MARMOR, WAYNE L. HOFFMAN,
THOMAS C. HEAGY

Introduction

Problems of medical care and issues of national health insurance are salient features of contemporary American politics. Within the larger public there is a broadly diffused sense of unease about the costs of illness and the reliability of access to medical services.[1] In the arena of national politics there has been visible attention to the details of competing national health insurance proposals and some searching for realistic appraisals of the effects of alternative interventions on problems of cost, quality and access. This is clearly an atmosphere in which informed understanding of other national experiences with governmental health insurance could aid policy discussion and choice.

Canada's experience, in particular, holds potentially important lessons for American decisionmaking. Canada's encounter with the effects of a national health insurance program, which predates but is closely akin to some current American proposals, offers a natural experiment that deserves careful examination. Our purpose is to use the Canadian experience as a model predicting both the *impact* on the medical care system of the enactment of national health insurance and the *reactions* of national policymakers and the general public to these changes.

The case for American scrutiny of Canadian national health insurance experience rests on at least two propositions. First of all, the health care concerns of the two societies are strikingly similar. Worry about the increased proportion of national resources going to medical care is widespread and some uncertainty about the marginal benefits of increased expenditures is visible among the public

From *Policy Sciences*, 6:447–466, 1975. Copyright ©1975 by Elsevier Scientific Publishing Co. Reprinted with permission. More recent data are taken from "National Health Insurance: Further Reflections on Canada's Path, America's Choices," in Ronald L. Numbers, ed., *Compulsory Health Insurance: The Continuing American Debate* (Westport, Conn.: Greenwood Press, 1982), pp. 77–96.

Other published versions include "NHI: Can the U.S. Learn from Canada?" in Spyros Andreopoulos, ed., *National Health Insurance: Can We Learn from Canada?* (New York: Wiley, 1975), pp. 231–250, and "National Health Insurance: Canada's Path, America's Choices" with Edward Tenner, *Challenge*, 20 (2): 13–21, 1977.

officials of both countries. Beyond resource costs, there is common concern about equal access financially, geographically, and socially. Among a relatively small but vocal group in each country there is substantial interest in questions of quality and organization of care, and ferment about regulating medical care providers. Finally, after many years of similar focus on expansion of medical care facilities and personnel, there are parallel Canadian and American efforts to reduce, particularly, the use of expensive hospital services and to resist any increase in the number of hospital beds, and, to a lesser extent, physicians and some other medical care resources.

Our second proposition, quite simply stated, is that Canada is enough like the United States to make the effects of Canadian health insurance policies rather like a large natural experiment. The industrial countries of the West share, of course, a great number of medical policy concerns, but major political, social, economic, or cultural differences raise questions about whether the United States would have similar experiences with similar public policy interventions.[2] These differences are far less marked with Canada. Our particular two-nation research design would be termed a "most similar systems" approach in the more technical social science literature on cross-national comparisons.[3] This paradigm requires that the nations compared share a broad array of factors which might be causally related to the narrower features of central analytic concern. This is the case for our comparison. Canada has extensive decentralization of authority with a tradition of dispute over federal power analogous, though by no means identical, to controversies over American federalism. The structure of the health industry and the history of voluntary health insurance in Canada and the United States are strikingly similar. American and Canadian hospitals are largely "voluntary" and not government-owned, and physicians in both are still paid under a largely fee-for-service system. The two countries adjusted similarly to the growth of health insurance, which was primarily private at first, but in the postwar period increasingly public in character.[4]

Two major differences between the American and Canadian experiences are often put forward against using Canada as a "most similar system." These are the greater independence of the Canadian provincial governments, and the different route followed by Canada to national health insurance. The major implication of the greater *independence*, both constitutionally and politically, of the Canadian provincial governments is that, to the extent United States policymakers build in a greater role for the states, *ceteris paribus*, the more the problems of cost control and national standards for the national government will imitate the Canadian experience. American planners, however, possess a policy option denied to the Canadian planners by constitutional stricture—the option of a centralized federal system. In the American context, the extent of state involvement is a matter for public choice.

Turning to the second major Canadian–American difference, observers recall that Canada's first big step toward national insurance came via the hospital sector in 1958, followed a decade later by full-scale coverage of physician services. In contrast, the United States' advance on the road to national health insurance has been an incremental extension of coverage to additional segments of the population, first the aged, then the poor, and perhaps finally the full citizenry. The implication of this difference for political characterizations of the welfare state debate in the two countries may be great, but the limitation it places on the likely consequences of a national health plan seems small. The routes to full coverage have been different, but, once arriving at the same point, the concerns and policy options that result from that public commitment are likely to bear a strong resemblance. In summary, the number of shared similarities makes Canadian experience with health policy instruments a valuable source of conditional predictions for the United States.

This paper addresses the implications of Canadian national health insurance experience for problems of rising cost and unequal access to medical care. Canadian policies have been several years ahead of the United States in attempting some measures for the control of costs and the fairer distribution of medical care. Our analysis shows that the United States health policies, though lagging, have been remarkably similar in outcome. The power of the comparison is enhanced by the fact that American outcomes matched the *predictions that could have been made on our knowledge of Canadian experience alone.* We can predict the consequences of policy choice not only in terms of the key indicators of health care inflation, utilization, access and distribution, but also with respect to the likely concerns such first-stage effects will generate among politicians and administrators. Such policy analysis may make the appraisal of similar instrumentalities in American proposals more realistic and informed than usual.

It is perhaps appropriate here to mention a serious difficulty in transplanting Canadian experience into the current American debate over national health insurance. Canada does not constitute a laboratory for the full range of health insurance programs. Without extensive coinsurance or deductibles, Canada does not allow us a test of such a national scheme in practice, though her reluctance to employ such policies may be relevant to the discussion. Further, the reputed advantages of prepaid group practice cannot be tested from Canadian experience nor can the way be seen for using national health insurance as a prod for the expansion of that delivery mode. Group practice, quite simply, has been too small a part of Canada's experience for exportation of lessons. It should thus be emphasized that the Canadian experience bears most directly on those American proposals that closely resemble it.

Historical background of Canadian national health insurance[5]

Fundamental to an understanding of health care legislation in Canada is the fact that the constitutional division of powers between the provinces and the federal government puts health care (with a few minor exceptions) squarely in the jurisdiction of the provinces. This jurisdictional factor has had a fundamental effect on the form, and, to a lesser extent, the content of all of the legislation leading up to and including National Health Insurance.

The National Health Grant Program, beginning in 1948, provided the financial basis for a nationwide program of hospital expansion. Unlike the similar program in the United States (under the Hill–Burton Act), this expansion of hospital facilities was specifically intended to prepare the way for national hospital insurance which was subsequently enacted in 1957, and implemented beginning in 1958; the last province, Quebec, joined in 1961. A program for insurance covering physician and related services was enacted in 1966 (the Medical Care Act) with the various provinces joining between 1968 and 1971.

Both programs (hospital and physician service insurance) provide for government subsidy (averaging 50%) of programs set up and administered by the provinces, provided the programs meet certain standards of universality, coverage, and administration. Although joining is optional for each province, the financial incentives for doing so proved to be irresistible and every province participates in both programs. The percentage of subsidy by the federal government varies for different provinces. It is higher for provinces that spend less per capita on covered medical services, the highest subsidy being about 80%.

The provinces are permitted (with considerable limitations) to utilize point-of-service charges to raise revenue or discourage unnecessary utilization, but these have been unpopular, and only three provinces (Alberta, British Columbia, and the Northwest Territories) currently use them. For most Canadians, national health insurance contains no deductible and no copayment up to the federally mandated standards. To go beyond the standards of the public program (especially the ward accommodation standard for hospitalization), many Canadians purchase supplementary coverage insurance.

Inflation and cost control policy

Broadly speaking, the striking fact about cross-national cost comparisons between Canada and the United States is their parallel experience. The trends of prices, utilization, and expenditures are similar and the proportion of national resources spent on health is almost identical[6] (see Figs. 1 and 2). By the late 1960s there was a sense of inflationary crisis in both countries and a common worry about ways to contain the inflation.[7] For simplicity, we will discuss Canadian cost experience with hospitals separately from physicians' services. (While it is convenient to treat these separately, it must be kept in mind that physicians have a major role in the determination of hospital expenditures.)

Hospitals

What are the implications of the growth of Canadian hospital expenditures and governmental efforts to restrain it? It should be noted that Canada and the United

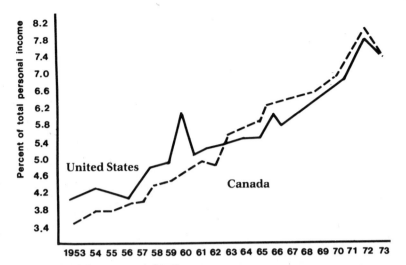

Fig. 1. Expenditures on personal health care in the United States and Canada, 1953–1973 (as a percentage of personal income).
Sources: United States—Reinhardt and Branson, "Preliminary Tabulation of Selected Comparative Statistics on the Canadian and U.S. Health Care Systems," (August 1974) mimeograph.
Canada—Robert G. Evans, "Beyond the Medical Marketplace: Expenditures, Utilization and Pricing of Insured Health in Canada," Table 3, p. 140, in Spyros Andreopoulos, ed., *National Health Insurance: Can We Learn from Canada?* (New York: John Wiley and Sons, 1975).

States proceeded in the postwar period from somewhat different starting points as to number and costs of beds; they have experienced very similar trends. Canada still remains more generously supplied with hospital beds per capita and has higher rates of hospital admissions, patient days of care and expenditures per capita[8] (see Fig. 3).

American interpreters of Canada must understand that national hospital insurance, in and of itself, does not seem to have caused rapidly increased use of hospitals in Canada. But it did bring more rapid increases in expenditures for hospital services.[9] Most of the postwar increases in hospital expenditures in both America and Canada are accounted for by growth in expenses per patient day, not increased per capita utilization. From 1953 to 1971, Canadian hospital expenditures per capita (in constant dollars) increased 259% while hospital patient days per capita only increased 29%.[10] Thus, increased utilization accounted for only a small part of the total increase in expenditures. The most important part of the increase in real expenditures on hospitalization can be attributed to the increase in the relative wages of hospital workers. Evans estimates that from 1953 to 1971, the average wage of hospital workers increased 68% more than the average wage of all industrial workers.[11]

R. G. Evans' interpretation[12] suggests that hospital admission is not very

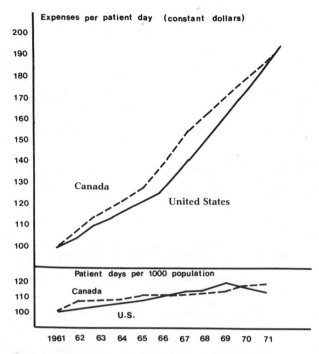

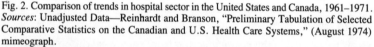

Fig. 2. Comparison of trends in hospital sector in the United States and Canada, 1961–1971. *Sources*: Unadjusted Data—Reinhardt and Branson, "Preliminary Tabulation of Selected Comparative Statistics on the Canadian and U.S. Health Care Systems," (August 1974) mimeograph.
U.S. Price Deflator (Consumer Price Index)—Bureau of Labor Statistics, *Monthly Labor Review* (various issues).
Canada Price Deflator (Consumer Price Index)—Statistics Canada, *Canada's Yearbook*.

sensitive to price; i.e., reduction in point-of-service costs of care did not lead to a large increase in utilization. Based on his view, it follows that copayment mechanisms designed to reduce costs by directing incentives at patients will have little effect on utilization, will redistribute costs to the ill, and, in hospitals, will not restrain increasing costs.[13] This interpretation of Canadian hospital inflation, for purposes of American discussion, raises doubts about the value of cost-sharing provisions in a number of current national health insurance proposals.

The fact that Canadian hospital cost increases were dramatic in the late 1960s, on the other hand, has serious implications for proposed methods of restraining hospital expenditures in the United States, such as detailed budget review, incentive reimbursement schemes with global (as opposed to line) budgeting and direct bed control. Canada has employed detailed budget review for more than a decade, and while it is apparently a good instrument for detecting fraud, it has not been judged a successful expenditure restraint and has been partially replaced in some provinces with global budgets and special incentives.[14] Indeed, it ap-

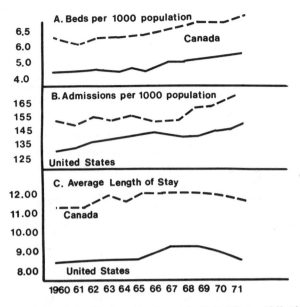

Fig. 3. Hospital utilization—Canada and the United States, 1960–1971.
Source: Reinhardt and Branson, "Preliminary Tabulation of Selected Comparative Statistics on the Canadian and U.S. Health Care Systems," (August 1974) mimeograph.

pears fair to conclude that Canadian officials have accepted a bed supply strategy of hospital expenditure control. The cutting off of national grants for hospital construction in 1969 parallels the interest in the United States in controlling hospital inflation by reducing the number of hospital beds or at least halting any increase in them. Both the use of supply controls and the concern for better incentive reimbursement schemes can thus be understood as responses to the failure of detailed review as a major cost-control measure.

Faced with the inability of budget review to limit cost escalation, Canadian officials experimented in the late 1960s with incentive reimbursement approaches to hospitals. The governmental task forces on the costs of medical care made much of the increases in efficiency which were thought to be available to the hospital sector. But according to two Canadian analysts,[15] incentives to better management as a technique of overall cost containment does not seem as powerful a policy variable as making hospital beds more scarce. This interpretation ought to be viewed in light of the faith so many American economists have in devising a reimbursement method which would make the hospital sector largely self-regulating.

The Canadian experience suggests that there are serious limitations to reportedly sensible reimbursement schemes, a caveat that could be of great import. Some American policy commentators firmly believe that "reimbursement patterns must be changed so that hospitals are no longer guaranteed that revenues will equal costs regardless of their productivity." They hold out the hope for an

> ...incentive reimbursement system...advocated to promote hospital efficiency and rationalize capital expenditures. Hospitals would be reimbursed on a case basis, taking account of the case mix of the hospital and its teaching program; the system would be based on a formula that assured the hospital of average efficiency recovery of operating and capital costs. Deficits would force inefficient hospitals to improve their management, change the nature of their operations, or shut down.[16]

Our Canadian interpreters provide evidence that such a system, however appealing theoretically, is very hard to implement. A number of actual conditions weaken the operation of a self-regulating reimbursement scheme: for political reasons, poorly managed hospitals are rarely allowed to fail; capital funds are supplied separately from operating budgets; case mix adjustments are not well worked out; and hospital managers do not seek "profits" as strongly as increased services and thereby larger budgets. Whatever the reason, the Canadian turn toward supply constraints[17] rather than reliance on fine-tuned management incentives is revealing.

National health insurance in the United States has been presented by some as the remedy to cost inflation and by others as a source of even greater inflation.[18] But, in the debate over the causes and character of and appropriate remedies for hospital inflation, a common thread has been the belief that hospitals are used inappropriately and that savings are possible by the more sensible use of these very expensive health items. This may be thought of as the "hospital substitute" theory: the view that insurance programs should have very broad benefits so as to discourage the use of expensive benefits like hospitalization for pecuniary rather than medical reasons. This rests in turn on the view that excessive hospitalization does take place, and that alternatives—whether nursing homes or outpatient clinics—would save money. Yet, according to Evans, "unless new facilities are balanced by withdrawal of the old, total costs rise." He cites Alberta's experience as evidence that well-developed out-of-hospital convalescent systems do not necessarily reduce hospital costs per capita and explains why "reimbursing agencies [may] fear...that attempts at partial efficiency [hospital substitution] may raise overall health costs."[19] In the United States, Martin Feldstein found that extended care facilities raise the cost per hospital *episode*. What is saved in lower acute care stays is lost in longer extended care stays.[20]

Even if increased nursing homes were matched by decreased hospital beds, it is not clear that any savings would be realized. The lower average costs per patient day of nursing homes compared to hospitals does not imply that it costs hospitals more than nursing homes to provide convalescent care. In fact, we would expect hospitals to be able to provide lower cost convalescent care than nursing homes because of economies of scale associated with having convalescent beds and acute beds in the same institution.

One can see, without understanding the full complexity of medical economics, why some infer that limiting the supply of beds is more effective in reducing unwarranted hospitalization than a hospital substitute strategy promoted by more comprehensive benefits to deal with the problem of unwarranted hospitalization. But the diagnosis that Canada has had "too many general hospital beds" which cost them a "great deal of money" must acknowledge the equally striking fact that, according to the then-Deputy Minister of Health and Welfare, "once a modern hospital is built, it is politically very difficult to close."[21]

Making hospital beds scarcer is a cost-control strategy with strong advocates in the United States. For the short term, at least, it appears that such crude policies are likely to be more effective than subtle management measures of theoretical force for which one cannot find large-scale instances of successful use and impact. Many Canadian interpreters judge detailed budget review a time-consuming, conflictual, and relatively inefficient means of restraining hospital expenditure increases. The continuing appeal of global budgeting is that, as an anti-inflation measure, it does no worse than detailed budgeting; as a device for disbursement of funds, it is less conflictual to administer. The failure of both the line-by-line and the global budget technique to control Canadian inflation provides a demonstration lesson for the United States. Short of direct government control over wages, there appear to be few policy alternatives to bed control that have much chance of success in controlling health expenditures in the hospital sector.

Physicians

There are at least three important topics in the American health care debate for which Canadian experience with medical insurance is strikingly relevant: complaints about the fees and incomes of physicians; the impact of their practices on the total costs of health care; and the controversy over different strategies to redistribute physician services by location and by speciality. The complaint in the United States is that we have too few doctors in the places or specialties of greatest need and that not only are fees and incomes quite high, but physicians also contribute to the escalation of health care costs in a number of indirect ways. One strategy that has been advanced in the United States—and is embodied in the fee schedule provisions of several national health insurance bills—is detailed specification of fees and peer review of the appropriateness of the pattern of care as well as of the appropriateness of the price per unit service. What can we learn from reported Canadian experience on the likely implications of such a strategy?

The comparative data on change in the ratio of the Physicians' Fee Index to the Consumer Price Index, presented in Fig. 4, show that, at about the time of the introduction of medical insurance, Canadian physicians' fees started a sharp decline relative to the other prices. Fig. 5 illustrates, for the same time period, the corresponding movement in the net income (in constant dollars) of Canadian

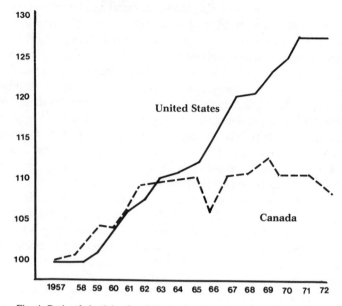

Fig. 4. Ratio of physician fees index to the consumer price index in the United States and Canada, 1957–1972 (1957 = 100).
Source: Reinhardt and Branson, "Preliminary Tabulation of Selected Comparative Statistics on the Canadian and U.S. Health Care Systems," (August 1974) mimeograph.

and United States physicians. The contrast of successful control of fee levels with continued growth of real incomes suggests that explicit fee schedules, as currently understood and implemented, will not restrain physician incomes nearly as much as the policy's most ardent backers have suggested.

This does not imply that open-ended fee reimbursement systems are superior or even acceptable. Rather, it points out that sufficient attention was not paid to the mechanisms by which average net physician incomes would rise markedly under Canada's Medicare program. Planners there sought to implement physician reimbursement at 85% or 90% of established fee schedules. They largely succeeded, but percentage reimbursement, predicated on the basis of a published fee schedule rather than on an estimate of actual average fees received before national health insurance, provided the mechanism by which large-scale increases in physician earnings were produced. According to R. G. Evans, "the single most prominent influence of health insurance in Canada has been to increase the earnings of health providers."[22] This is somewhat obscured in Fig. 5 because of the various dates different provinces entered the Medicare (physicians' services) program. By standardizing the provinces on the dates they entered the program, Table 1 shows how large the impact of National Health Insurance really was on physician income. The average increase in net physician income (deflated by the Canadian Consumer Price Index) was more than twice as great during the transi-

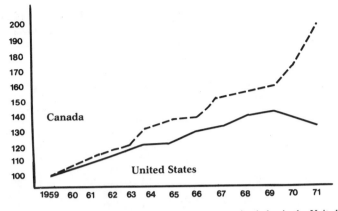

Fig. 5. Ratio of physician net income to consumer price index in the United States and Canada, 1959–1971 (1959 = 100).
Sources: United States—Unadjusted Data, *Statistical Abstract of the United States*, U.S. Department of Commerce, Bureau of the Census (various issues).
Price Deflator (Consumer Price Index)—*Monthly Labor Review*, Bureau of Labor Statistics (various issues).
Canada—Unadjusted Data, R.G. Evans, in Spyros Andreopoulos, ed., *National Health Insurance* (New York: John Wiley and Sons, 1975), p. 70.
Price Deflator (Consumer Price Index)—Statistics Canada, *Canada's Yearbook*, 1972.

tion to National Health Insurance as the increase in the immediately previous period. Studies in Quebec show absolutely no increase in the number of physician visits per capita after Medicare.[23] While comparable data are not available for other provinces, there is no reason to expect substantial differences. Thus it does not appear that the increase in physician income can be attributed to increased workloads.

The American discussion of fee-for-service reimbursement under national health insurance should clearly indicate the indirect mechanisms by which net physician earnings are likely to rise. There are at least two of importance. The first and simplest is the reduction of bad debts under national health insurance. The financial impact of bad debt reduction varies with the proportion of bad debts and expenses that physicians face. The main point, however, is that the introduction of the debt reduction mechanism will cause incomes to rise without an increase in workload, because of both the elimination of the bad debt losses and the reduction of expenses associated with debt collection.

The second mechanism by which physician incomes may rise is closely akin to the first. Physicians have traditionally varied their fees somewhat in relation to income and insurance coverage. Under conditions of national health insurance they try to establish their highest rates as "customary" even though those rates are not necessarily the average fee received or even the most frequently asked fee. If national health insurance reimburses at the highest rate, net earnings will increase and, just as with bad debt reduction, will not show up as official fee increases.

Table 1. *The effect of national insurance on net physician earnings [divided by the consumer price index]. Percentage change over two-year periods.*

Province	First full year of province's participation in a program covering physician services	Period ending with first full year of province's participation		Immediately previous period	
Saskatchewan	1963*	32.5%	(1961–63)	2.7%	(1959–61)
British Columbia	1969	5.3	(1967–69)	16.5	(1965–67)
Newfoundland	1970	26.2	(1968–70)	21.4	(1966–68)
Nova Scotia	1970	34.4	(1968–70)	21.1	(1966–68)
Ontario	1970	12.5	(1968–70)	17.0	(1966–68)
Manitoba	1970	37.1	(1968–70)	12.3	(1966–68)
Alberta	1970	10.6	(1968–70)	26.5	(1966–68)
Quebec	1971	42.1	(1969–71)	8.2	(1967–69)
Prince Edward Island	1971	60.5	(1969–71)	1.0	(1967–69)
New Brunswick	1971	26.6	(1969–71)	10.6	(1967–69)
Average		28.8%		13.7%	

* Saskatchewan adopted a provincial health insurance plan prior to National Health Insurance.
Sources: Nominal Data, Spyros Andreopoulos, ed., *National Health Insurance: Can We Learn from Canada?* (New York: John Wiley and Sons, 1975), p. 70.
Price Deflator (Consumer Price Index), Statistics Canada, *Canada's Yearbook*, 1972.

What is at issue is the appropriate standard for fee-for-service remuneration under national health insurance. It seems clear that average fees received should be the appropriate standard and not so-called customary charges. But that standard requires detailed information on the actual fees of physicians broken down by specialty and region. Such information is not currently available in the United States.

Further, we should anticipate from Canadian experience that physician incomes will be a contentious public issue, not simply between the profession and the government but involving considerable public clamor. Disputes over physician incomes in British Columbia, Ontario, and Quebec (among others) have been among the most conspicuous of the postenactment politics of national health insurance. All American discussants are prepared for controversy concerning the level of fees in a national health insurance program, the question of direct or assignment billing and the variation in fees by education or location. But few have extensively considered how fees should be adjusted when a government program removes bad debts and "reduced" fees completely. Canadian experience highlights this issue which American policymakers should consider as payment methods and levels are debated.*

[*Author's note.* There is some evidence that negotiations about fee structures and reimbursement policies are now yielding some protection from physician prerogatives to increase their income. From an all-time high in 1970, physicians' relative incomes fell steadily until 1978 (R.G. Evans, "Is Health Care Better in Canada Than in the U.S.?," paper presented at the University Consortium for Research on North America Seminar, Cambridge, Mass., Dec. 2, 1980, p. 19).]

A related remuneration issue involves professional review of the patterns of service. "Peer review" is already a heated issue among American physicians. The Canadian concern about patterns of costly service which do not show up in extra billing, but in extra servicing, is parallel. One apparent lesson drawn from Canada is that a claims review procedure works well for the egregious cases of excessive and inappropriate claims but that the fee-for-service system's tendency toward increased units of care and altering the mix of procedures is very hard to control. It is worth noting at this point a paradox regarding the insistence on fee-for-service payment in societies like Canada and the United States and the increased threats to professional independence which the governmental review of such a payment method entails. Brian Abel-Smith suggests that

... world experience has shown, as the United States experience is also beginning to show, the paradox underlying attempts to preserve the free and independent practice of medicine. At first sight, fee-for-service payment enables private free-market medicine to be readily combined with health insurance. In practice, it is not long before interference with medical practice becomes much greater than occurs or needs to occur when physicians are salaried employees in government service. Physicians are made answerable for each of their acts. Because there are incentives for abuse, restrictive and punitive safeguards are established to prevent abuse from occurring. Sometimes the punishment falls on the physicians, but sometimes it falls on the patient.[24]

Whatever world experience has shown about the problems of fee-for-service payment, Canadian experience suggests that, for America, this mode of payment will predominate in the post-national health-insurance world. Indeed, the problems of making fee-for-service regulation appropriate without its being excessively punitive should occupy the attention of planners more than imagining general shifts from present fee-for-service methods to other forms like capitation and salary.[25] Concern for wholesale transformation may drive out discussion of marginal improvements in the present dominant method of payment, or of ways to adjust national health insurance to other less traditional remuneration methods.

For some American health care discussants, increasing the supply of physicians is a strategy for improving both the distribution of physicians and for restraining doctors' fees through competition. That strategy appears, from Canadian experience, to lack promise on either count. And, to the extent physicians determine the use of other medical care services, it presents additional inflationary problems. The common sense view that increasing the supply of physicians will greatly improve either the distribution or the price is challenged now by a number of Canadian commentators, and the national government publicly expresses concern that a "saturation point for certain specialties is very close or has been reached in a number of provinces."[26] While there appears to be some improvement in supplying physicians to under-doctored areas, dramatic increases in physician numbers apparently do not restrain fees through competition. Given the nature of medical care which inhibits patients from questioning the price or quantity of services provided, and the existence of widespread private insurance, the ability of competition to limit physician income was weak even before the start of national health insurance. It may well be that the role of "national health insurance [in Canada has] been to relax further any market constraints on how physicians manipulate utilization to generate income."[27]

British Columbia, as Evans points out, is typically near the top in the levels of fees and near bottom in average physician incomes, which is related to its being the province with the largest number of doctors per capita. Increasing physician supply apparently is a weak and expensive instrumentality for coping with the problems of cost increases and the maldistribution of physician manpower.

Copayment

While one suggestion for controlling costs is increasing the supply of doctors prior to implementing national health insurance, another prominent suggestion is that patient financial participation—through either deductibles or coinsurance—will introduce a needed and efficacious degree of cost-consciousness. Canadian analysts take a much less enthusiastic view of significant patient copayment. Where modest copayment was tried under Canadian Medicare—in Saskatchewan during 1968 to 1971—its effect on expenditures is unknown. But its impact on utilization was disproportionately felt by the poor and the old.[28] Moreover, there is little evidence in Canada that copayment reduced the "least medically necessary" care, and hence, there are distributional grounds for questioning this policy instrument. Finally, some commentators hold that the patient, once in the medical system, is dependent on the physician's judgments about further care and consequently that patient copayment is mis-targeted away from the doctor, the "gatekeeper" to further medical services. What copayment does do, as Evans has pointedly written, "is reduce program costs by transferring them back to the ill rather than forward to taxpayers," and to reduce disproportionately patient-initiated physician contacts compared to physician-initiated ones. In Canada, he judges, this is "politically highly unpopular, and consequently co-payments as a means of cost-control appears...a dead issue."[29]

Copayment is most clearly not a "dead" issue in the United States; indeed, all of the current major proposals rely on family copayment for the great bulk of current average family health expenditures. Two considerations shape the United States discussion differently from Canada's. One is the effort to make copayment more equitable by varying the amounts with family income, thus trying to reduce the disproportional burden which fixed dollar copayments represent for the poor. The difficulty here is that the likely supplementation of national health insurance proposals of either the 1974 Nixon or Kennedy–Mills type would reduce the out-of-pocket expenditures of the middle and upper income groups buying supplementary insurance.[30] The major effect of copayment under those plans would be to reduce government program costs. In addition, it is certain that the supplementation by private insurance, with the resulting distribution of actual cost-sharing, would be sharply different from that of the formal proposals.

The second American consideration is the search for ways to limit substantially the federal program costs of national health insurance, one means of which is the substantial patient cost-sharing just noted. In the political discussions of 1974, considerable efforts have been made to show limited amounts of "new" federal expenditures, even if such arrangements represent misleading labelling of required non-governmental expenditures as "private."[31] On the other hand, paying for the total United States personal health care bill through governmental budgets does have an impact on the opportunities for other governmental initiatives. The current Canadian emphasis on holding down medical expenditure increases illustrates the perception that governmental opportunities for other programs are severely constrained by the increasing share of the public budget devoted to health insurance.*

[*Author's note*: Administered by the provinces with heavy federal subsidy, the Canadian system initially lacked both the appropriate means and powerful incentives to control inflation. Because of the federal subsidy, the provinces lacked sufficient incentives, particularly in the early years; because of provincial administration, the federal government lacked the means. In 1977 the federal government established upper limits on the percentage increases of hospital- and medical-care insurance cost that it would share, leaving each province the responsibility of paying costs beyond the federal subsidy. This action has apparently provided sufficient incentive for the provinces to take measures to contain costs. The figure presents graphic proof of the success of these incentives.]

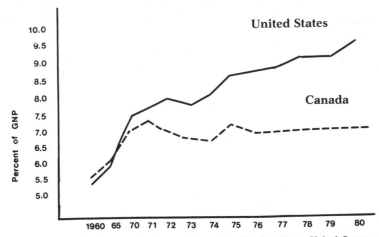

Health expenditures as a percentage of the gross national product, United States and Canada. From "National Health Insurance: Further Reflections on Canada's Path, America's Choice," in R.L. Numbers, ed., *Compulsory Health Insurance: The Continuing American Debate* (Westport, Conn.: Greenwood Press, 1982).
Sources: Department of National Health and Welfare (Canada) *National Health Expenditures in Canada, 1960–1975*, Information Systems Branch (Ottawa: January, 1979); Department of National Health and Welfare (Canada) *National Health Expenditures in Canada, 1970–1978* (unpublished, provisional), Health Information Division (Ottawa: August, 1980); Department of Health, Education, and Welfare (United States) *Health United States, 1979*, DHEW Pub. (PHS) 80-1232 (Washington, D.C.: Government Printing Office, 1979).

Access to care

What are the implications for the United States of Canadian findings about the impact of national health insurance on access to medical care services? What does national health insurance mean for the utilization of medical care services generally? What, further, does the Canadian experience teach us about the distributional consequences of national health insurance on access by income class? These questions are important in the current American national health insurance debate. There is the hope that lowering financial barriers will distribute access to care much more fairly than our present arrangements and help reduce the striking inequalities in the probabilities that similar medical problems will receive equal medical attention by race, income, location, age, and connection with physicians. Both projections must be carefully considered because the Canadian experience offers mixed results.

First, on the basis of Canada's experience, we should expect relatively modest changes in the overall utilization of medical care services. In both the hospital and physician sectors changes in use were relatively modest in the wake of national insurance.[32] The fears of run-away utilization resulting from "cheap" care thus appear unrealistic and ignore the impact of pre-existent health insurance, the barriers to care which financing will not change, and the rationing which doctors will impose. This is an issue where the findings of the natural experiment—Canada—conflict with projections of sharply increased use (or crowded offices) based on estimates of the elasticity of demand for medical care in the United States.[33] Canadian findings, while discomforting about rising expenditures, are certainly less alarming on the issue of overall increases in actual or attempted utilization.

One's judgment of the impact of Canadian national health insurance on the distribution of access depends very much on initial expectations. Reported evidence suggests that national health insurance reallocated access to some extent from "rich" to "poor." This is true in the Beck study of Saskatchewan. Measuring access by the proportion of nonusers of medical care services by income class, the findings were that nonuse by the lowest income class declines substantially and nonuse by other income classes remains stable. The Enterline et al. study in Quebec shows not only an increase in the use of physician care by income groups under $5,000, but a decline in physician visits for income groups above $9,000. Table 2 provides the summary of the redistributive effect reported by Enterline and his colleagues.[34] But the evidence is not that such redistribution took place everywhere nor that national health insurance eradicated differences in access by income class. Disparities in access remain. Observers emphasize that the problem of access remains only partially solved in the wake of national health insurance. As Castonguay suggests in his emphasis on the problems remaining, "achieving access to care is not strictly a financial problem; physical and psycho-social barriers are also of significant importance."[35]

Table 2. *Redistributive effects of Medicare measured by
average annual visits to a physician by income group before
and after Medicare, 1969–72. (In Montreal metro area.)*

Income in dollars	Average number of visits	Percent change in visits
$0–3,000	7.8	+18
$3,000–5,000	6.0	+9
$5,000–9,000	4.7	no change
$9,000–15,000	4.9	−4
$15,000 and over	4.8	−9
All income groups	5.0	no change

Source: Modified from Castonguay, Table 4, p. 117, in Spyros Andreopoulos,
ed., *National Health Insurance: Can We Learn from Canada?* (New York:
John Wiley and Sons, 1975).

We should note, however, the direction of redistribution in favor of the less
advantaged. A recent critique of American Medicare by Karen Davis argues that
equal entitlement to program benefits has unequal results with greater benefits
for the higher income aged and that income-conditioned programs like Medicaid
partially redress the balance. Because American Medicare has significant cost-
sharing, we should approach this interpretation with caution. It may well be that
America's better-off aged are less deterred by cost-sharing, use more expensive
services, and are much more likely to buy supplementary insurance. If that is the
case, and if Medicaid reduces those out-of-pocket expenditures for the poorest,
one should expect that the poorest and the richest would use disproportionately
large shares of the Medicare budget.[36] The Canadian case suggests that where
out-of-pocket costs are almost zero, equal benefits are associated with increasing
access for the disadvantaged.*

There seems agreement that removing financial barriers through national health
insurance is insufficient for producing equal access to care. One should distinguish between equal use by income class, region, and sex from equal access
measured by the likelihood of identical medical responses to similar health
conditions. Canada has not, it appears, achieved equality on the first count; in
contrast, there is evidence in the United States that the poor (under $3,000/year)
see doctors as much as or more often than their Canadian compatriots. But the
probability that a given symptom will stimulate care varies markedly with socio-

[*Author's note. A 1979 report on the distributional and redistributional aspects of the
Canadian health-insurance program confirmed these earlier conclusions; it concluded that
after appropriate adjustment for family size and demographic factors, low-income people
receive more hospital and medical care than upper-income people. (J.A. Boulet and D.W.
Henderson, *Distributional and Redistributional Aspects of Government Health Insurance
Programs in Canada*, Discussion Paper No. 146 (Ottawa: Economic Council of Canada,
1979).]

economic characteristics. What Canada suggests is that national health insurance contributes to greater equalization of access, but that it neither solves the problem nor eradicates concern for further amelioration. We should note the increases in availability of medical care personnel where financial incapacity was a problem before national health insurance; LeClair reports that in Newfoundland, the supply of medical practitioners in relation to population increased between 20% and 30% in the first three years of the Medicare program.[37]

The issue of access highlights an interesting difference in the focus of current American and Canadian discussions of medical care. Canadian commentators now sharply distinguish between access to good health and access to medical care services. The 1974 pamphlet *A New Perspective on the Health of Canadians*[38] illustrates the distinction and emphasizes that Canadians cannot expect substantial improvements in their health status through medical care. Though this argument is made in the United States, it is often employed to discourage national health insurance itself. Yet it makes an enormous difference whether one highlights the non-medical care determinants of health status before or after the introduction of national insurance. The arguments for national health insurance concern the access to and consequences of medical services use as much as—if not more so than—the means to healthiness. Canadians take for granted now that illness no longer is associated with fears of destitution; they hardly mention that one of the most central impacts of national health insurance was the improved access to protection against financial catastrophe. Once that is accomplished and it is recognized that access is dependent upon variables other than income, it may well be that American leaders will also focus on trying to influence environmental factors as the "key to better national health and reduced rates of increases in health costs."

Acknowledgments

An earlier version of this paper was presented at the 1974 Sun Valley Health Forum and subsequently published in S. Andreopoulos, ed., *National Health Insurance: Can We Learn From Canada?* (New York: John Wiley and Sons, 1975). A number of colleagues and institutions—notably the University of Chicago's Center for Health Administration Studies—gave valued assistance to the senior author at that stage.

This collaborative essay reflects a thorough revision of the earlier formulation and the painstaking editorial efforts of Lynn Carter of the University of Chicago's School of Social Service Administration, Sherry Russell, Michel Thibault, Pahlavi Universities, Iran, and Peter deLeon, one of the special editors of this issue of *Policy Sciences*. Seldom do authors receive such sustained intelligent advice with polite persuasion. We are grateful to them and especially to Evelyn Friedman for giving expression to such improvements in a seemingly unending succession of drafts. Finally, we want to thank the Robert Wood Johnson Foundation for support during 1974–75 in drawing American health policy implications from the Canadian experiences.

Notes

1 The nature and magnitude of this public worry has been analyzed by Ronald Andersen et al. "The Public's View of the Crisis in Medical Care: An Impetus for Changing Delivery Systems?" *Economic and Business Bulletin*, Vol. 24, No. 1 (Fall 1971), pp. 44–52.

2 There is evidence, in fact, that a variety of health care concerns—rising costs, interest in rationalization, worry about efficacy and patient satisfaction—are evident throughout Western Europe and North America irrespective of the details of medical care's public financing modes. See Anne R. Somers, "The Rationalization of Health Services: A Universal Priority," *Inquiry*, Vol. 8 (1971), pp. 48–60.

The enumeration of health care concerns is extraordinarily extensive in both Canada and the United States. Note particularly, however, the interest in similar Canadian health insurance concerns and experience by the U.S. Congress' Committee on Ways and Means in its review of issues of national health insurance: "The material on Canada is in considerably more detail than that presented for other nations since the Canadian experience seems more relevant to U.S. policy." Committee of Ways and Means, *National Health Insurance Resource Book* (Washington, D.C.: Government Printing Office, 1974), p. 111.

3 A concise discussion of comparative research design useful for cross-national policy study, including the "most similar system" and "most different system" approach, is found in Adam Przeworski and Henry Teune, *The Logic of Comparative Social Inquiry* (New York: John Wiley and Sons, 1970).

4 There is a large literature on Canada's movement toward national health insurance. Among the more helpful brief interpretations, see Malcolm G. Taylor, "The Canadian Health Insurance Program," *Public Administration Review*, Vol. 33, No. 1 (Jan./Feb. 1973), pp. 31–39; J. E. F. Hastings, "Federal-Provincial Insurance for Hospital and Physicians' Care in Canada," *International Journal of Health Services*, Vol. 1, No. 4 (Nov. 1971), pp. 398–414. For fuller treatment, the basic source is the *Report of the Royal Commission on Health Services* (Hall Commission; Ottawa: The Queen's Printer, 1964) and supporting studies. For the physician sector more generally, see B. R. Blishen, *Doctors and Doctrines: The Ideology of Medical Care in Canada* (Toronto: University of Toronto Press, 1969).

For similar information on the U.S. from a comparative perspective see Odin Anderson, *Health Care: Can There Be Equity? The United States, Sweden, and England* (New York: John Wiley and Sons, 1972), and T. R. Marmor, *The Politics of Medicare* (Chicago: Aldine, 1973).

5 The information in this section came from Maurice LeClair, "The Canadian Health Care System," in Spyros Andreopoulos, ed., *National Health Insurance: Can We Learn from Canada?* (New York: John Wiley and Sons, 1975), pp. 11–42. This is a collection of papers by participants in the Sun Valley Health Forum on National Health Insurance.

6 See, for example, *National Health Expenditures in Canada, 1960–71 with Comparative Data for the United States*, Health Program Branch, Ottawa (Oct. 1973), and the documentation presented by Stuart Altman in "Health Care Spending in the U.S. and Canada," in Andreopoulos, op. cit. For the proportion of national resources expended in health, see Altman, pp. 193–94.

7 The Canadian alarm was fully expressed in the *Task Force Reports on the Cost of Health Services in Canada* (Ottawa: The Queen's Printer, 1970), 3 vols. Concern about the rate of inflation in the health care field was plain as well in the Economic

Council of Canada's Seventh Annual Review, *Patterns of Growth* (Sept. 1970). The parallel American preoccupation with rising medical care costs was perhaps best evidenced by the production in the first Nixon Administration of a "white paper" on health which catalogued familiar diagnoses of the ills of the industry.

These same concerns were apparent in the hearings on national health insurance before the Ways and Means Committee in Oct./Nov. 1971; 93rd Congress, 2nd Session, 11 volumes (Washington, D.C.: Government Printing Office, 1971).

8 See for the period 1966–72, Maurice LeClair, "The Canadian Health Care System," in Andreopoulos, op. cit., Table 3; for the earlier period, see Andersen and Hull, "Hospital Utilization and Cost Trends in Canada and the United States," *Medical Care*, Vol. 7, No. 6 (Nov./Dec. 1969), special supplement, Table 5, p. 13; compare Altman in Andreopoulos, op cit., p. 198, and Table 5. Canada has been and continues to be a heavier spender in the hospital sector.

9 This information is consistent with that of Andersen and Hull, op. cit., and R. G. Evans' chapter, "Beyond the Medical Marketplace: Expenditure, Utilization and Pricing of Insured Health Care in Canada," in Andreopoulos, op. cit.

10 The nominal data are from R. G. Evans, ibid., pp. 138–142. The price deflator is the Canadian Consumer Price Index from: Statistics Canada, *Canada's Yearbook* (1972).

11 R. G. Evans, ibid., p. 146.

12 R. G. Evans to R. A. Berman, letter, July 2, 1974, on the subject of major issues to be highlighted for Sun Valley conference on Canada's experience with national health insurance.

13 The inability of increased copayment mechanisms to restrain costs arises only partly because hospital utilization is relatively insensitive to price. Equally important is the fact that the patient's copayment represents only a very small part of his total cost of hospitalization, which includes not only the direct cost of hospital services, but also physicians' fees, foregone earnings, and general inconvenience.

14 For a discussion of the reliance on detailed, line-item budget review as the mechanism of budgetary control during the first decade of Canada's national hospital insurance, see Evans, and LeClair, in Andreopoulos, op. cit., pp. 151–155 and 57–58, respectively. For the arguments justifying less detailed budget review, see Claude Castonguay, "The Quebec Experience: Effects on Accessibility," in Andreopoulos, op. cit., pp. 106–107, including an explanation of global budgeting.

15 Compare the comments of R. G. Evans, and M. LeClair, in ibid., pp. 151–155 and 64–65, respectively.

16 Judy and Lester Lave, *The Hospital Construction Act: An Evaluation of the Hill-Burton Program, 1948–1973* (Washington: The American Enterprise Institute for Public Policy Research, 1974), p. 3.

17 For discussion of this policy change, see Robin Badgley et al., *The Canadian Experience with Universal Health Insurance.* Third annual report, Department of Behavioral Science, University of Toronto (August 1974), p. 135 f (unpublished).

18 See chapter 3 in this volume.

19 Evans, in Andreopoulos, op. cit., p. 154.

20 Martin Feldstein, "An Econometric Model of the Medicare System," *Quarterly Journal of Economics*, Vol. 85, No. 1 (Feb. 1971).

21 M. LeClair, in Andreopoulos, op. cit., p. 15.

22 Evans, in ibid., p. 133.

23 Castonguay, in ibid., p. 116.

24 Brian Abel-Smith, "Value for Money in Health Services," *Social Security Bulletin*, Vol. 37, No. 7 (July 1974), p. 22.

25 For evidence on the practically invariant relationship between dominant methods of physician remuneration before and after the enactment of universal government health programs among western industrial democracies, see William Glaser, *Paying the Doctor: Systems of Remuneration and Their Effects* (Baltimore: Johns Hopkins Press, 1970), and Marmor and Thomas, "The Politics of Paying Physicians...," *International Journal of Health Services*, Vol. 1, No. 1 (1971), pp. 71–78. The actual working-out of these common constraints in the Canadian case is mentioned in all of the papers in Andreopoulos, op. cit.

26 LeClair, in Andreopoulos, op. cit., p. 76. The "super-saturation-spillover" approach is criticized in John R. Evans, "Health Manpower Problems: The Canadian Experience," prepared for the Institute of Medicine, Washington, D.C., 1974, p. 15.

27 R. G. Evans, in Andreopoulos, op. cit., p. 162.

28 Discussed in LeClair, in ibid., pp. 48–49 and Table 7, based on R. G. Beck, "The Demand for Physician Services in Saskatchewan," unpublished Ph.D. thesis, University of Alberta, 1971. The major conclusion of Beck's study is "that co-payment provisions reduce the use of physician services by the poor by an estimated 18 per cent. The impact upon the poor, it was observed, is considerably greater than the reduction of service experienced by the entire population, which has been estimated at 6 to 7 percent."

29 Evans letter to Berman, July 2, 1974; see also LeClair, ibid., p. 79, for discussion of the physician as the "gatekeeper" of medical care expenditures.

30 This prediction is based on the experience under the Medicare program and the substantial incentives to buy health insurance in the current tax laws. For a discussion of these incentives and the magnitude of their impact see Mitchell and Vogel, "Health and Taxes: An Assessment of the Medical Prediction," *Southern Economic Journal* (April 1975).

31 This issue is clearly defined by Karen Davis in the chapter on "National Health Insurance," in Blechman, Gramlich, and Hartman, *Setting National Priorities: The 1975 Budget* (Washington, D.C.: The Brookings Institution, 1974). See also, T. R. Marmor, "The Comprehensive Health Insurance Plan," *Challenge* (Nov./Dec. 1974), pp. 44–45.

32 For the hospital sector, see Evans, in Andreopoulos, op. cit., Table 4, p. 142, and the report that "hospital utilization rates rose steadily from 1953 to 1971 at about 1.4 percent per year increase in patient days per 1000 population and about 1.3 percent per year in admissions" and that the main increase in these rates came in the period before national health insurance, pp. 3–4 of discussion of issues paper. See LeClair, Table 5, discussed at p. 88, on changes in per capita physician use, all "consistent with the view" that government medical insurance did not generate a surge of patient-initiated demand.

33 See, for instance, Newhouse, Phelps, and Schwartz, "Policy Options and the Impact of National Health Insurance," *New England Journal of Medicine*, Vol. 290, No. 24 (June 13, 1974), pp. 1345–1359.

34 R. G. Beck, "Economic Class and Access to Physician Services Under Medical Care Insurance," *International Journal of Health Services*, Vol. 3, No. 3 (1973), pp. 341–355; P. E. Enterline et al., "The Distribution of Medical Care Services Before and After 'Free' Care—The Quebec Experience," *New England Journal of Medicine*, Vol. 289, No. 22 (Nov. 28, 1973); R. F. Badgley et al., "The Impact of Medicare in Wheatville, Saskatchewan, 1960–65," *Canadian Journal of Public Health*, Vol. 58, No. 3 (Mar. 1967).

35 Castonguay, in Andreopoulos, op. cit., p. 100.

36 See Karen Davis, op. cit., pp. 214–217.
37 Leclair, in Andreopoulos, op. cit., p. 75.
38 Marc Lalonde, *A New Perspective on the Health of Canadians*, Government of Canada, Ottawa, Apr. 1974.

10. Rethinking national health insurance

THEODORE R. MARMOR

Most Americans, the polls report, are alarmed by a "medical-care crisis." Yet most are also satisfied with their own medical treatment. This paradox suggests that the admittedly serious problems of American medicine—its cost, availability, and quality—are not the only concerns. Part of the difficulty is the rhetorical exaggeration of medical-care problems and the unrealistic expectations for the proposals for national health insurance. Any sensible national-health-insurance plan must balance conflicting purposes. It must be fiscally possible, administratively manageable, politically feasible, and capable of improving the health of Americans without accelerating the worrisome rate of medical inflation (14 percent in 1975). Yet many proponents of national health insurance misleadingly suggest that the problems of cost, access, and quality can be relieved simultaneously; few realistically show how to meet the conflicting constraints of cost control, administrative simplicity, and medical effectiveness. In what follows, I will try to chart a course between the clichés of impending doom and the smug complacency that American medicine is healthy.

Americans are understandably alarmed about medical care because their leaders—and the media—have alarmed them. Speech after speech, article after article, and program after program have cited the crisis of rising costs, maldistributed services, inefficient organization, and poor-quality care. Bipartisan promotion of the sense of crisis has come from public figures as diverse as Richard Nixon, Edward Kennedy, and George Meany. Just six months after assuming his first term in office, former President Nixon warned of a "massive crisis" that could lead within two or three years to a "breakdown in our medical care system... affecting millions." Senator Kennedy's book on American health care was point-

From *The Public Interest*, 46:73–93, 1977. Copyright ©1977 by National Affairs, Inc. Reprinted with permission. A number of versions of this paper have been published and reprinted. The most frequently cited are: "The Political Economy of National Health Insurance: Policy Analysis and Political Evaluation" (with Kenneth Bowler and Robert T. Kudrle), in Kenneth E. Friedman and Stuart H. Rakoff, eds., *Toward a National Health Policy* (Lexington, Mass.: Heath, 1977), pp. 153–188, and in the *Journal of Health Politics, Policy and Law*, 21: 100–133, 1977; "The Politics of National Health Insurance Analysis and Prescription," *Policy Analysis*, 3(1): 25–48, 1977, reprinted as "National Health Insurance," in T.R. Marmor and J.B. Christianson, eds., *Health Care Policy: A Political Economy Approach* (Beverly Hills, Calif.: Sage, 1982), pp. 83–124.

edly titled *In Critical Condition*, suggesting the imminence of disaster. Even the sober editors of *Fortune* placed American medicine "on the brink of chaos" in 1970. No wonder that labor leaders can treat the "crisis" as "generally accepted."

Opinion surveys suggest that a large majority of Americans agree there is a medical crisis, but don't regard it as affecting them. Three-quarters to four-fifths of the population, depending on the survey and the questions asked, are satisfied with the care they receive and with their doctors—despite misgivings about the "system." Fewer than 10 percent are dissatisfied with their own health care, though nearly 40 percent are worried about high costs and perceived inaccessibility. But these discrepancies in attitudes may be understood as simultaneously reflecting personal experience on the one hand, and the acceptance of the conventional wisdom of vocal elites who insist on using the rhetoric of crisis, on the other hand. Probably the specific complaints of Americans depend in part on economic status. The rich don't like waiting, and pay to avoid it; the poor don't like high costs, and wait to avoid paying them; and the middle class dislike both. All would like, in time of need, easier access to personal physicians. But few would require wholesale changes to satisfy their specific complaints.

Why do our politicians magnify these concerns into an impending crisis? Do reformers assume that only the rhetoric of disaster can spur public action? In the effort to awaken social interest, have they misled us into regarding American health care as declining on all fronts? The "issue-attention" cycle that starts with doomsaying is surely partly to blame. But whatever its origins, the rhetoric of crisis hinders realistic appraisal of what competing national-health-insurance proposals might do about the problems of health care in the United States.

The problems of American medicine

It should be stated at this juncture that concern about the cost, access, and quality of care is certainly warranted. Cost heads the list of concerns. The rising price of medical services has inflated both private and public health-insurance bills; there are really two cost problems, one individual, the other social.

As Martin Feldstein has pointed out, existing insurance plans cover expenses that many families could pay from current income, and a large proportion of these plans run out precisely when insurance is essential—in financially catastrophic cases.[1] In fiscal year 1975 Americans on average spent $558 per person on health care, up from $485 in 1974. In total, health-care expenditures consumed some $118 billion in 1975—or 8.3 percent of the GNP. Adjusted for inflation, the share of GNP for medical care has increased more than 80 percent over the past quarter-century, up from 4.6 percent in 1950. In the last five years alone, the rate of increase has been explosive, which is clearly reflected in the rising expenditures for hospital care, now eight times greater per capita than they were in 1950.

This increase in hospital costs—the most heavily insured medical service, accounting for some 40 percent of current health expenditures—also explains most of the rapid expansion of the government's public insurance programs. Medicare and Medicaid now spend $25 billion on services for the elderly, those on welfare, and the medically needy. Medicaid pays for services for about 25 million low-income Americans, and Medicare covers some 23.5 million elderly and disabled. But despite this extensive coverage, the needs of the poor and the elderly have increased under worsening economic conditions, and the real value of Medicaid benefits has declined. The present inflation has squeezed the poor, elderly, and unemployed even though the expenditures for current programs have increased in terms of nominal dollars. Thus the present 14 percent rate of medical inflation threatens not only family income after expenses, but government programs as well. We may soon have a Department of Health, Education, *or* Welfare.

American medical care is also said to be disorganized and badly distributed. Some critics have called our medical-delivery units too "small, too specialized, too fragmented to be economical or even to deliver the quality of medical care our physicians are capable of." They are sure that such fragmentation "is bad for the quality of medical care," and results in patients lost "between the units." In fact, it is not clear that quality suffers from decentralization, or that flow charts and organizational reform would improve it. But the shortage of doctors in the countryside and in the inner cities is a serious problem. So is the dearth of old-fashioned family doctors: Only approximately 70,000 of the 295,000 practicing physicians in this country are pediatricians or general practitioners.

The quality of medical care is a subject of controversy, as well. The issue regularly reaches the public in the furor over malpractice—the suits themselves, the costs of malpractice insurance, and the physicians' outrage at paying it. But malpractice—errors of omission or commission—may be rarer and may do less social harm than *questionable* and *inefficient* practices. Questionable practices risk injury to patients in exchange for insufficient medical benefits—for example, overprescribing drugs or performing unnecessary surgery. (To the English expert Brian Abel-Smith, America is the land where "so many people lose their appendices, their wombs, or their tonsils...without good cause.") Inefficient practices either are needlessly expensive (hospitalization for testing) or divert medical resources to very costly care (renal dialysis, cardiac bypass surgery) from more cost-effective uses (immunizations, prenatal checkups for mothers).

From criticism of questionable and inefficient practices it is but one short step to skepticism about all sophisticated medical care. This attitude is revealed in the attention given to iatrogenic (physician-caused) disorders; in the emphasis on environmental reform, anti-smoking campaigns, and highway-safety programs; and in the interest in an expanded role for paraprofessionals in medicine. In this view, concern should not be focused on national health insurance, which to some critics is a "giant step sideways," if not an actual health hazard itself. Thoughtful critics worry that we will put scarce public resources into traditional and costly medical care at the very time that other ways of improving our health are available.

All of these criticisms—many of which have merit—lend plausibility to the fear that the present health-care system will break down. However, the litany of problems suggests more agreement among critics than, in fact, exists. The proposals for national health insurance reveal conflicting standards for assessing American medicine, and represent genuine disputes about how best to deal with the competing demands for greater access, improved quality, and less rapid increases in medical costs. But even if the problems were similarly assessed, there would be little reason to predict that similar national-health-insurance plans would be offered as solutions.

In fact, however, there is not even any agreement about the problems of health care *except* concerning high and apparently uncontrollably rising costs. The various other "problems" are merely difficulties that any sensible analyst would recognize, but do not justify a fear of disaster. This is particularly true concerning the difficulty of access to medical care—the gap between the rich and the poor has been substantially reduced in the past decade (Table 1). But the popularity of crisis rhetoric has promoted hopes of a rapid solution that have been frustrated by the prolonged political struggle over national health insurance.

Competing proposals

All sides agree on at least one thing: the need for a larger governmental role in the financing of medical care. Some groups—most notably the American Medical Association (AMA)—have concentrated on increasing financial accessibility to health care. The AMA Medicredit proposal was designed as a federal subsidy of health-insurance premiums in hopes of stimulating broader insurance coverage. It would have replaced the present tax deduction for medical-care expenditures with a tax *credit*, to offset in whole or part the premiums of (qualified) insurance policies. The amount of the credits would have varied inversely according to income-tax bracket: the higher the taxable income, the lower the tax credit.

All the major proposals now before Congress call for more intervention in the health-insurance industry than Medicredit. The most ambitious is the Kennedy-Corman bill, which proposes a government monopoly of the medical-insurance business. To insure that "money would no longer be a consideration for a patient seeking any health service," the Kennedy-Corman plan would establish a national-health-insurance program with universal eligibility and an unusually broad coverage of services, financed jointly by payroll taxes and general revenues. There would be no cost-sharing by patients, so that care under the plan would be "free"

Table 1. *Access to health care by race and economic status,* 1964 and 1973

	1964	1973
Short-stay hospital discharges per 100 population per year		
Total		
Poor	13.8	19.0
Nonpoor	12.6	12.5
White		
Poor	15.3	20.2
Nonpoor	12.9	12.6
All other		
Poor	9.9	15.3
Nonpoor	9.6	11.6
Percent of population with no doctor visits in past two years		
Total		
Poor	27.7	17.2
Nonpoor	17.7	13.4
White		
Poor	25.7	16.8
Nonpoor	17.1	13.2
All other		
Poor	33.2	18.5
Nonpoor	24.7	15.3
Number of doctor visits per person per year		
Total		
Poor	4.3	5.6
Nonpoor	4.6	4.9
White		
Poor	4.7	5.7
Nonpoor	4.7	5.0
All other		
Poor	3.1	5.0
Nonpoor	3.6	4.3
Number of dental visits per person per year		
Total		
Poor	0.8	1.1
Nonpoor	1.8	1.8
White		
Poor	0.9	1.2
Nonpoor	1.8	1.9
All other		
Poor	0.6	0.7
Nonpoor	1.2	1.1

Source: Ronald W. Wilson and Elijah L. White, "Changes in Morbidity, Disability, and Utilization Differentials Between the Poor and the Nonpoor; Data from the Health Interview Survey: 1964 and 1973," table reprinted in *Journal of Health Politics, Policy and Law*, Vol. 1, No. 2 (Summer 1976), p. 160.
* Definition of poor and nonpoor is based on annual family income. For 1964: poor, under $3,000; nonpoor, $3,000 and over. For 1973: poor, under $6,000; nonpoor, $6,000 and over.

at the point of service, with the federal government directly paying the providers of the services. Further provisions of the bill address the problems of cost escalation, by limiting the total budget for medical care; distribution, by creating incentives for comprehensive health-service organizations and for health personnel in underserved areas; and quality, by enforcing standards for care.

Politically fashionable are plans that would provide protection against financially catastrophic expenses, while allowing other governmental programs and private health-insurance companies to cope with the remaining problems of the medical-care industry. The catastrophic-protection portion of the Long-Ribicoff bill covers hospitalization beyond 60 days and annual medical expenditures over $2,000. The major-risk-insurance (MRI) proposal made by Martin Feldstein would protect against financial disaster, while requiring direct payment by patients for most medical expenses—thereby, it is hoped, reducing the rate of medical inflation. MRI is a comprehensive, universal health-insurance policy with a very high deductible—it would pay all medical bills that exceed 10 percent of annual income.[2] Quite similar, though administered by the Internal Revenue Service as a tax-credit scheme for major medical expenses, was the bill sponsored by Senator William Brock of Tennessee.

Catastrophic insurance is effective and cheap (typically predicted to be less than $5 billion in federal cost), because its objective is limited. It is concerned with financial catastrophies rather than with reorganizing the health sector. The Long-Ribicoff proposal, for example, leaves almost intact the rest of the present system—as does MRI, with one major qualification. In suggesting the removal of current tax incentives for insurance, Feldstein attempts to shift the burden of medical-financial decisions from physicians to the cost-consciousness of patients. The use of a high deductible in relation to average yearly medical expenditures—but short of catastrophic expenses—is similarly intended to combat medical inflation with consumer restraint. But if these plans were fully implemented, they would reintroduce the financial barriers to care that many national-health-insurance advocates see as the problem in the first place.

Mixed strategies

Finally, there are mixed strategies that call for increased government regulation and partial federal subsidy of the present medical-care system. The Ford Administration, for example, proposed a Comprehensive Health Insurance Plan (CHIP) to expand insurance through mandated employer offerings, to rationalize Medicaid by requiring larger financial contributions from welfare families as their incomes rise, and to control costs through state regulation and the encouragement of prepaid group practice.

The mandated employer plans are a way of insuring vast numbers of families for health expenses with a minimum impact on the federal budget. Employers under CHIP, for example, would be required to offer policies with broad benefits and to pay three-quarters of the premium. The employee would pay one-quarter of the premium and be responsible for substantial sharing of costs at the time of use. There would be more modest payment scales for families in lower-income categories. Whatever the specific features, such plans distribute the current health expenditures among patients, employers, and the government; they do not lower health costs (unless they result in less care)—although they appear to because the federal price tag is so much lower than, for example, under Kennedy-Corman. Saying that CHIP costs $45 billion and Kennedy-Corman $100 billion is misleading. It would be accurate only if unions dropped their present benefits and accepted the cost-sharing of CHIP. More likely, under CHIP there would be employer supplementation of the federally mandated plan, in which case total health expenditures under CHIP would differ little from those under Kennedy-Corman, and would not differ from the present $118-billion total.

Very similar to CHIP is the 1974 Kennedy-Mills proposal, which shares with CHIP the structure of benefits and out-of-pocket payments. Where it differs most sharply is financing. The Kennedy-Mills proposal would be run by the Social Security Administration (as is Medicare), using the insurance industry as a fiscal intermediary. A four percent payroll tax (up to $20,000) would finance the program, with the employer nominally paying three percent, and the employee not more than one percent. In addition, there would be a 2.5 percent tax on self-employment and unearned income up to $20,000, a one percent tax on family welfare payments, and miscellaneous state and federal contributions. With such financing, the estimated *federal* cost of the Kennedy-Mills plan, $77 billion, vastly exceeds the $43 billion of the CHIP plan, though both are lower than the estimated $103 billion federal cost of the Kennedy-Corman plan (1974 estimates by the Secretary of Health, Education, and Welfare).

What is striking is how the political debate over these alternatives, which are relatively close in content, exaggerates their differences. The ideological influence on the shape of the various bills makes comparison of their substantive proposals difficult. The proponents of the various plans are likely to claim more for their bills than is justified. One bill cannot solve all the shortcomings of the health industry. Not only are the problems complicated, but the solution to any one of them often conflicts with the solution to another. One may disagree with the proposals of the AMA, but the organization has recognized that improving "any system of medical care depends basically on balancing three strong and competing dynamics: the desire to make medical care available to all, the desire to control cost, and the desire for high quality care." The competition among these goals must be substantial, since any two of them together work against the third.

The current debate over national health insurance, in fact, recalls the virulent but superficial controversy surrounding Medicare in the late 1950's and early

1960's, which obscured the problems of implementing any major government health-insurance program. One can blame polarization, distrust, and reluctance to compromise. All sides used ideological name-calling to discredit their opponents, and profited little from legitimate criticisms.[3] The problem now is how to avoid a similar battle over national health insurance.

Common sense and the Canadian experience

The current proposals should be judged by their probable results, not their legal form. An informed understanding of the experiences of other nations with governmental health insurance would aid us in the prediction of these outcomes. The Canadian experience is particularly relevant because both Canadian society and its health-care concerns are strikingly similar to ours, and can serve rather like a large natural experiment.[4] For example, would any of the proposals for national health insurance reduce the more than $10-billion annual increase in the national medical-care bill? The example of Canada is not promising. Canada and the United States have experienced remarkably parallel trends in the price, utilization, and expenditure for medical services. The proportion of national resources spent on health is almost identical, despite the fact that Canada began its national program in 1958. In Canada, large-scale public financing has not reversed the upward spiral in prices and expenditures, partly because financing is dispersed among different levels of government.[5] Canada's other efforts to control costs— budget review, incentive reimbursement schemes with global budgeting—have also failed to control inflation.

There is evidence that where financing is concentrated at one governmental level and providers of service are paid directly (rather than reimbursed by insurance), expenditures and the rate of medical inflation are lower. In the last 15 years, with its National Health Service, England has spent a third less of its resources on medical care, and experiences roughly a third the rate of inflation of Canada, Sweden, or the United States. To the 22 percent of Americans who favor putting doctors on salary in an English-style system, this will be a welcome piece of evidence. But even to others, the British experience suggests that concentrated financing is desirable in a future national-health-insurance program.[6] Thus the "conservative" goal of controlling inflation may be best accomplished by a greater degree of governmental centralization than even many "liberals" favor.

Of the leading American plans, the Kennedy-Corman bill—with its concentrated federal financing—theoretically affords the best prospects for curbing inflation. But to be effective, it must be fully implemented, which is unlikely at present. The Feldstein plan is also aimed at controlling inflation, by placing the financial responsibility on patients. But to work it must discourage supplementary insurance by removing current tax incentives—a challenging political task.

Hence, the most promising anti-inflation proposals are politically the least likely to emerge in the United States.

The most likely is CHIP or some other mixed plan that would offer more business and further subsidies to health-care insurers and providers, without strict central budgetary control. Such a fiscally decentralized plan would be inflationary, and would also still leave major gaps in coverage—thus combining the worst of both worlds.

National health insurance is likely to be more successful in improving access than in containing costs. Americans hope that lowering financial barriers will distribute access to care much more fairly than our present arrangements, and promote more equal medical attention to different race, income, regional, and age groups. The Canadian experience offers mixed evidence. First, on the basis of that experience, we should expect relatively modest changes in the overall utilization of hospitals and physicians. The fears of runaway utilization resulting from "cheap" care thus appear unrealistic and ignore the impact of preexisting health insurance, the barriers to care that financing will not change, and the rationing that doctors will impose. One's estimate of Canadian success in redistributing access depends very much on initial expectations. The evidence suggests that national health insurance moderately reallocated access from "rich" to "poor." A study in Quebec shows not only an increase in the use of physician care by income groups under $5,000, but a decline in physician visits for income groups above $9,000.

But financial barriers are only part of the problem. Equally serious is unavailability of care, resulting from the poor distribution of physicians, both geographically and across the range of medical specializations. No proposed remedy has worked well in the United States—not exemption from repaying educational loans in exchange for practicing in under-served areas, nor substitution of medical service in rural or ghetto areas for physicians' military obligations, nor direct subsidies for medical centers in under-served locales. Other Western democracies have learned that poor distribution remains even after the medical purchasing-power of poor city neighborhoods and remote rural areas is improved. Only forced assignment to regions and specializations would work; otherwise young doctors have good professional and social reasons for continuing to prefer specialized medical practices in affluent suburban neighborhoods.

What Canadian experience suggests is that universal health insurance raised public expectations of accessible medical care and increased pressures on the government to address the problem of redistributing services, particularly in rural areas. Canadian analysts report some redistribution of physicians to poorer areas; in Newfoundland the physician/population ratio improved nearly 30 percent in the first three years of national medical insurance. The Canadian evidence is not that such redistribution took place everywhere, nor that national health insurance eradicated differences in access by income class. But Canadian experience does suggest that national health insurance without cost-sharing promotes a more equitable distribution of care.

The quality of care

National health insurance, whether fiscally centralized or decentralized, will probably do little to improve the quality of care. It may provide incentives for preventive care.[7] But it cannot check malpractice or doubtful practice any better than present institutions do, and it may actually stimulate the demand for costly and inefficient procedures. The quality of medical care depends much more on professional self-regulation and consumer awareness than on any conceivable health insurance plan. Adequate financing cannot insure that the care we get is good.

This prediction of minimal impact is supported by Canadian experience. In Canada, national health insurance seems to have had little or no effect on the incidence of medical abuse. It also appears that Canada has employed traditional measures to deal with cases of patient abuse. Peer review and malpractice litigation continued as the *ex post facto* deterrent, and licensing remained the standard method of assuring quality by screening unqualified personnel and facilities.

But this sober assessment of the capacity of national health insurance to reform our medical-care arrangements is no excuse for inaction. The major task of insurance is to calm fears of financial disaster. The issues of quality, prevention, and reorganization are peripheral to that concern. The argument that more traditional medical care will not markedly improve our health is beside the point when the question is whether the current burden of medical care expenses is fairly distributed.

Recognizing the conflicting objectives in national-health-insurance proposals is the beginning of prudent choice. We must ask whether we should spend a larger share of the nation's resources on medical-care services, through the federal government or otherwise. Should efforts be made to make care more accessible (and perhaps less fancy), substantially higher in quality (and therefore more expensive), more humanely delivered (and therefore objectionable to some currently satisfied providers of services)? Should the use of medical care be independent of the ability to pay (and therefore likely to be more costly in the aggregate)?

These will not be the questions asked if ideology continues to distort our understanding of doctors, patients, and national health insurance. When Republicans lock horns with Democrats over the role of the private and public sectors, the public is not well served. For the crisis in American medicine lies as much in our thinking as in our medical-care arrangements.

What is to be done?

The sense of crisis expresses political strategy more than medical-care reality. But ignoring it entirely would be a mistake, for two reasons. First, most of the problems cited are real, if not truly critical—especially the relative inflation in medical-care prices and expenditures. Second, once voters have been "sold" on the existence of a crisis, the path of least political resistance in the United States is a mixed plan. By this I mean a compromise, on both financing and administrative centralization, that would disperse regulatory and financial responsibility among citizens and patients, governments and private insurance companies, states and federal government. The CHIP bill is a good example of such a politically appealing mix, and the 1974 Kennedy-Mills proposal was very similar in financial, if not administrative, dispersion.

But compromises in medical-care financing bring together the worst of the private and public worlds. Ironically, a mixed plan will continue the inflation problem and so institutionalize that aspect of the crisis, as the Swedish and Canadian experiences suggest. In fact, whenever insurance—public or private— is offered as a cure for medical inflation, it becomes iatrogenic—the disease of which it purports to be the cure.

National health insurance will increase inflationary pressures under the best of circumstances. Plans that mix private, state, and federal financing—and regulation— offer the least hope for resisting inflation while expanding access. We need instead a plan that provides ample protection against disastrous medical costs, encourages worthwhile preventive care, offers incentives to efficient practice, and, for the sake of political feasibility, does not suddenly cost $118 billion.

The typical response of national-health-insurance advocates to fiscal constraints has been to vary the richness of the benefit package, not to change the beneficiaries. In Canada, developments took place by type of service—first national hospital insurance in the late 1950's, and then national medical insurance a decade later. But the American pattern so far has been to phase in programs by age and income groups, as with Medicare and Medicaid in the 1960's. A comprehensive health insurance program for all preschool children and pregnant women—combined with universal catastrophic protection—could in the near term be a sensible and traditional American way to introduce national health insurance in the face of the current budgetary restraints.

Health insurance for children

Children are worth our attention for a number of reasons. First, poor children enjoyed less of the redistribution of medical-care services made during the 1960's than poor adults. For similar illnesses, upper-income children are many times more likely to receive care than children from poor homes. Second, the care children need most is easily produced, relatively cheap, and in the case of preschoolers, reasonably likely to improve their current and future health. Immunization is an example of inexpensive but effective preventive care that liberals and conservatives alike know is important. It is also an example of an area where the current allocation of responsibility has left glaring inadequacies—up to 50 percent of the children in some counties have not been immunized against dread diseases. Preventive care in such cases can help—in individual, social, and financial terms.

Consider infants with low birth weights. About 240,000 of them are born every year in the United States. One-fifth of them will not survive the first five months of life, and those who do often suffer permanent impairments. But we have research results that show how to reduce such occurrences: prenatal intervention programs, improved diagnostic techniques, methods to delay the onset of labor, and special attention to groups, such as teenaged mothers, with a high risk of having a low-birth-weight infant. Preventive care could do more for infants than for any other age group.

A comprehensive health insurance program for preschool children and pregnant women could be relatively cheap. Medical care costs less for children than for any other age group in the population: about one-sixth of the total expenditures for the elderly, for example. In 1974, per capita expenditures for those under 19 years of age were $183, compared to $420 for those aged 19 to 64, and $1,218 for those 65 and over. A third of the population, children, account for about 15 per cent of all health expenditures. From these figures one can readily see that a comprehensive program for children is within our *fiscal grasp*. Per capita payments of $200 a year per child under six would total about $4 billion; the cost of prenatal and postnatal care for approximately 3.2 million births per year would probably cost some $2 billion a year. Thus, something on the order of $6 billion annually would pay for Kennedy-Corman benefits for preschool children and pregnant women.[8] (After giving birth, women would then be covered under the catastrophic portion of the plan, as is everyone else.)

Not only would the total initial cost of such a plan be modest, but the chances of an unpredictable inflationary surge are less with young children. Most of their care is predictable, relating to prevention (immunization), well-baby checkups, and routine procedures for common illness. The expenses associated with pregnancy, though not modest on a per case basis, are relatively uniform and predictable, and hence less susceptible to the danger of overuse under national health insurance.

A program for pregnant women and young children could be reimbursed on a capitation basis—the yearly payment of lump sums for medical care—and thereby further this widely praised method of remunerating doctors. American doctors generally favor the traditional fee-for-service payment, but one can imagine far less medical objection to capitation if it is limited to obstetrical and pediatric care. We already have an existing pattern of prepaid lump-sum payments for obstetrical care (including prenatal care), encouraged by the predictable character of the required medical services. The familiar nature of the required care for pregnant women and infants makes the review of quality and costs easier for this group than for any other. The serious problem with capitation is the possibility that it will discourage needed care. Capitation provides economic incentives either to keep patients well or to deprive them of expensive care; depriving them is the (unethical) alternative to prevention and efficient services. But widely understood standards of ordinary care make it easier to monitor whether providers of services who receive capitation payments are underserving or abusing their patients. Child care is an area in medicine with fairly clear standards of what constitutes adequate service.

The routine nature of so much pediatric care has another virtue for using child care to help reform our current medical-care system. Routine care can be delivered quite easily by physician substitutes and nurse practitioners, who deliver most of the services in other parts of the world. In America, pediatric nurses, as many mothers know, are extensions and sometimes substitutes for physicians. So there exists the possibility of providing medical services more efficiently through physician substitutes; per capita payments make this financially attractive to pediatricians and family physicians. It should be noted that the number of preschool children will decline over the next quarter-century, though it will continue to increase for the next few years. Critics might contend that substituting nonphysicians in a dwindling market will raise strong medical objections. But this problem is manageable in at least two respects. First, the number of unmet needs among preschoolers, particularly the poor, is significant; meeting them will keep the physicians busy even as the number of kids declines. Further, family physicians, who deliver more than half the care to children, can adjust their practices among the different age groups. It still makes sense for them individually to hire assistants to do more routine work, if there are other patients or other problems to deal with.

A possible program

The nature of children's medical problems and care makes a "kiddie care" national-health-insurance plan a sensible first (or last) step toward extending financial access to medical services through government action. Many have urged smaller benefits for the entire population as an initial public step; my view is that such steps (whether CHIP or the 1974 Kennedy-Mills bill) are fiscally irresponsible, expanding the demand for medical services by groups whose most pressing health needs are not for conventional medical care, and whose most serious concern is financial catastrophe. These reasons must also influence the shape of a child-care plan: The nature of the benefits must meet children's real needs, and a catastrophic-protection plan must be offered to ensure that the adult population, especially the childless, do not regard children as their public-policy nemeses.

Children's needs will not be met by a plan that requires substantial cost-sharing by their parents. The reasoning behind patient cost-sharing (co-insurance, co-payments, and/or deductibles) hardly applies to children. The simple and largely preventive procedures of routine child care should not be rationed according to complex financial constraints. Since the overall budget for children's medical care is relatively low, cost-sharing to ease the government's budget burden (the real rationale in the Kennedy-Mills and CHIP plans) is politically less necessary. Cost-sharing to reduce unnecessary utilization is less important because of the more limited risk of "overuse." To the extent such risk exists (tonsillectomies, unnecessary hospitalization, drug prescriptions) it can be reduced by capitation: The examples of the Kaiser plans in California and the Group Health Cooperative of Puget Sound illustrate the reduction in the rates of hospitalization and surgery in prepaid as compared to fee-for-service plans. It is worrisome that American children are four times more likely than British to have their tonsils surgically removed, but a plan to pay for child care need not encourage such questionable practice. Indeed, the concentration of financing in government hands will increase the incentive to discourage harmful practices.

In the light of these considerations, starting with children (with catastrophic protection for all of them) is a reasonable approach to national health insurance. The present economic and political context requires attention to forms of national health insurance that can be administered, that are less costly to the federal treasury than the Kennedy-Corman bill, and that are unlikely to increase the rate of medical inflation. Plans for child care provide compelling alternatives to the muted versions of the universal proposals that the current debate has thrown up. Children rightly have political appeal as deserving recipients of medical dollars, and the relatively limited costs of even a comprehensive "kiddie care" plan address the demand for fiscal restraint.

The great appeal of other plans lies in their suggested ways of putting a lid on health expenditures—a specific feature of the Kennedy-Corman proposal, which also eschews cost-sharing and strongly supports capitation payments. All of these features are maintained in a Kennedy-Corman program for preschoolers, though the expenditure ceiling would apply only to children. "Kiddie care" would not in itself restrain medical inflation across the board; other measures in connection with Medicare, health-planning legislation, and facility control would have to be (and now are) employed. But "kiddie care" would assist in this effort, not undercut it.

Those who seek far-reaching changes in the overall organization of health care have been saddled with the political burden of being responsible for the $118-billion health budget. At a time when concern about the size of the federal budget is so widespread, a reform alternative with limited costs is appealing. "Kiddie care" meets that standard, and can be supplemented by a universal catastrophic credit income-tax scheme costing less than $3 billion. Such a joint plan could be financed by $8 to $9 billion of gross federal expenditures. We should remember that almost half of this could be financed by the current tax expenditures for health—the $3.5 billion for medical-care deductions from the taxable income of individuals who now spend more than three percent of family income on medical care, and the nearly equal amount lost by the federal government through subsidizing health-insurance premiums. Tax reform, in short, could make the cost of child-health care and universal catastrophic-insurance protection no greater than what we are now spending.

Catastrophic protection is not added to the proposal merely because it is politically fashionable. That is an additional feature, but a responsible national-health-insurance program should respond to the widespread fears of financial ruin from ill-health, fears that the plans for "kiddie care" do not address. A catastrophic protection program would address those fears; it is a crucial ingredient in an overall plan. If fewer than one percent of the populace have expenses more than $5,000 per year, such a scheme is fiscally possible if the deductible is set high in relation to average expenditures, and low in relation to economic ruin. As Table 2 makes clear, the Internal Revenue Service could implement such a plan with the great political appeal of benefiting everyone (through insurance protection), while actually paying only a few directly. Further, such a plan would have the great substantive advantage of reforming the tax treatment of medical costs in a more equitable and efficacious manner.

Planning for child care

Here are the features of a joint child-care and catastrophic program, beginning with pregnant women and preschoolers.

1. *Benefits*: The benefit package would be inclusive—partly preventive in nature, including prenatal care for mothers, fertility benefits, *dental care*, such kinds of nutritional and well-baby care that seem to work, immunizations, setting broken bones, etc. Neonatal intensive care, renal dialysis, and heart surgery would be included, as would all conventional, minor acute care.

2. *Provider Reimbursement*: The only form of payment would be capitation. The federal government would offer perhaps $200 per year, per child—possibly adjusted for regional differences—to any qualified provider, individual or organization, capable of providing the benefit-package. Providers would sign up children, just as general practitioners in Britain sign up families. Those wishing to buy care in the regular fee-for-service system would be free to do so, but not with government subsidy. Pregnant women would be included, and pregnant teenagers could enroll in their own names, even though they are minors.

Table 2. *Amount of reduced tax under current personal-income-tax provisions*[1]

Adjusted annual gross income	Out-of-pocket medical expenses:			
	$500	$1,000	$2,000	$5,000
$ 5,000	$ 0	$ 0	$ 0	$ 0
10,000	55	150	334	806
15,000	33	141	361	957
20,000	38	123	373	1,093

[1] *Source:* Karen Davis, "Tax Credits for Health Relief for Working Class, Unemployed, and Disadvantaged," revised version of a paper presented to the National Health Council Annual Forum (Orlando, Florida, March 18, 1975). Tax reductions are based on a family with four exemptions. The calculations assume that families with incomes under $5,000 take the standard deduction, and that other families have itemized deductions of $1,500, plus medical expenses. Of the medical expenses, $150 is assumed to be fully deductible as health-insurance premiums, the remainder is subject to an exclusion of three percent of adjusted gross income. Calculations are based on tax law in effect in 1974.

Table 3. *Amount of tax credit under proposed plan*[1]

Adjusted annual gross income	Out-of-pocket medical expenses:			
	$500	$1,000	$2,000	$5,000
$ 5,000	$ 0	$250	$750	$4,000
10,000	0	0	500	3,000
15,000	0	0	250	2,000
20,000	0	0	0	1,000

[1] *Source:* Same as Table 2.

3. *Patient Cost-Sharing*: No cost-sharing at the time of receiving services would be required, excepting perhaps some nominal payment for drugs or other care where the serious possibility of overuse exists.

4. *Quality Review*: A quality-monitoring mechanism would be established, based on the work of David Kessner, Robert Brook, and others, designed to reduce the likelihood that providers will offer too little care for the fixed per capita price.

5. *Financing*: There would be straight, general revenue financing, with the following tax adjustment: either reduction in the $750 exemption for children as partial payment for the benefit, or half the tax credit for children at the median income as partial payment. Tax adjustments should provide approximately half the cost, and should be adjusted as costs increase.

6. *Cost*: At $200 per child, per year on average ($4 billion), plus prenatal and postnatal care for an estimated 3 million births ($3 billion), the total would be an estimated $7 billion per year.

7. *Administration*: The child and maternal health-insurance program would be administered by the local health boards specified in the Kennedy-Corman legislation. The setting of capitation rates and broad policy would fall to the National Health Security Board specified in the 1975 version of Kennedy-Corman. The catastrophic tax-credit program would be the administrative responsibility of the Internal Revenue Service, managed by the division that implements the medical expense deductions under current tax law.

8. *Research and Development*: Some attempt should be made to link expenditures on research to reducing the need for the services covered by the children's program, and to producing technology for delivering those services more efficiently. Among the possibilities: contraceptive research; funding of demonstrations of better manpower utilization, such as pediatric assistants; further research on prenatal care and well-baby care to determine effectiveness and to modify program benefits accordingly; a research and statistical effort comparable to that of Medicare, so we can learn from doing.

The catastrophic tax-credit program

The child and maternal health-insurance program can be supported by a universal national catastrophic plan. The proposal briefly described here calls for the incorporation of catastrophic protection into a reformed tax policy for medical expenses.

1. *Benefits*: Comprehensiveness of covered services is important for a catastrophic program. That is, practically all medical care expenses should be eligible for tax credits, though the amount of the deductible, coinsurance, and maximum out-of-pocket liability could vary. One promising schedule, whose distribution of benefits by income levels (in Table 3) is compared with our current regressive tax-deduction policy (in Table 2), has a deductible of 10 percent of taxable income, and 50 percent coinsurance up to a maximum family expenditure of 20 percent of taxable income. For this purpose taxable income would be more broadly defined than under current law. One wants to prevent incorporating loopholes into this plan, where the very definition of catastrophe depends upon the relative burden of medical expenses on family wealth.

These benefits, it should be emphasized, provide only minimal protection against burdensome health-care expenses. The tax credit works like a catastrophic health-insurance plan that requires families to pay up to 10 percent of their taxable income before the insurance benefits begin. By providing 50 cents for each dollar of further expense up to the maximum family liability, the plan shares expenses with families having high costs, and places a ceiling on their medical liabilities, short of financial disaster. Further, it does so progressively, so that at higher income levels, benefits decline gradually. And it is progressively financed, as Karen Davis of Brookings has emphasized, through foregone revenues—income tax revenues.

The payments of benefits would be integrated into the current tax cycle. That would mean annual adjustments for most, or quarterly assessments for those who chose to report their income and expenses in that manner. The schedule shown in Table 3 illustrates how the tax credit for out-of-pocket expenses (including health-insurance premiums) would affect families at different income levels. A family with an income of $5,000 and ruinous expenses of $5,000 would be entitled to a tax credit of $4,000. The credit would decline for families with the same expenses but higher incomes. For a family with an income of $15,000 and with the same $5,000 medical expenses, the tax credit would amount to $2,000 for the year.

A credit against one's tax bill would work for those with incomes high enough for the Internal Revenue Service to tax. A credit in the form of a cash rebate would be paid in April for those—like pensioners on social security—who have little or no taxable income. There is concern among some critics of this plan over the problems health providers might have in getting prompt payment of their bills from the poor and the elderly. This plan would not address that difficulty directly. It is insurance protection for individuals, not protection against the cash-flow problems of hospitals, doctors, and nursing homes. On the other hand, the assurance that beyond a reasonable limit no patient would be destitute from medical expenses constitutes substantial underwriting of the working poor and the medically impoverished and, in that sense, assistance to the providers of services. What is more, the possibility of using quarterly declarations and year-end tax adjustments might go a long way to allay such fears.

2. *Staging*: The child insurance program would be expanded, if desired, on a manageable basis each year for the *first five years*. Adding two years to the child-eligibility level each year would mean that children under 15 would be completely covered then. This option leaves open whether at that time the child-health-insurance policy should be extended to the rest of the population. Over the period of implementation—extending into the 1980's—the rest of the population, and most particularly the unemployed, aged, and working poor, would be relieved of the worry that medical expenses could bankrupt them. Medicare and Medicaid would be left in place for further protection.

The nation's health

The United States remains one of the few industrial nations in the world where destitution can result from medical-care expenses. Some four percent of the population spend more than a quarter of their income on illness. Up to four million are potential candidates for coronary bypass surgery, an expensive new procedure costing (according to government estimates) about $7,000 per operation. So catastrophic protection would relieve a burden that now falls most heavily upon the sick, aged, unemployed, and poor.

It is undeniable that political considerations make a combination of child and catastrophic insurance appealing. Catastrophic insurance deals with the serious concern about impoverishment, particularly from cancer, stroke, heart disease, and mental illness. But both plans can be accomplished fiscally, and are now within our political and administrative grasp. The deductible provisions of the tax-credit plan limit its costs, and the introduction of a Kennedy-Corman plan for children is aimed at the very group who will not use an enormous amount of resources in the expensive hospital-surgical area of medical care.

The child program, moreover, involves pediatricians and family practitioners, a group far easier to monitor and less likely to oppose the capitation mode of payment. This plan would not apply to those insistent on fee-for-service medicine. The financing for both plans would come largely from the current tax expenditures for medical care, but would be far more progressive in effect. An additional source of funding is some portion of the yearly child-allowance now paid by the Internal Revenue Service in child tax credits or deductions, which could be earmarked for child health insurance—reminding parents everywhere that medical care is not free even if the sick don't have to pay every time they use medical services. Finally, at a time when the country is beset by the fear of failure in government and discouraged by the competence of our governors, a plan that is manageable but effective would do much for the health of the political order.

Notes

1 The remarkable growth of interest in catastrophic protection—in both private plans and new state insurance programs during the past two years—indirectly supports Feldstein's criticism of American health insurance in the early 1970's as woefully "shallow." Fewer than one percent of the population spend more than $5,000 on health care in any one year, but the fear of catastrophic illness is universal.

2 Martin Feldstein, "A New Approach to National Health Insurance," *The Public Interest*, No. 23 (Spring 1971), pp. 93–106. This is only one version of Feldstein's MRI. A variant is to have a lower deductible (five percent of family income), followed by 50 percent co-insurance over a further 10 percent of family income. The advantage of this more complex scheme is to keep persons partly responsible financially over a wider band of medical expenditures. See T. R. Marmor and Robert Kudrle, "National Health Insurance Plans and Their Implications for Mental Health," prepared for delivery at the Symposium on Political and Community Problems in Mental-Health Care (Northern Illinois University, April 22–23, 1975), p. 12.

3 At that time the major question before Congress was whether to enact a health-insurance program for the aged, financed by social security. During the hearings, almost all the attention was focused on whether such an idea was politically attractive. Those who found it appealing discovered almost nothing of practical worth in opposing arguments.

Those who opposed social security financing of health insurance found little worthwhile in the Medicare proposal. The consequence was that two large, well-financed, warring camps fought in full public view for more than a decade. The tragedy was that each side learned so little from the other. This intemperate policy debate was followed by serious operational difficulties that emerged after the program began in 1966. See Richard Harris, *A Sacred Trust* (New York, New American Library, 1966); Herman and Ann Somers, *Medicare and the Hospitals* (Washington, D.C., Brookings Institute, 1967); and T. R. Marmor, *The Politics of Medicare* (Chicago, Aldine, 1973).

4 Most of the countries of the West share similar health concerns, but major political, economic, or cultural differences raise questions whether the lessons of health insurance in those countries would apply to the United States. With Canada, however, the differences are far less marked. While the parliamentary system presents an obvious political difference, Canada has extensive decentralization of authority, with a tradition of resisting federal power analogous, though by no means identical, to American federalism. The structure of the health professions, the hospitals, and the history of voluntary insurance are also strikingly similar, especially as contrasted with France or Great Britain. Both Canada and the United States have voluntary hospitals not owned by the state, a medical-care profession largely under fee-for-service remuneration, and a pattern of partial adjustment to the intervention of insurance—mainly nonpublic at first, but in the postwar period increasingly more public in character. For a more detailed examination of the Canadian national-health-insurance experience, the reader is referred to chapter 9.

5 Chapter 3 of this volume discusses the problem of inflation; chapter 9 presents more recent data from Canada that conflict with this 1977 factual portrait. See author's note on page 179.

6 By "concentrated financing" I mean that a single unit of government pays the bill—the Health Security Board, in the case of the Kennedy-Corman bill. By contrast, our present medical financing is dispersed among patients, numerous insurance carriers, and federal, state, and local government agencies.

7 It should be noted that there is little evidence to support the general enthusiasm for preventive care. There are indications that prenatal care effectively prevents some maternal and infant problems. But there is also evidence that mass screening programs and even annual physical checkups are wasteful, and only occasionally detect conditions that are aided by early treatment. Economists Burton Weisbrod and Ralph Andreano conclude that preventive care can increase costs without significantly raising the level of health. They attribute apparent cost-savings in the Kaiser-Permanente plan (which is often cited as a model of the medical and financial efficacy of prevention) to "various factors, many of which are unrelated to preventive care." Even apart from the question of whether prevention is effective or not, however, it could be argued that the issue is peripheral to the debate over national health insurance. Is it really necessary that a plan focus on preventive care? Some have argued that national health insurance without incentives for preventive care is not worth having, but would anyone seriously argue, for example, that automobile insurance is not worth having if it doesn't prevent accidents?

8 Compare this cost with the $7 billion now spent on medical care through the medical-expense deduction and other tax breaks for health insurance. In fiscal year 1976–77 the cost of Medicare alone will increase by an estimated $5.4 billion.

11. Patient cost sharing

DOUGLAS CONRAD, THEODORE R. MARMOR

Patient cost sharing, the direct payment by consumers of some share of the costs of medical care at the time of use, has been a topic of controversy throughout the continuing American national health insurance debate. Cost sharing has received particular attention in recent months as observers have become increasingly concerned with the inflationary potential of national health insurance and increasingly pessimistic about the probable success of regulatory efforts. The debate over costs has enhanced the appeal of all measures promising economy; as a result, many national health insurance proponents have taken pains to show how their provisions for patient cost sharing would avoid excessive use of medical services, thus combining widened insurance coverage with economy measures. The theoretical appeal of a policy should not, however, obscure potential problems in implementation of that policy. This chapter identifies and explores problems likely to arise if national health insurance should put cost sharing into effect.

The three types of cost sharing are deductibles, coinsurance, and copayment. Deductibles require a patient to pay all costs up to a specified maximum, such as the first twenty-five dollars of a hospital stay. With coinsurance, the patient's liability is fixed as some percentage of a medical bill. Copayments, in contrast, are fixed charges per unit of service, for example, two dollars per office visit. Coinsurance and copayment obligations can be unlimited or kept within some specified maximum or percentage of income.

A variety of approaches to cost sharing are included in past and current national health insurance proposals. A number of plans—particularly the major risk insurance proposal of Martin Feldstein, the Nixon-Ford administrations' Comprehensive Health Insurance Plan (CHIP) and the Kennedy-Mills proposal of 1974—propose cost sharing as a central policy tool for containing medical costs while expanding insurance coverage. The CHIP bill offers perhaps the most comprehensive approach to cost sharing. Individuals qualifying for the Employee Health Care Insurance Plan (EHIP) would face a $150 deductible with a $450 family maximum and 25 percent coinsurance. The maximum out-of-pocket payments would be $1,500 per family. Families and individuals covered

From J. Feder, J. Holohan, and T.R. Marmor, *National Health Insurance: Conflicting Goals and Policy Choices* (Washington, D.C.: The Urban Institute, 1980), Chap. 8. Copyright © 1980 by The Urban Institute. Reprinted with permission.

by the Assisted Health Care Insurance Plan (AHIP) would face a schedule of premiums, deductibles, coinsurance rates, and limits to liabilities that increased with income. Deductibles would begin at zero and rise to $50 for prescription drugs and $150 for all other services for individuals with incomes greater than $7,000 and families with incomes greater than $10,000. Coinsurance rates would begin at 10 percent for the lowest income class and rise to 25 percent for the two highest classes. Liability for expenditures would be limited to 6 percent of income for individuals with incomes less than $1,750 and families with incomes less than $2,500. Maximum liability would increase to 15 percent of income for individuals with incomes greater than $5,250 and families with incomes greater than $7,500.

The Kennedy-Mills plan proposes a $150 per person deductible with a $300 maximum per family, 25 percent coinsurance, and maximum per family liability of $1,000. No cost sharing would be imposed on individuals with incomes less than $2,400 or families with incomes less than $4,800. Individuals and families with incomes above these levels would be liable for cost sharing, and maximum liabilities would increase with income. For example, maximum liability for a four-person family with an income between $4,800 and $8,800 would equal 25 percent of the difference between their income and $6,800.

Other plans give cost sharing a prominent role, but clearly not as a device for restraining demand. The Long-Ribicoff-Waggonner bill, for instance, prescribes large deductibles—sixty days of hospital care and $2,000 worth of medical expenses—but at the same time attempts to induce beneficiaries to supplement or pay all of these amounts through health insurance coverage.

Finally, some plans—the Kennedy-Corman plan and the Dellums bill, most strikingly and explicitly—reject cost sharing as a major means of cost containment, on grounds that substantial patient cost sharing is both an inequitable way to restrain medical care use and an ineffective mechanism for reducing inflation in the health industry's most inflationary sector—the hospital.

Clearly a wide range of cost-sharing mechanisms have been proposed. In examining the problems of putting any patient cost-sharing plan into effect, this chapter particularly attempts to anticipate gaps between proposals and performance. It is assumed that cost sharing would deter some service use and thus *could* affect the cost of national health insurance. Hence the chapter concentrates on exploring the practical consequences of employing complicated cost-sharing provisions within a national health insurance program. It is hoped that understanding the actual forms of cost-sharing policies when implemented will contribute to more realistic policy assessment.

The chapter first reviews the range of arguments for and against cost sharing. Then it considers the administrative feasibility of cost sharing, examining particularly the complicated provisions for relating cost sharing to family income, the main device most NHI proposals offer for making sure that rationing of care by patient costs would not fall disproportionately on lower-income families. The main concern is to discover if these provisions can be put into effect, and at what price in administrative complexity and dollars. The chapter then investigates the possibility of private supplementation of national health insurance, that is, the purchase of private insurance to cover costs that patients would be required by national health insurance to share (as well as some uninsured services). The more extensive the supplementation, the less that patient cost sharing under national health insurance would affect the use of service under an NHI program.

Cost-sharing arguments: pro and con

Several arguments can be used to justify patient cost sharing. First, it is most often advocated as a way to make consumers cost-conscious—discouraging unnecessary use of services while encouraging search for inexpensive care. The assumption is that consumers will use more health services when their out-of-pocket costs are low. When a third party pays all of a physician's or hospital's bill, the services are free to recipients, so they can be expected to use more services than would be the case if a price were attached. According to this reasoning, the demand for free care is limited only by transportation costs, the cost of lost time (in wages or leisure), and the pain sometimes associated with the consumption of medical care. The conclusion is that cost sharing would reduce the total amount of care demanded and might lead to a substitution of less expensive forms of care.

The effect of various levels of cost sharing on demand for health services will depend on how well the population is insured for particular services before enactment of national health insurance and how responsive individuals are to charges for those services. Newhouse, Phelps, and Schwartz have completed an extensive review of available research on the demand for hospital and ambulatory care and have used that evidence to estimate the costs of different NHI cost-sharing arrangements.[1]

They estimate that an NHI plan with a coinsurance rate of 25 percent could increase demand for hospital inpatient services by as much as 8 percent, depending on the current configuration of coverage. An NHI plan offering full coverage could increase demand for inpatient services from 5 percent to 15 percent. Given current hospital occupancy rates, the authors argue that the capacity of the system would not be seriously strained. Thus, barring successful control through other mechanisms, increases in demand for inpatient services would probably be reflected in utilization. Because current hospital inpatient services (including inpatient physician services) already account for approximately 55 percent of health service expenditures, however, even these small percentage increases would be quite important.

Because insurance now covers ambulatory services less comprehensively than it covers hospital care, the percentage change in ambulatory service demand generated by national health insurance would be considerably greater than the changes in demand for inpatient services. Newhouse and associates project the demand for ambulatory services to increase by 75 percent under a full-coverage plan and by 30 percent under a plan with a 25 percent maximum coinsurance rate. They estimate demand for ancillary services to increase by about half, or about 35 percent to 40 percent, under a full-coverage plan and by about 15 percent under a plan with a 25 percent coinsurance rate.

Increases in *demand* for ambulatory services, however, would probably not be translated into increases in *utilization* because of existing supply constraints. Newhouse and associates conclude that without cost sharing, the demand for ambulatory care would dramatically increase, and that other rationing devices, with their own cost implications, would have to be imposed. Cost sharing for ambulatory care, they argue, is the only alternative to delays in obtaining appointments, increased waiting time, reductions in time physicians devote to individuals, and higher physician fees. These researchers assume Americans would not tolerate such rationing devices and would press for expansion of ambulatory services. Thus they conclude that cost sharing must be seriously considered as a measure for restraining the growth of ambulatory medical expenditures.

A second justification for cost sharing is that it makes the medical system easier to "police." According to this argument, cost-conscious patients can limit abuses such as unnecessary laboratory tests and X-rays, excessive referrals to other practitioners within a clinic, and excessive prescribing of drugs. These well-publicized abuses are easily perpetuated when patients bear none of the financial costs of care. Without cost sharing, the burden of monitoring the appropriateness of care is borne almost entirely by third-party payers, whose efforts to control abuse thus far appear decidedly ineffective. By limiting such abuses, cost sharing would contribute to national health insurance's political acceptability as well as to cost containment goals.

In this connection, it should be noted that in some West European countries, patients pay almost a quarter of the costs of ambulatory medical visits, not primarily to restrain medical inflation, but to remind patients about the costs of using medical services, particularly those services for which use is typically initiated by patients (such as individual psychotherapy or eyeglasses). It may be that such services are particularly suited to continued financial participation by patients. That question thus far has been peripheral to discussion of national health insurance in the United States, but the matter is directly relevant to the issues of implementing complex provisions of cost sharing and estimating private supplementation.

A third argument in favor of cost sharing is that it would permit NHI plans to cover a broader range of services than would otherwise be possible. Cost sharing is but a single example of a general search for ways to reduce public insurance program costs in reaction to a growing sensitivity to the size of the federal budget. Cost sharing is said to offer a method of reducing third-party program expenditures that is fairer than other prominent alternatives, such as rigid limits on benefits that exclude certain infrequently needed services or deny payment for hospital care beyond a fixed number of days. Cost sharing could be designed to apply only to routine services and thus be broadly shared among beneficiaries, thereby avoiding the effects of measures that fall most heavily on persons with severe but specific needs for services. Theoretically, cost sharing also could be related to family incomes, with little or no sharing of costs for low-income families and increasingly greater shared costs as income rises.

In response to these arguments in favor of cost sharing, there seems little doubt that cost sharing would deter utilization, perhaps substantially, for *some* services, but it is less clear that cost sharing would deter utilization equitably or efficiently. To begin with the equity question, programs with uniform deductibles or coinsurance rates impose relatively greater burdens on low-income families than on high-income families. As a result, it is argued, use of medical services varies not solely with illness but also with income.

Karen Davis has provided evidence that Medicare's equal cost-sharing terms have supported continuing discrimination by income affecting the elderly's access to medical care.[2] Enterline and associates have argued that the absence of cost sharing in Canadian national health insurance has eliminated this problem and in fact has redistributed physician services toward the poor.[3] These views have led some NHI planners to reject cost sharing as a major policy tool and others to propose tying cost sharing to family income levels. Unless cost sharing is linked to income, increasing access to medical care for persons currently underserved—one of the major stated aims of national health insurance—is unlikely.

As for the efficiency of cost sharing, authorities disagree. A further problem is that if cost sharing is to control costs, providers must collect cost-sharing payments and consumers must adjust their level of utilization. If cost-sharing payments proved difficult to collect, as might be the case with low-income populations, or if cost sharing had significant deterrent effects on utilization, the incomes of physicians and other providers would suffer. Physicians might well respond by increasing their delivery of services they initiate to compensate for any reduction in incomes.[4]

Some argue that patients have insufficient knowledge to make rational calculations of benefits and costs of their medical choices (can patients judge what is "unnecessary" care?), and that physicians and other providers who presumably possess adequate information are only indirectly affected by the prices facing consumers. Cost sharing, it is argued, might deter people, especially the poor, from seeking necessary care early, thereby adversely affecting health and leading to greater use of services in the long run.

Having presented just the outlines of the cost-sharing debate, this chapter now turns not to the details of the debate but rather to a precondition of that debate—an assessment of whether cost-sharing proposals can be put into effect as their designers intend. If they cannot, debate about the consequences of cost sharing is premature if not irrelevant. Two arguments against cost sharing pose the most serious obstacles to its use as a cost control mechanism. The first is a claim that administration of patient cost sharing in a national program would be extremely costly and perhaps unworkable, particularly if the system should attempt to minimize inequities by linking cost sharing with income. Second, it is argued that individuals and groups would purchase supplementary insurance to cut their out-of-pocket expenses at the time of service use, thereby undermining cost containment objectives. The remainder of this chapter reviews the evidence supporting and opposing each of these views.

Administrative implementation of cost sharing under national health insurance

Implementation of patient cost sharing would impose several kinds of costs. Uncertainty about coverage, for example, can lead to actual loss of benefits. A beneficiary can be uncertain about the services or expenses that count toward a deductible, the point at which a deductible is met, the copayment or coinsurance associated with a particular service, or the claims payment—patient or program—at a given time. Beyond uncertainty are actual administrative costs: The patient has to keep track of bills, the provider has to bill and collect from two sources, and finally, the program has to process claims.

Obviously, the actual costs of cost sharing—and the determination of who will bear them—depend on a plan's specific terms. Opponents of cost sharing, particularly opponents of income-related cost sharing, argue that the more complex the terms, the more reason to question whether cost sharing is administratively feasible. To assess the validity of this concern, this section addresses a specific set of administrative issues: (1) claims processing and collection when cost sharing is not related to income and (2) methods of income determination in an income-related system.

Even without income determinations, claims processing for cost sharing involves several detailed steps. For each claim it may be necessary to determine patient eligibility, service coverage, medical necessity, the "reasonableness" of the charge, satisfaction of the deductible, any limits on out-of-pocket expenses, and the amount of copayment or coinsurance. Although these tasks are numerous and complex, they are currently being performed by both public and private third-party payers for the bulk of the population. Some payers undoubtedly perform better than others, but the tasks themselves are clearly feasible.

A national health insurance plan, however, could increase the detail involved in one or more claims-processing decisions—for example, eligibility, medical necessity, or provider charges. If claims processing were handled by a multitude of carriers (either as underwriters or government agents), considerable variation in the determination of patient liability would probably result. Variation of this sort has occurred in determining charges under Medicare.[5] The result is that, contrary to the statute's intent, different program beneficiaries pay different cost-sharing amounts. Processing could be centralized to avoid this result, but centralized processing would probably slow claims payments. In either case, mistakes are inevitable. Although these mistakes might be no more severe under national health insurance than under current insurance arrangements, they might well attract more attention. These problems do not suggest that cost sharing is infeasible, only that it would compound the problems a new program like national health insurance would have to confront.

The collection of cost-sharing payments would depend on the national health insurance program's approach to claims payment. When physicians bill patients, who, in turn, submit claims for reimbursement under commercial insurance plans, cost-sharing payments are collected as part of the total bill. Whatever collection problem exists applies to the total charge and is not unique to the cost-sharing portion. To reduce collection problems, Blue Cross-Blue Shield has introduced a different approach to paying claims. Providers submit bills to and receive payment from the plan, but the insurer's payment usually does not cover any cost-sharing payments. When cost sharing is required, the provider must bill the patient as well as the insurer. In addition to having to bill twice, the provider also must wait until the third party pays the claim to know the patient's cost-sharing obligation. To avoid these burdens, physicians might decide to bill all patients directly and try to avoid serving anyone who appeared to pose a financial risk.

Credit mechanisms have been proposed for national health insurance that would reduce collection burdens and associated access problems. The health credit card, suggested in both the Kennedy-Mills and CHIP bills, would allow patients to "charge" their entire expenses. The program—or carrier—would pay to the provider the full charge, including the patient cost-sharing portion, and then collect the cost-sharing portion from the patient. By shifting the collection burden to the program, proponents of the health card seek not only to reduce barriers to access but also to encourage physicians to accept reimbursement from the program as payment in full. This transfer to the public sector of the collection task would increase the visibility of the administrative costs of patient cost sharing.

The credit card's capacity to achieve its objectives at reasonable administrative cost is open to question. Carriers would be required to take on collection responsibilities with which they have had no experience, to have the reserves available with which to advance credit, and to absorb bad debts. Carriers may be reluctant to undertake these responsibilities, and there is no reason to assume that they would perform them more efficiently than providers have done.

An even greater problem posed by the credit card is the proposed treatment of beneficiaries who defaulted on their cost-sharing obligations.[6] Following commercial practice, the NHI bills propose to deny credit to persons who default. Carriers would be responsible for identifying and notifying these persons. Once credit was withdrawn, providers would be responsible for collecting whatever cost-sharing payments defaulters incurred. As a result, not only would the administrative burden imposed by the credit card increase, but also providers would inherit the very collection tasks the card was intended to eliminate. Inasmuch as defaulters are estimated to make up as much as 15 percent of the population,[7] it is appropriate to consider whether the credit card ultimately would raise more problems than it would solve. Alternative approaches to credit are presented in the following discussion of income-related cost sharing.

The most striking feature of income-related cost sharing is that it has never been tried before. To minimize program administrative costs, a national health insurance program would probably retain the current system of income determination for individuals whose income is now determined by a government agency. This practice, which follows the assumptions of actuary Gordon Trapnell,[8] would reduce the incremental costs of administering national health insurance. Even with this conservative assumption, however, approximately 26 million new income determinations would be required under the CHIP bill. To put this task into perspective, consider the 8 million income determinations that the current welfare programs—AFDC and SSI—together now require.[9] Using the estimates of the Social Security Administration with some adjustments, the incremental administrative costs of income testing proposed under CHIP would have cost about $740 million in 1975.[10] This amount is approximately equal to the total costs of administering Medicare during fiscal 1975. The real resource costs of implementing just this aspect of national health insurance cost sharing are obviously not trivial. Nevertheless these costs are only a small fraction—less than 1 percent—of total expenditures. Clearly, the desirability of these administrative expenses depends on the amount of savings in total expenditures cost sharing might produce.

The question of which time period to use for determining beneficiary income is important for program administration. Generally, income-related cost sharing is designed to distribute progressively the burden of out-of-pocket medical expenses across socioeconomic groups. To enhance redistribution, cost-sharing obligations ideally would be based on a measure of permanent income rather than current income, which is subject to random, transitory disturbances. Out-of-pocket medical costs, however, pose an immediate consumer budgeting problem, which suggests reliance on a measure of current income.

There are several ways to measure current income. One is the face-to-face interview, or means test, which is currently employed for welfare and Medicaid.

Given the number of income determinations required, however, this approach appears to be prohibitively expensive for national health insurance. The Social Security Administration estimated that to obtain initial income declarations for CHIP, this approach for 39 million filing units would cost at least $1.5 billion and require more than 65,000 employee-years. Costs would rise if changes in income and family status were incorporated during the year.[11]

It may be reasonable to continue the interview approach for the population on welfare, but it seems advisable to consider alternatives for the rest of the population. CHIP proposed that each person not on welfare who wanted to establish eligibility for lower-than-standard premiums or cost-sharing payments should file an application with the appropriate authorities. (Normally these applications would be taken by providers and forwarded to the public agency.) Subsequent declarations of income during the calendar year would be recorded by state or federal income tax authorities, and income tax forms would provide for year-end refund claims related to national health insurance premiums and cost-sharing payments.

Income-related cost-sharing rates for the entire population not on welfare could be established on the basis of the previous year's income as reported to the Internal Revenue Service (IRS). The IRS, or the NHI administration agency using IRS data, could inform individuals of their cost-sharing obligations for the coming year, based on their previous year's tax returns. To avoid hardship for families with fluctuating incomes, an exceptions process could be introduced. Choosing the criteria for exceptions would require a balance between two program objectives: avoiding excessive financial burdens for beneficiaries and maintaining an acceptable administrative workload. In considering a similar option, the Social Security Administration noted that defining "significant variance" between current and previous year's income—that is, variance that warrants a change in cost-sharing obligations—as a positive or negative 20 percent would minimize the frequency of exceptions.[12] The credit card could be used to minimize burdens on beneficiaries. Rather than denying credit to defaulters, the IRS could add unpaid cost-sharing payments to income tax obligations at each year's end.

Reliance on the income tax system has several advantages. First, this method of determining income requires far less time and fewer personnel than the interview method. Second, it builds on an established, unstigmatized mechanism for income determination, the Internal Revenue Service, rather than developing a new and perhaps duplicative system. Third, it simplifies administration for the carriers. Because they could accept the IRS determinations of patient income levels, they would not have to make detailed income investigations or eligibility queries. The complexity of employing different cost-sharing terms for each beneficiary, however, would remain.

Involving the Internal Revenue Service, however, would pose several policy choices.[13] First is the definition of income employed. If the national health insurance program were to determine cost-sharing obligations on the basis of taxable income, it would reinforce inequities created by loopholes and subsidies in the income tax system. To avoid this result, cost-sharing rates could be based on gross incomes, an alternative approach that is itself not free from problems.

Second is the issue of comparability of IRS and NHI filing units. The "family" unit on which maximum cost-sharing liabilities are based may not correspond to the unit filing an income tax return. If two persons who were married to each other filed separate returns, for example, the IRS would not identify them as a family unit. Combining returns to correspond to NHI categories might constitute an unwieldy task. It may therefore be necessary to make NHI cost-sharing terms correspond to IRS filing units.

A third problem with reliance on the IRS is the burden it might pose on the tax-collecting agency. Using the tax system to handle individuals in default would lower the direct costs of collecting cost sharing, as an upward adjustment of withholding taxes could be used to "collect" the amount in default. However, one must weigh the political and administrative consequences of employing the income tax mechanism in a nontax function against the potential savings in direct administrative costs. By involving itself in the collection of NHI cost sharing, the IRS might become a party to litigation in cases in which default is challenged by program beneficiaries.

Another risk to the IRS approach is the possibility that individuals might choose to underreport their income and defer their cost-sharing obligations, particularly if a credit card were used to provide easy credit. The Social Security Administration has noted that

secondary uses of tax data may create incentives detrimental to the integrity of the basic system. IRS personnel contend that the basic declaration of income could be strongly influenced by external incentives encouraging the underreporting of income. Although the accuracy of this contention cannot be evaluated, current estimates indicate that income is now underreported by 20 percent.[14]

It is not clear how realistic concerns of this kind are; they could simply reflect the reluctance of agency personnel to take on new and different tasks. In any case, they must be addressed if an NHI program is to use the IRS as a monitoring agency for cost sharing. Even if the IRS were able to collect all debts retroactively, the administrative burden and the credit demanded of the program could be so great as to raise questions about the fiscal integrity of a national health insurance program. In addition, such extensive use of credit might eliminate the deterrent effect of cost sharing. Such a risk must be considered in deciding the amount of credit the program should make available.

In sum, using the tax system to determine cost-sharing obligations appears feasible but poses political risks. If through insufficient monitoring the Internal Revenue Service should allow taxpayers to shirk their cost-sharing obligations under national health insurance, not only would the integrity of the NHI program be undermined, but also compliance with the entire income tax system could be jeopardized. Policy makers should weigh these contingencies in appraising income-related cost sharing.

Private supplementation of national health insurance

The principal argument against extensive use of cost sharing is that many individuals and families would buy supplementary insurance policies. Such policies would pay the deductibles and coinsurance, as well as extend coverage to services such as drugs or dental care that were not included in the national health insurance plan. Extensive supplementation of the first kind would work against the efficiency and cost-containing objectives of cost sharing. If persons who bought supplementary policies were to face little or no cost sharing at the time of service use, they would have little or no incentive to consider the cost of the service or of alternatives. Moreover, individuals who purchased supplementary policies could be expected to have higher incomes than those who did not. Thus, widespread supplementation would contribute to inequities in access; the wealthy would face lower prices at time of use than would the poor.

A basic principle of insurance is that one seeks to insure against events that are unlikely to occur but are very costly when they do. Supplementary insurance policies that cover deductibles, coinsurance, and, in some cases, uncovered services probably would not meet this criterion. In most cases, price would exceed the expected medical payments from the supplementary policies, sometimes by a wide margin. This apparent economic irrationality has led to the argument that significant supplementary insurance purchases would occur only if the current system of tax subsidies for private insurance were permitted to continue. This section argues, on the contrary, that supplementary insurance might thrive for other reasons, including pressure in the unions' collective bargaining process and the public's general aversion to risks.

To identify areas in which supplementation is likely, we first describe the current structure of the U.S. insurance industry. We then consider possible reasons for supplementation under national health insurance. Empirical evidence regarding the purchase of supplementary insurance under national health insurance in Canada and Medicare in the United States is presented.

U.S. private health insurance industry

The private health insurance industry in the United States includes many competing firms and broadly covers the population for hospital, surgical, and some physician services. Table 1 summarizes private health insurance coverage in 1976. Although gross enrollment has grown steadily for hospital, physician, and other types of care over the past decade, the percentage of expenditures met by

Table 1. *Estimates of number of persons covered by private health insurance and percentage of population covered, by age and specified type of care (December 31, 1976)*

Type of service	All ages		Under age 65		Ages 65 +	
	No. ('000s)	%	No. ('000s)	%	No. ('000s)	%
Hospital	164,235	76.8	149,643	78.5	14,592	62.8
Physician:						
Surgical	162,179	75.8	149,262	78.3	12,917	55.6
In-hospital visits	155,548	72.7	145,470	76.3	10,078	43.4
X-ray and laboratory exams	150,897	70.6	142,942	75.0	7,955	34.2
Office and home visits	124,124	58.0	118,522	62.2	5,602	24.1
Dental Care	46,578	21.8	45,808	24.0	770	3.3
Prescribed Drugs (out-of-hospital)	150,222	70.2	145,440	76.3	4,782	20.6
Private Duty Nursing	147,311	68.9	142,668	74.8	4,643	20.0
Visiting Nurse Service	145,863	68.2	140,841	73.9	5,022	21.6
Nursing Home Care	70,422	32.9	65,560	34.4	4,862	20.9

Note: Health Insurance Association of America estimates included in the *Social Security Bulletin* table are excluded here, but they are roughly similar to the SSB estimates.

Source: Marjorie Smith Carroll, "Private Health Insurance Plans in 1976: An Evaluation," *Social Security Bulletin* 41 (September 1978), Table 1, p. 4.

private health insurance has grown steadily only for physicians' services and for other types of care. In 1974, private health insurance met the following proportions of consumer expenditures, broken down by type of care: 77 percent for hospital care, 50.6 percent for physicians' services, and 7.4 percent for all other types of care.[15]

This pattern of coverage reflects both relatively little market penetration by private insurers beyond hospital and physician care, and little depth of coverage. Insurance companies generally offer policies for physician services performed outside a hospital with relatively high coinsurance and deductibles. Economically, such policies lower actuarial cost by shifting to the insured the liability for the low-risk and relatively discretionary component of medical care expenses. Unless NHI were to substantially alter the demand or cost conditions for covering these expenses, there would be little reason to expect supplementation in these areas.

It is useful to note the areas in existing coverage that offer the greatest potential for expansion. First, dental care coverage is probably the fastest-growing form of private health insurance, estimated net enrollment having increased approximately elevenfold between 1965 and 1974.[16] Perhaps more important, from the standpoint of our interest in tracing the mechanism by which supplementation probably would occur under national health insurance, of the 5 million to 8 million beneficiaries added in 1975 alone, the majority obtained dental insurance through new benefits added in collective bargaining. Despite the rapid growth of dental coverage in the past decade, Table 1 reveals that only 24 percent of the population who are not elderly currently have dental coverage. Thus this area offers considerable room for expansion, but that fact by itself does not imply that high growth rates will continue.

Although Table 1 indicates that out-of-hospital prescription drug coverage is widespread in the United States, private insurance actually meets only about 7 percent of all prescription drug expenses. The high net enrollment probably reflects the inclusion of these benefits within most major medical policies, but the low fraction of expenses covered reflects the use of deductibles and coinsurance, plus the limited coverage of the elderly.[17] Clearly there is considerable potential for more intensive coverage of existing enrollees, but the extent of such benefit expansion is hard to predict.

Finally, a significant gap exists in current policies for cash benefits for short-term disability not related to work. Insurance and sick leave provisions together cover little more than one-third of the potential income loss due to illness.[18] There is substantial scope for expansion in income replacement, to increase the number of beneficiaries (extensive) and the depth of protection (intensive). One might predict greater growth in the number of beneficiaries, because even with less than 100 percent protection, income replacement is subject to moral hazard—that is, having the insurance is likely to encourage the occurrence of the insured event.

Several factors that have contributed to the growth of insurance coverage would undoubtedly affect supplementation under national health insurance. Group policies now constitute a substantial share of all private insurance sold. Because of the potential role of group policies in supplementation, it is important to understand group policy structure. Group plans are less costly than individual policies because of (1) economies of scale in terms of administrative function such as marketing, underwriting, and processing claims; and (2) reduction of risk through minimization of adverse selection by individuals. Insurers have difficulty getting adequate information for estimating the expected losses of particular individuals. Not only is it costly for insurance companies to acquire the information, but insured people have an incentive to understate their own risk.

To compensate for this problem, the insurer asks a surcharge. This surcharge is mitigated in the group policy for three reasons: (1) Because of the law of large numbers, insurers can price a group policy with better foresight than they can price individual policies. (2) Because individuals presumably do not choose among employment opportunities solely on the basis of the health insurance contract offered, the risk of adverse selection is diversified in the group setting. (3) In the case of an employee group policy, the very fact of employment is a signal of reasonably low health risk.

Income also affects the purchase of health insurance. In families with an employed head, the enrollment rate for private health insurance is 41 percent among those with incomes below $3,000, as compared with 98 percent for those with incomes greater than $15,000. The data do not allow us to separate independent effects, but income and coverage are linked by the following factors: (1) the fact that demand for insurance increases with wealth as well as with income; (2) the availability of Medicaid to the poor as a substitute for private health insurance; and (3) the positive relationship between income level and tax subsidies for purchase of private health insurance.[19]

Tax subsidies generally favor income tax payers in relatively high brackets both because of the increasing marginal rates of income taxation and the larger volume of insurance purchased by higher-income families. (It is not clear to what extent the latter results from the marginal tax subsidy or causes it.) Mitchell and Vogel estimate that the tax subsidy for deductions from personal income tax for unreimbursed medical expenses rises gradually until adjusted gross incomes of $15,000, thereafter increasing more rapidly with income. Despite the fact that no one can deduct his or her medical expenses from taxable income until expenses exceed 3 percent of income, the effect of progressive income taxation is to render the tax subsidy regressive with respect to income. Table 2 illustrates the distribution of the tax subsidy for employer and employee contributions to health insurance premiums by income class. (The table excludes deductions for unreimbursed medical expenses, in order to highlight the subsidy only to purchase health insurance.) Karen Davis has estimated total subsidies for 1975 at $3.4 billion due

Table 2. *Tax subsidies for health insurance premiums, by income class*

Family income, 1969	Tax reduction per family due to employer contribution exclusion, 1969	Adjusted gross income, 1968	Tax reduction per taxpayer due to deductions for individual premium payments, 1968
Less than $1,000	$12.10	Less than $1,000	
$ 1,000—	19.58	$ 1,000—	
2,000—	21.13	2,000—	$ .61
3,000—	24.28	3,000—	1.17
4,000—	26.50	4,000—	1.88
5,000—	29.44	5,000—	2.44
6,000—	38.65	6,000—	3.72
7,000—	37.70	7,000—	3.80
8,000—	29.57	8,000—	5.07
10,000—	37.18	9,000—	6.28
15,000—	46.98	10,000—	9.51
25,000+—	58.81	15,000—	11.98
		20,000—	16.55
		25,000—	25.91
		50,000—	29.54

Source: The table is constructed from Tables 2 and 6 in Martin S. Feldstein and Elizabeth Allison, "Tax Subsidies of Private Health Insurance: Distribution, Revenue Loss and Effects," Health Care Policy Discussion Paper No. 2, Harvard Center for Community Health and Medical Care, Program on Health Care Policy, Boston, Massachusetts, October 1972, pp. 5 and 13.

to employer premium contributions and $2.7 billion due to personal income tax deductions (the latter includes deductions for individual premium payments and for unreimbursed medical expenses in the ratio of six to thirteen).[20]

Tax subsidies have encouraged insurance coverage. The total tax subsidy for employer and individual premium contributions to health insurance actually exceeds the administrative costs of health insurance (measured as total earned premiums minus benefits paid).[21] In other words, the cost of insurance to the consumer net of the subsidy is on average actually less than the expected benefits. Thus the purchase of medical care by insurance is cheaper than out-of-pocket purchase. This fact helps explain the purchase of coverage beyond what would be expected if insurance simply served to spread risks.

If such subsidies were to continue under national health insurance, one would expect "upper-end" coinsurance burdens to be privately insured. As for supplementation for first-dollar deductibles, net loading costs (e.g., administrative costs and profit, as a fraction of expected benefits) are appreciable even in the presence of tax subsidies. What private insurance supplementation does occur can be expected to cover a broader range of services in greater depth as the income level of the individual increases, because the tax subsidy is regressively distributed with respect to income. Supplementation also is likely to be concentrated in group insurance plans.

The current structure of the private health insurance market raises important questions about how and where supplementation would develop under national health insurance. Currently, private health insurance makes substantial use of deductibles and coinsurance, and offers only limited benefits for drugs, dental care, or income replacement. The most obvious explanation of this pattern is that the value of insuring such benefits does not exceed the costs, despite group insurance and tax subsidies. If this is true in the absence of national health insurance, why should we expect private insurance to cover these services once national health insurance exists?

In assessing the probable extent and character of private supplementation under national health insurance, at least four issues require review. First, to the extent that an NHI plan reduces patients' out-of-pocket expenditures, two effects would follow: (1) The use of medical care services would be less sensitive to costs of care; and (2) certain services would be in greater demand because of national health insurance's effects on relative medical care prices. Reducing patients' sensitivity to the price of care encourages increases in hospital charges, professional provider fees, and other prices. The consumer could gain by purchasing a supplementary policy against the financial risk created by this price change if the premium (net of expected medical payment) was less than the benefits derived from insurance.[22] Reduction of the out-of-pocket price for hospital and physician care increases the demand for services that normally accompany this care. It is plausible to predict that coverage of hospital and physician services will increase the demand for drugs and for replacement of the income losses due to illness. Consequently, the private demand for insuring such expenses might increase, suggesting a range of supplementation even if national health insurance were to cover part of these services.

Second, national health insurance would alter the distribution of income. The configuration of premiums, payroll taxes, corporate income taxes, and personal income taxes that now finance both private and public health insurance probably would be quite different from the financing of national health insurance. The incidence of the tax and premium burden also would probably be quite different; that is, some income groups would gain and others would lose. The demand for insurance of uncovered benefits would increase if the increase in demand by those who gained exceeded the reduction in demand by those who lost. (Clearly, if, on balance, incomes net of taxes and premiums declined, then demand for supplementary insurance could fall.)

Third, if national health insurance preempted the private health insurance market, the range of market opportunities to insurance entrepreneurs would narrow considerably. Firms would have an incentive to search out alternative productive activities once national health insurance was enacted. If they found better methods of calculating risks and administering claims, the new coverage would be marketable even if demand for that coverage did not increase. It is certainly reasonable to expect the search for new opportunities to be concentrated in areas closely related to previous insurance coverage—drugs, dental care, and income replacement.

The fourth rationale for supplemented insurance relies less on economic calculation than on the visibility of benefits from collective bargaining.[23] If a substantial range of fringe benefits were removed from the bargaining table, union representatives would be pressured to replace those benefits with an equivalent set. Thus, benefits that were less desirable before the advent of national health insurance might be included afterward.

Supplementation would occur only if at least one of these four factors assumed importance. All else being equal, the demand for supplementary policies would be greater with tax subsidies than without them. In the absence of tax subsidies, supplementation would occur if these factors proved great enough to compensate for the reduced demand for insurance following the elimination of tax subsidies. For example, the importance to union representatives of the "visibility" of fringe benefit packages must be great enough to compensate for the lessened economic attractiveness of including them. The same would be true for changes in risk aversion, income, and so on.

Evidence from Canada

This section examines insurance supplementation in Canada following enactment of national health insurance. This particular natural experiment on a national scale suggests the direction and magnitude of the private insurance sector's response under institutional arrangements roughly similar to those in the United States. Before further discussion, two characteristics of Canadian policy need to be mentioned. First, Canadian national health insurance offers very comprehensive benefit coverage; in addition, there are no deductibles or coinsurance on covered services. Thus supplemental insurance is not needed to cover cost-sharing liabilities. The supplemental insurance market is limited to drugs, dental care, private hospital rooms, and income replacement. Private insurance by law may not provide supplemental coverage of an NHI benefit.

Second is the Canadian treatment of health insurance premiums. In Canada, employee premium contributions to voluntary, nongovernment medical care plans are treated as a legitimate medical expense for tax purposes. Medical expenses, which are defined to include expenses for drugs, dental care, hospital/medical care, eyeglasses, and health insurance premiums, are deductible on either of the following bases: (1) One can take the standard $100 deduction for medical expenses and charitable contributions, or (2) one can deduct an amount equal to total unreimbursed (by private or public plan) medical expenses minus 3 percent

Table 3. *Key dates in the development of Canadian national health insurance*

Date	Event
1956	Federal government offered program of conditional grants toward half the cost of basic hospital services if majority of provinces with a majority of population agreed to implement universal, publicly administered programs.
1961	By this year, all provinces had established hospital care plans and had excluded private carriers except for insuring differential cost of private or semiprivate rooms.
1962	Saskatchewan implemented government-operated, compulsory medical care insurance.
1963	Alberta adopted an insurance company-operated medical care insurance plan (based on an intercompany risk pool), which offered basic medical insurance to all willing to buy it, with premiums for low-income persons to be paid either partially or totally by the government.
1968	Implementation of federal conditional grants was begun to share provincial costs of physicians' services.
1971	By this date, all provinces had established a universal medical care insurance plan.

of net income. Employer premium contributions are treated as a legitimate business expense, and thus are deducted from taxable corporate income. As in the United States, payments an employer makes to a group sickness or accident plan are not regarded as taxable to the employee. But when the plan begins to pay benefits, the employee pays tax on all benefit payments that exceed accumulated premiums that the employee has paid into the plan. If the employee paid no share of the premium (the employer having paid it all), the result would be the same as if the employer simply gave the employee taxable income to pay for medical care. In contrast, disability insurance premiums are treated differently, with neither premiums nor benefits taxable to the employee, so there is a tax incentive for these disability benefits.[24]

In sum, the Canadian tax treatment of the employee's premium contribution is virtually identical with the U.S. treatment of such contributions. But, in contrast to the United States, the employer premium contribution to voluntary health insurance plans in Canada receives only a small implicit tax subsidy. Thus, to the extent that we can observe private supplementation in Canada, given only a small tax subsidy to employer premium contributions, we predict (on the tax effect alone) that even greater private health insurance supplementation would occur under national health insurance in the United States than has occurred in Canada.

Table 3 documents key dates in the development of Canadian private and public coverage. These dates are significant for understanding the relationship between the private market and national health insurance. Canada's national health insurance program developed in two stages: the implementation of hospital coverage between 1956 and 1961 and enactment of the physicians' services component in 1968.

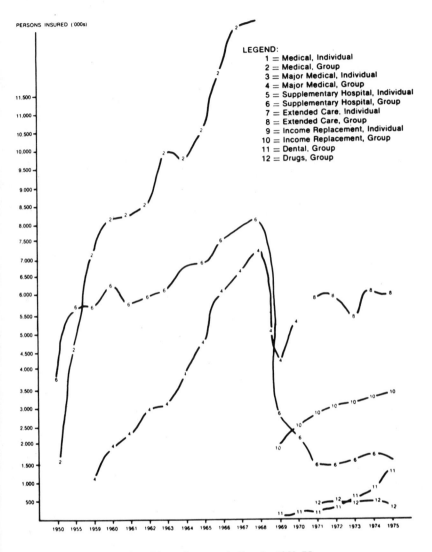

Figure 1. Number of insured persons in Canada, 1950–75.

Figures 1 and 2 show the relatively rapid growth in private health insurance, particularly group medical and major medical policies, in the period after NHI hospital coverage was enacted.[25] Interestingly, supplementary hospital coverage not only was maintained, but experienced gradual growth during this period.

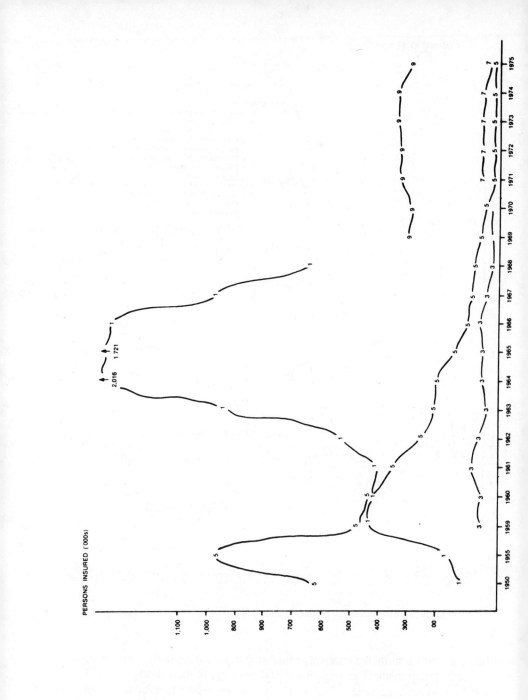

In the post-1968 period the pattern of private health insurance changed. With the addition of physicians' services benefits to the NHI package, the market for private insurance was reduced substantially. But, even though the NHI plan required no cost sharing, private insurance remained and some benefits grew. Supplementary hospital policies declined but were largely offset by the emergence of extended care plans in the private sector. Major medical and basic group medical policies diminished after 1968. Most of the growth in private health insurance during this time was concentrated in drugs, dental care, extended care, and income replacement. Roughly 6 million Canadians, 30 percent of the population, have purchased extended care policies. Subscribers to income replacement plans have increased from 2.0 million in 1969 to 3.3 million in 1975.

Explanatory notes to Figures 1 and 2

1. From 1962 on, information distinguishes between supplementary and comprehensive major medical contracts. Part of the swing to major medical coverage was accomplished by rewriting existing surgical and medical coverages into broader, more comprehensive contracts. Notice that our major medical categories total supplementary plus comprehensive coverage.

2. Until 1962, our medical category is for medical coverages only. It should be noted that the number of persons insured for medical expense is almost equal to the number covered for surgical expense, and either category provides a rough estimate (because of the large majority being covered simultaneously for surgical and medical expense) of the number of persons covered for both medical and surgical. After 1962 the medical column is defined to include all persons insured for surgical and medical simultaneously, plus those with surgical only and medical only.

3. As of 1964, Trans Canada Medical Care Plans first began reporting individual and group medical-surgical contracts separately, so there is a possible error in pre-1964 comparisons of group vs. individual coverage. However, the *total* of the two categories should be accurate for both periods.

4. Beginning in 1965, the medical category includes figures from the British Columbia Medical Plan and the Alberta Medical Plan, both of which are voluntary, but the Saskatchewan Medical Care Insurance Plan is excluded because it is compulsory.

5. As of 1967, the figures from the Ontario Medical Services Insurance Plan, which is voluntary, are included in the medical-surgical category of our table.

6. After 1968, when the federal Medical Care Act was enacted, the medical-surgical category of the Survey of Voluntary Health Insurance is discontinued, because the previous variety of voluntary medical care plans began to erode.

7. After 1968 only "supplementary" major medical is included for the major medical categories.

8. For 1970 extended care benefits are explicitly included in the major medical category.

9. The extended care category overlaps substantially with the class previously called "major medical."

Source: Canadian Association of Accident and Sickness Insurers (CAASI), "Survey of Voluntary Health Insurance in Canada 1960–75," Toronto, unpublished data.

Group dental and drug plans covered approximately 1.3 million and 300,000 persons, respectively, in 1975.[26]

Figure 3 provides information on the changes in private insurance premiums written in Canada before and after the two stages of NHI implementation. The total for all group insurance (line 1b) indicates that the volume of private premiums has grown dramatically both before and after national health insurance.[27]

Income replacement policies (the benefit that is subsidized by the tax system) now dominate the supplementary insurance market. Income replacement policies are believed to yield benefits clearly in excess of their costs, but it is hard to determine how extensive income replacement—and thus total supplementation insurance—policies would have become in the absence of the subsidy. Yet the tax subsidy for income replacement policies existed before national health insurance was enacted, and income replacement policies were not important then. This fact suggests that the tendency toward supplementation is independent of the tax system.

The desire to supplement can be explained by any or all of the hypotheses proposed earlier: change in relative prices, income, or supply factors; or replacement in the collective bargaining process. The latter hypothesis is particularly persuasive in light of evidence from Canada. When medical insurance was introduced there between 1968 and 1971, Canadian employers shifted funds to provide additional benefits rather than to reduce health and welfare fringe benefits.[28] Similar collective bargaining arrangements are in place in the United States, and the same incentives would encourage the provision of supplementary benefits in this country, particularly if the United States should retain its tax subsidies to private insurance. In addition, because the purchase of supplementary policies increases with income, the income distribution of the out-of-pocket burden of health care consumption will be partially reversed from that intended by the framers of income-related cost-sharing proposals.

Failure to examine the Canadian evidence on private supplementation could easily lead one to overemphasize the importance of tax incentives for private health insurance. Indeed, if the Canadian data teach us one thing, it is that factors *other than* the tax subsidy to employer premiums (the largest component of United States tax subsidies) are driving the general trends in supplementation. A competing explanation for the broad trends in supplementation should begin with the strong pressures on union leadership to maintain the size of health and welfare fringe benefits.

In anticipating the private purchase of policies covering deductibles and coinsurance in the United States, policy makers must remember that the outcome would still depend largely on the value of those policies relative to their costs. Policies designed to cover large deductibles and coinsurance might be more or less economically rational than the Canadian income replacement, dental care, or extended care policies. It is hard to tell a priori because many factors are in-

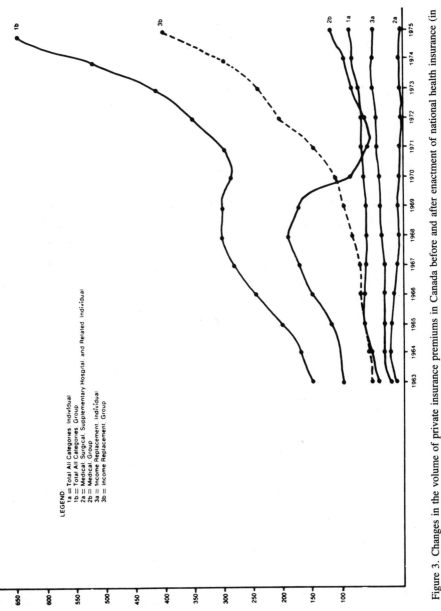

Figure 3. Changes in the volume of private insurance premiums in Canada before and after enactment of national health insurance (in millions of Canadian dollars).

Table 4. *Time spread of net enrollment as a percentage of total aged population*

Year	Hospital care percentage enrolled	Surgical care percentage enrolled
1962	54.1	46.2
1967	45.0	44.1
1970	51.4	46.7
1972	56.4	52.9
1974	57.9	54.0
1976	62.8	55.6

Sources: Data for 1962–74 are from Marjorie Smith Mueller and Paula A. Piro, "Private Health Insurance in 1974," *Social Security Bulletin* 39 (March 1976): Table 6, p. 8; for 1976, Marjorie Smith Carroll, "Private Health Insurance in 1976," *Social Security Bulletin* 41 (September 1978): Table 1, p. 4.

volved: the size of the deductible, the maximum liability, the tax subsidy, and so on. The Canadian evidence suggests, however, that analysts cannot ignore the role of negotiation over fringe benefits.

U.S. experience with private insurance

The experience of the elderly with private insurance to supplement the Medicare program provides further evidence on supplementation. In contrast to the Canadian NHI program, Medicare employs deductibles and coinsurance and leaves several services uncovered. In addition, most private insurance coverage is purchased by the elderly as individuals, or through senior citizens' groups that are not employment-related. Hence the economies of employee group purchase and generous tax subsidies are not present. The costs of supplementary insurance coverage, therefore, are very likely to exceed their expected benefits. Two questions must be asked if supplementation occurs: What motivates the purchase of supplementary insurance, and why is private insurance purchased in the presence of a public insurance program that was not purchased before its enactment? In drawing inferences from the Medicare program for other population groups, one must be cautious because of differences in health risk and income of the population groups.

Table 4 shows the time trend of net enrollment as a percentage of total aged population. Private health insurance is presented in separate columns for hospital and surgical care. During the first full year of Medicare, individuals cut back on private insurance coverage, but thereafter they steadily increased coverage for hospital and surgical care. Even so, the share of per capita personal health care expenditures of all types met by private health insurance remained virtually constant between 1967 and 1975, ranging only betweeen 5.9 percent (1967) and 5.2 percent (1972). In 1975, private health insurance paid 5.4 percent of the elderly's expenses.[29]

This relatively small and consistent percentage reflects the limited services covered by private insurance policies for the elderly. Beyond hospital and surgical services, coverage is quite limited. Because out-of-hospital services represent almost half of the elderly's health expenses, a major gap in insurance protection exists. In 1975, less than one-third of the elderly had coverage for physician home and office visits; about one-fourth had coverage for visiting nurse services; about one-fifth had coverage for nursing home care, out-of-hospital prescription drugs, and private duty nursing; and about 3 percent had coverage for dental care. Statistics on other services are not generally available. The limited available information on insurance policies currently offered suggests that insurers offer benefits for services not covered by Medicare (custodial care in nursing homes, drugs, home nursing, dental care, vision and hearing aids, etc.) far less frequently than they offer benefits for noncovered costs of covered services (hospital and physician care). Insurance for hospital care generally covers the Medicare deductible and coinsurance, but not the costs beyond what Medicare covers. Insurance for physicians' services (predominantly in-hospital) is more difficult to characterize. In 1967, about two-thirds of Blue Cross–Blue Shield individual policies reportedly paid Medicare's deductible, while somewhat more covered the 20 percent coinsurance. It is not clear how many policies then or now covered physician charges that exceeded the level Medicare deems reasonable.[30]

Previous assessments of supplementation may have underestimated the likelihood of first-dollar coverage. Keeler, Morrow, and Newhouse[31] estimate that only 11 percent of eligible Medicare beneficiaries have purchased private insurance against the Part B deductible for physician services. The authors argue that in the absence of special tax subsidies, private insurance supplementation of deductibles for out-of-hospital services would be negligible under national health insurance. We suggest caution in using Keeler's evidence to forecast first-dollar supplementation under national health insurance. First, the sample from which the 11 percent figure is constructed is limited to Part B enrollees who were not hospitalized in 1969. Although that group is numerically large (80 percent of enrollees), its financial risk for health losses is clearly less than the risk for enrollees who were hospitalized, since the latter presumably would use more ambulatory services as a by-product of hospital episodes. Keeler and his associates concede that 11 percent may be an underestimate, but additional data are required to determine the degree of understatement.

Keeler, Morrow, and Newhouse present direct evidence from the Current Medicare Survey for 1970 which is consistent with greater than 11 percent supplementation against the Part B deductible: 38 percent of Medicare Part B

Table 5. *Private health insurance, percentage of persons age 65 +, civilian noninstitutional population, enrolled by service type and by family income, 1974*

Family income	Private hospital insurance, percentage enrolled	Private surgical insurance, percentage enrolled
Less than $3,000	39.7	35.6
$3,000–$4,999	55.1	50.3
$5,000–$6,999	67.5	63.4
$7,000–$9,999	69.9	65.8
$10,000–$14,999	70.3	65.2
$15,000 +	68.3	65.4

Source: Unpublished estimates from Marjorie Smith Mueller.

beneficiaries meeting the $50 deductible used private insurance to pay all or part of the deductible or coinsurance amounts, while 14 percent of those not meeting the deductible did so.

The small size of the Part B deductible plays a crucial role in these writers' conclusions regarding first-dollar coverage. Even granting the rough accuracy of the 11 percent figure, a $50 deductible is quite small, particularly to a nonhospitalized population. If deductibles ranged from $150 to $450, the implications for national health insurance would be very different.

In sum, it appears that enactment of Medicare did not lead to new areas of insurance coverage. On the contrary, insurance coverage is concentrated on the cost sharing for covered services, often not including open-ended or catastrophic expenses. First-dollar coverage is expensive to administer because it consists of a large volume of small claims. When first-dollar coverage is offered in individual policies, for which marketing costs are high, a large percentage of the premium dollar goes to administrative costs rather than to benefits.

What, then, explains supplementary insurance purchases by the elderly? Turning to answers offered above, the popularity of such insurance can perhaps be explained in terms of a change in the absolute and relative success of health services to the elderly and higher disposable incomes. The expansion of employment-related group benefits extending into retirement also would have an effect.

The Current Medicare Survey and unpublished figures from the Health Interview Survey of the National Center for Health Statistics show that supplementary private insurance enrollment as a proportion of the eligible population over age sixty-five increases with income level. Table 5 illustrates this finding for private hospital and surgical care insurance by family income.

The positive relationship between percentage enrollment and family income reflects the close tie between income and demand for insurance, the tax subsidy for individual premium payments, and the positive relationship between labor force participation and, therefore, employer premium contribution and resulting family income. Supplementary demand is weakened by Medicaid buy-in arrangements for the purchase of private health insurance among eligible, low-income elderly. But even with Medicaid, almost 40 percent of elderly persons with incomes below $3,000 purchased supplementary policies.

Caution must be exercised in using the Medicare experience to predict probable supplementation of coinsurance and deductibles under national health insurance. The elderly may be more averse to risk than are younger people, and may have less information to make cost-effective choices in the complex supplementary market. Furthermore, as consumers supplementing Medicare, the elderly are in a position different from the position younger people would occupy under national health insurance. The availability of Medicare—financed through taxes paid by the working population—frees income for persons reaching age sixty-five who previously purchased private health insurance. Although these people could use this income in a variety of ways, its continued use for health insurance is not surprising. Under a national health insurance program, younger people might be paying (or having paid for them) as much for national health insurance, through taxes and premiums, as they now pay for private health insurance. Hence supplementation could be less likely. Finally, it is important to recognize that most elderly people have not purchased (or have not been able to purchase) supplementary health insurance for physician office visits, a service for which cost sharing may have its greatest deterrent effect. This fact suggests that such policies might not arise under national health insurance.

Even allowing for these considerations, the widespread purchase of insurance policies for which premiums exceed the expected return suggests substantial aversion to risk among the elderly population.

Conclusions

In sum, cost sharing, even in its most complex form, appears to be feasible, but difficult to administer and increasingly expensive when tied to the income of insurance beneficiaries. Private insurance supplementation would probably be significant under national health insurance, particularly in a plan that assumed large amounts of patient cost sharing. Should extensive private supplementation of national health insurance occur, however, it would vitiate the constraint on the use of service that patient cost sharing would be expected to have under a national health insurance program.

Reliance on cost sharing to control service use under national health insurance makes sense only under two conditions: (1) that cost sharing can be effectively administered and (2) that people do not buy private insurance to pay for whatever services national health insurance does not cover. In this chapter, we explored the administrative feasibility of income-related cost sharing, the most equitable cost-sharing arrangement. If this arrangement were to be operated in conjunction with the income tax system, we concluded that it would be workable. There is some risk in this approach, however. Poor administration of NHI cost sharing could undermine public confidence not only in national health insurance but in the entire income tax system. This risk should be considered carefully in assessing cost sharing's desirability.

Supplementation poses what may be more serious obstacles than administration to cost sharing's effectiveness. Neither Canadian national health insurance (which has no cost sharing for covered services) nor Medicare (which is limited to the elderly) is directly analogous to the NHI plans with major deductibles now under consideration in the United States. But experience in Canada and in this country under Medicare suggests that factors other than the cost-effectiveness of risk spreading or the incentives created by a tax subsidy drive the purchase of supplementary insurance. These factors include the effects of national health insurance on employees' and employers' disposable incomes, on the public's attitude toward insurance, on insurance market practices, and, perhaps most important in the American context, on collective bargaining. In our view, strong pressures on union leadership to maintain the size of health and welfare fringe benefits make supplementation particularly likely. The higher the cost sharing an NHI plan imposes, the greater the likelihood of supplementation. If policy makers fail to take the likelihood of private supplementation into account before adopting an NHI plan, their expectations for cost sharing as a cost containment device are unlikely to be realized.

Cost sharing nevertheless remains a potential source of NHI financing. Whether this is a sensible form of financing is a question quite separate from the effectiveness of cost sharing as an allocative device.

Notes

1 Joseph Newhouse, Charles E. Phelps, and William B. Schwartz, "Policy Options and the Impact of National Health Insurance," *New England Journal of Medicine*, (June 13, 1974): 1345–59.
2 Karen Davis, *National Health Insurance: Benefits, Costs and Consequences* (Washington, D.C.: The Brookings Institution, 1975).
3 Philip E. Enterline et al., "The Distribution of Medical Services Before and After 'Free' Medical Care—The Quebec Experience," *New England Journal of Medicine* 289 (May 31, 1973):1174–78.
4 These problems are discussed in detail in John Holahan, "Physician Reimbursement," in J. Feder, J. Holahan, and T. Marmor, eds., *National Health Insurance: Conflicting Goals and Choices* (Washington, D.C.: The Urban Institute, 1980), pp. 73–128.
5 Charlotte F. Muller and Jonah Otelsberg, "Interim Research Findings on Physician Reimbursement Under Medicare," Department of Health, Education, and Welfare (DHEW) Contract No. 600–76–0145, Center for Social Research, City University of New York, 1978.

6 For a detailed discussion of these issues, see "National Health Insurance Administrative Alternatives—Option Papers for the Secretary; Healthcard," Memorandum from the Commissioner of Social Security to the Assistant Secretary for Planning and Evaluation, DHEW, January 10, 1975.

7 Ibid., pp. 3–4.

8 Gordon Trapnell, *A Comparison of the Costs of Major National Health Insurance Proposals*, prepared for the Office of the Assistant Secretary for Planning and Evaluation, DHEW, September 1976.

9 "National Health Insurance Administrative Alternatives—Option Papers for the Secretary; Income Determinations," Memorandum from the Commissioner of Social Security to the Assistant Secretary for Planning and Evaluation, DHEW, January 10, 1975, p. 1.

10 This figure was derived from reference estimates in Comptroller General, *Report to the Congress: Potential Effects of National Health Insurance Proposals on Medicare Beneficiaries* (Washington, D.C.: U.S. Government Printing Office, February 24, 1977). We assumed salary costs per staff-year of $12,307, fringe benefit and other costs per income determination of $7.18, approximately 26.7 million independent income determinations per year, and 1/600 staff-years per income determination.

11 "National Health Insurance Administrative Alternatives—Option Papers for the Secretary; Income Determinations," p. 1.

12 Ibid., p. 3.

13 Ibid.

14 Ibid., p. 2.

15 Marjorie Smith Mueller and Paula A. Piro, "Private Health Insurance in 1974: A Review of Coverage, Enrollment, and Financial Experience," *Social Security Bulletin* 39 (March 1976):18.

16 Ibid., pp. 3–20.

17 See chapter 11, pp. 521–565, "Prescription Drugs," by Robert Kudrle and Karen Lennox in Feder, Holahan, and Marmor, *National Health Insurance*, note 4, supra.

18 Daniel N. Price, "Cash Benefits for Short-Term Sickness, 1948–1972," *Social Security Bulletin* 37 (January 1974):19–30.

19 Charles E. Phelps, "Statement Before the Subcommittee on Public Health and the Environment," in *National Health Insurance Implications*, Hearings before the Subcommittee on Public Health and Environment, House Committee on Interstate and Foreign Commerce, 93rd Congress, Sessions 1 and 2, 1974, pp. 357–61.

20 Davis, *National Health Insurance*.

21 Phelps, "Statement Before the Subcommittee on Public Health and the Environment."

22 In the case where the NHI carrier (whether underwriter or fiscal intermediary) and the supplementary insurer were the same, the company could derive economies by jointly processing NHI and supplementary claims for a given health care episode. The dampening effect of coordinated processing on administrative cost would enhance the marketability of supplementary policies.

23 William Vickrey, "Comment: Group Health Insurance as a Local Public Good" in Richard N. Rosett, ed., *The Role of Health Insurance in Health Services Sector* (New York: National Bureau of Economic Research, 1976), pp. 113–14.

24 W. Gassira, personal communication, February 14, 1977.

25 The extent of the private market is understated in these figures and in Figure 3 since the Canadian Association of Accident and Sickness Insurers 1960–75 data omit subscribers of Blue Cross and Blue Shield Plans.

26 CAASI, "Survey of Voluntary Health Insurance in Canada."

27 Inflation in consumer prices accounts for some of this growth and these figures have not been deflated. Nonetheless, substantial real growth in premiums and persons covered has occurred.

28 Lewin and Associates, Inc., *Government Health Care Systems, the Canadian Experience: Supplementary Health Insurance in Canada*, HRP–0009349 (Washington, D.C.: National Technical Information Service, 1976).

29 Robert H. Gibson, Marjorie Smith Mueller, and Charles R. Fisher, "Age Differences in Health Care Spending, Fiscal Year 1976," *Social Security Bulletin* 40 (August 1977): Table 5.

30 The preceding paragraph was based on Judith Feder and John Holahan, *Financing Health Care for the Elderly: Medicare, Medicaid, and Private Health Insurance* (Washington, D.C.: The Urban Institute, February 1979).

31 Emmett B. Keeler, Daniel T. Morrow, and Joseph P. Newhouse, *The Demand for Supplementary Health Insurance, or Do Deductibles Matter?*, R–1958–DHEW (Santa Monica: The Rand Corporation, July 1976).

Epilogue

12. Medical care and procompetitive reform

THEODORE R. MARMOR, RICHARD BOYER,
JULIE GREENBERG

I. Introduction: reform without regulation

During the 1970s the focus of debate about national health policy shifted from issues of access to medical care and the distribution of the cost of care to concern about controlling the total cost of care. The rapid rate of growth of expenditures on medical care during that decade far exceeded the rate of inflation in the general economy, with the result that an increasing proportion of the gross national product (GNP) is now expended on medical care. In 1970 the United States spent 7.6% of its GNP on health care;[1] by 1980 the proportion had increased to over 9.1%.[2]

The conclusion that the marginal cost of care is greater than the resulting marginal health benefits is more distressing to some observers than the rate of growth itself. As a consequence, politicians and policy analysts alike have scrutinized medical expenditures severely. This impulse to scrutinize is startling when one remembers the public and elite attitudes about medical care that prevailed from after World War II until the mid-1960s. During that period, medical care and its providers were held in almost unparalleled esteem. There was faith in medical progress and broad agreement about the value of social investment in medical care. Today, however, our faith in medicine has been rudely and probably irrevocably shaken by evidence that medicine's real influence on the quality of our lives probably reached its zenith with the decline of infectious disease mortality.

Critics of national health policy with diverse political and disciplinary persuasions have now reached a broad consensus that the methods used to distribute the individual costs of medical care unacceptably increase social costs.[3] In particular, present forms of financing offer perverse incentives to deliver a quality and a quantity of care that, in the absence of those incentives, would not be provided. Briefly, the present financing system is dominated by third-party payments, either from private insurers, who in 1978 paid approximately 27% of all personal health care expenditures, or from public entitlement programs, which pay approximately 39% of all expenditures.[4] Third-party payments reduce incentives for consumers and providers to economize in consumption. In addition, three provisions in the tax system subsidize, and therefore encourage, the purchase of health insurance and medical care. First, employer contributions to employee accident and health insurance plans are specifically excluded from gross employee income for federal income tax purposes. Second, an individual can deduct one-half of his or her out-of-pocket expenditures on private health insurance, up to $150, from personal income. Last, a taxpayer can deduct all out-of-pocket personal health and medical expenditures above 3% of adjusted gross income from personal income.[5] Tax subsidies make a contribution equal to 12% of the national total expenditures on health care. In total, more than one-half of all medical care expenditures are financed either directly through tax subsidies or indirectly through public entitlement programs.[6] Any major reform of the financing and delivery of American medical care must therefore address not only questions of entitlement to services, but also the problems of cost containment.

Proposals for reform vary widely, but each proceeds from this common starting point.[7] For those who seek change with minimal or no expansion of governmental authority, moral exhortation to reduce demand and more sensible economic incentives are appealing. Those who favor modest intervention would rely partly on moral exhortation and economic incentives, but would also impose sanctions such as health system planning or even budget caps. Those who promote more governmental intervention favor centralized budgeting and bargaining structures to negotiate medical fees and rates. At the far end of this continuum, those who advocate maximum intervention would advance a national health service in preference to any combination of public or private insurance and regulation. It is those at this left end of the political spectrum who are silent now.

The minimal intervention—or "procompetitive" approach—currently has considerable political and rhetorical appeal.[8] Rising government budgets, coupled with increasingly frequent charges of waste and inefficiency in government bureaucracies, have encouraged some to propose that social service delivery systems be structured to accommodate market incentives. In medical care, those procompetitive proponents predict that a "return" to the market will lead to cost containment, more equitable allocation of scarce medical resources, the creation of a more rational delivery system, and delivery of more appropriate and perhaps better medical care. Indeed, the appeal of procompetitive arguments is so broad that the President's Commission for a National Agenda for the Eighties argued confidently that "an expansion of the role of competition, consumer choice, and market incentives rather than government control is more likely to create the much needed stimulus toward greater efficiency, cost consciousness, and responsiveness to consumer preferences so visibly lacking in our present arrangements for providing medical care."[9] Similar claims have received widespread coverage in trade journals,[10] the popular press,[11] and on Capitol Hill.[12] Yet this vision of reform through competition is uncommon among industrialized nations.

The positions advanced under this banner, while labelled procompetitive, are, in fact, diverse and distinguishable. They vary in the degree of change proposed for American medicine, the rationale for such change, and their mechanisms, implementability, and effects. Nevertheless, while three separable threads of procompetitive logic run through these positions, all have interrelated elements.

The first approach would enhance consumer sovereignty. Advocates of this approach believe that the absence of significant consumer cost sharing in insurance is the major problem in medical care. Near-complete prepayment for medical care removes the necessity for both the consumer and the provider to make tradeoffs among different medical services and between medical care and other desired economic goods. It is asserted that even if the consumer is not fully at risk for the cost of medical care, the use of deductibles, coinsurance, and co-payment[13] will lead consumers to elect more economically appropriate forms of care. The second view contends that the medical system provides too few acceptable alternatives to "fee for service" (FFS) payment.[14] Medical competition exists within FFS medicine, not between FFS and other delivery and financing models, as would be preferable. Reforms under this second view would encourage the development of groups of physicians, primarily in prepaid group practices (PPGP),[15] as alternatives to FFS medicine. The proponents of the third and last view advocate aggressive antitrust rulemaking and litigation to reduce the market power of the present medical providers.

As was stated, these three broad approaches need not be fully independent. Antitrust action could be used to eliminate barriers to the development of competing groups of providers, a result compatible with the provider reorganization approach. The cost sharing approach may be required to allow existing FFS reimbursement to compete with prepaid group practice.

Procompetitive proposals share questionable analyses of the effects of current command and control regulation; they typically compare present circumstances of regulatory disarray with future circumstances of uncorrupted competition. They draw analogies between regulation in health care and regulation in other industries when projecting the impacts of their proposed changes. These analogies, however, ignore or downplay the differences between the market for medical care and the markets for other economic goods, as well as the many different forms of regulation that pervade the medical care sector. In fact, although procompetitive proposals all reject present and proposed command and control regulation, all require "market correcting" regulation[16] to improve the workings of the market so admired. The aim of this essay is to sort out the distinguishable reform alternatives grouped under the procompetitive rubric. The concern here is to demonstrate not only the important differences among these positions, but the differences in the arguments on which they rely for support.

II. Background

Economic market approaches to medical system reform are not intrinsically concerned with cost containment. Rather, they are intended to generate a more appropriate level of medical care utilization uninfluenced by perverse economic incentives. If competitive conditions[17] exist in a market environment, an equilibrium in price and consumption results. This equilibrium is in some sense an ideal allocation of goods and services, technically termed "Pareto optimal."[18]

Attainment of this perfect allocation in the medical care market is frustrated by the fact that the market fails to meet numerous conditions for ideal competition. For example, because of the coverage afforded by health insurance, the decision to consume medical care is not made with limited financial resources. Health insurance purchases are themselves not fully constrained by market mechanisms, since tax subsidies allow market "decisions" on insurance coverage to be made with pre-tax dollars. Moreover, employer-provided group health insurance prevents consumers from making individual market decisions about the desired level of health insurance coverage, because the consumer-employee accepts the insurance package offered as a perquisite of employment. Many of these conditions that result in market failure might be rectified through procompetitive reform.

Medical care market failures reflect, to some extent, the nature of medical care itself. Medical care *is* different. Improved health, the anticipated outcome of medical care, has positive externalities. This makes medical care a merit good, and, unlike many other economic goods, one that should not be allocated solely on the basis of ability to pay. Equity considerations must enter into any discussion of the allocation of medical care. Market allocation, while more "efficient" in allocating resources in response to "dollar votes," is not directed at equitable distribution. Even subsidies to the poor included in some market-oriented reform approaches may not fully mitigate inequity.

Informed choice by consumers is a precondition to the successful operation of the competitive market. Several characteristics of the medical market, however, work against easy access by consumers to information. First, one can never know when and if illness and recovery from illness will occur. Also, medical care is not a fixed, precise good; its outcome is uncertain, and the treatments associated with a particular set of symptoms or diagnoses can differ substantially.[19] Professor Arrow contends that an economic system cannot operate fully rationally under conditions of uncertainty.[20] One response to uncertainty in the medical care market and the risk it entails has been a demand for insurance. A second response is the creation of an agency relationship between consumers and physicians in which physicians are estimated to influence or control 70% of all demand decisions.[21]

Just as differences exist between the medical market and other economic markets, the regulation of the medical care industry differs from the regulation of other sectors of the economy. These differences do not lie in the regulatory tools themselves as much as in the number and diversity of regulations emerging from different governmental bodies and affecting the same health actor. Hospitals, for instance, must deal with a series of agencies concerning regulations tied to the subsidy and reimbursement programs on which their existence often depends.[22] Public regulatory bodies review capital expenditures (certificate of need), rates (state rate commissions), and utilization (Professional Standards Review Organizations or PSROs). In addition, medical care providers are subject to standards and licensure requirements imposed by both public and private bodies.

The role of government is further complicated by its monopsonistic purchase of medical care for some segments of the population and the regulation tied to this purchase. This mix of direct regulation and regulation through finance or subsidy is very different from that faced by other industries or economic sectors. Although aspects of health regulation may resemble regulation of public utilities or licensing of television stations, in its totality it has a complexity all its own. While any single comparison of regulatory activity in another economic sector may have some relevance, the sum of multiple and sometimes conflicting regulatory activities in the health care market is on the whole not analogous to that in any other industry.[23]

III. Procompetitive proposals: examining the differences

The three classes of procompetitive proposals listed earlier[24] differ in their assumptions about the medical care market, the medical product, health care goals, and appropriate policy mechanisms. Each of the three views is expressed in current legislative proposals, although the first appears to have passed its peak of popularity, and some proposals incorporate elements of more than one.[25]

A. Enhancing consumer sovereignty in medical care consumption decisions

It is widely acknowledged that "market failure" exists in medical care. Opinions differ, however, about whether the primary basis for market failure is inherent in the nature of medical care itself or is generated by present financing policies. Those who advocate consumer sovereignty adhere to the latter claim. They argue that medical markets fail because consumers never directly face the economic consequences of their consumption decisions. This market failure would be rectified by dramatically reshaping the role of insurance to make patients and doctors cognizant of costs at the time of use of medical care. One instrument to reshape insurance is extensive patient cost sharing through use of deductibles, copayment, or coinsurance.[26] Theoretically, making the consumer responsible for significant proportions of the cost of care at the time of use would generate economizing alertness in both patients and doctors, since presumably the need for alertness would be communicated from the patient to the doctor.

A second way to make consumers aware of the true cost of medical care is to reduce or eliminate the federal tax subsidy that now encourages the purchase of health insurance by employers.[27] Health insurance purchases would then be made with after-tax dollars, as are the purchases of other goods.[28]

Support for these forms of enhanced consumer sovereignty rests on two premises about incentives in medical care. First, the existence of massive prepayment for medical care through health insurance is, in this view, the prime cause of overuse. Because the purchase of insurance represents both a prepayment and a preallocation of consumer resources toward the purchase of medical care, consumers do not have to trade off the cost of medical care against the cost of other desired goods and services at the time of use.[29] From this perspective, first-dollar health insurance—insurance with a very low or nonexistent deductible—is not properly insurance. It does not really spread the risk of high cost, low probability illness, but prepays relatively common, highly discretionary services.[30] Second, tax subsidies lead to the provision of excessive levels of health insurance.[31] Eliminating the tax subsidy for the provision of health insurance by employers will lead consumers to purchase an "economically rational" level of coverage. This level of coverage, combined with cost sharing, will translate into more appropriate levels of demand for and utilization of medical care.[32]

The intellectual appeal of the cost sharing component of the consumer sovereignty approach depends partially on one's view of the elasticity of demand for medical services. The elasticity of demand clearly varies for different types of services. Low cost, high probability, discretionary services have the highest elasticity; their use varies considerably depending on costs to patients. The elasticity of demand for high cost care, however, is low, with physicians dominating consumption choices. Given these elasticities, one would expect that cost sharing would primarily affect demand for services of the first type. Nevertheless, low cost, discretionary services are not necessarily the type to be limited. High cost, high technology, high intensity services are partially, and perhaps primarily, responsible both for the rapid rise in medical sector expenditures and for the doubts about the worth of such expenditures. Cost sharing would not directly alter the major pressures toward consumption of this type of care since most episodes of high cost care exceed the limit of any feasible deductible.

The appeal of cost sharing can also vary with one's views on the need for equity in the distribution of care. Cost sharing amounts to a tax or user fee imposed on the sick and is a de facto transfer of wealth from the sick to the healthy. If cost sharing obligations are determined without regard to income, a fixed sum liability will have a greater impact on lower income than higher income groups: "[C]harges whose aggregate levels for a given family are direct functions of utilization only will involve perverse wealth transfers—from the ill to the healthy and, to the extent that the poor (including a significant share of the aged) are less healthy than the rich, from low- to high-income classes."[33] The income-related cost sharing plans do not create this vertical inequity, but they do retain the peculiar horizontal inequity of transferring wealth from the sick to the healthy within income classes.

The major impact of cost sharing may well be on the demand for preventive care. Demand for this type of care is the most highly responsive to price, because it is the most discretionary. The California Medicaid program's experiment with copayments demonstrated that "[t]he inhibiting effect applied to office visits—the bedrock of general medical care—and also to typical diagnostic tests (urinalyses), to preventive procedures (Pap smears), and to drug prescriptions."[34]

Admittedly, coinsurance may have some desirable cost constraining effect if consumers question the utility of increasing service intensity in the form of increased bed days and superfluous tests. In the absence of upper limits on consumer liability, however, this form of cost sharing imposes serious financial burdens on the catastrophically ill. Enthoven, a champion of restructured competition, contends that cost sharing not only fails to reduce overutilization, but its timing is inappropriate:

The individual episode of medical care is usually not good material for rational economic calculation. If the patient is in pain or urgent need of care, the transaction is not entirely voluntary. The sick or worried patient is in a poor position to make an economic analysis of treatment alternatives. When my injured child is lying bleeding on the operating table is hardly the time when I want to negotiate with the doctor over fees or the number of sutures that will be used.[35]

Consumers may prefer, and be prepared to pay for, first-dollar health insurance coverage precisely because they do not want to make decisions about economic tradeoffs while under care. When dealing with potentially life and death decisions, which almost invariably involve discomfort, consumers do not want to use economic criteria.[36] "[T]he evidence in Canada and in Medicare in this country is that consumers with their own money will supplement even weak deductibles; the evidence of labor group bargaining, individual health insurance policies, and the Federal Employees options is that people want comprehensive insurance, not strongly cost-shared insurance."[37]

One major effect of mandated consumer cost sharing would be that those who can afford supplementary insurance will choose to purchase it and circumvent cost sharing provisions. Supplementation leads to cost spreading among the affluent, which shifts the burden of payment to insurers and to the low income patients and potentially reduces equity in access. Those unable to afford supplementary insurance will be subject to the barriers of access imposed by cost sharing.

The powerful consumer preference for health insurance unconstrained by cost sharing also implies that reducing tax subsidies may have little effect on the aggregate level of health insurance coverage. While no doubt affected by tax incentives, the level of first-dollar coverage may not depend solely on that subsidy. Failure to consider properly the Canadian experience with private supplementation in the absence of tax incentives[38] could lead to an over-emphasis of the importance of tax incentives to choices on coverage. If the level of insurance remains unchanged after reducing tax subsidies, that reduction raises the rate of taxation on employment. If reducing the tax subsidy does lower the level of insurance purchased, employees' salaries should be increased to compensate for this loss. This too would represent an increased tax on employment.[39]

A final question regarding the consumer sovereignty approach relates to its structural effects—that is, how the various elements of the approach would affect competition between providers. The competitive market relies on consumer choice between providers on the basis of prices that reflect differences in the provision of services. While cost sharing consumers would be aware of the costs of their decisions and might be deterred from consumption, they would face no incentives to shop for a more efficient medical provider when the charges they pay are uniform for all providers. "The major weakness of the uniform-charge plans as cost control mechanisms is that uniformity allows no scope for price-sensitive consumers to affect provider market shares."[40]

B. Encouraging alternative organization of providers

The second class of reforms would provide incentives to restructure medical care, primarily by encouraging the development of competing groups of physicians. The class is best illustrated by three proposals: Enthoven's Consumer Choice Health Plan (CCHP),[41] McClure's broadened definition of health plans,[42] and Elwood's Health Maintenance Organizations (HMO) strategy.[43] These proposals acknowledge that it is socially necessary both to insure against uncertainty and to provide needed access to medical care without requiring patients to make economic decisions at the time care is needed. They propose that consumers be free to choose between annual packages of comprehensive health care, and to either retain the savings accrued if they choose a package offered at a price beneath the payment their employer or the government is willing to contribute for benefits, or pay the difference if they elect a more expensive option. This approach would put the existing FFS form of medical care payment in competition with alternative financing and delivery mechanisms—primarily prepaid group practices—on the basis of their ability to deliver adequate services for a competitive premium price.

Proponents of alternative forms of delivery have several slightly different conceptions of the optimal structure for these alternative organizations. Frech and Ginsburg argue that "HMOs are likely to change the nature of the market for medical care toward greater competition."[44] Moore advocates Primary Care Networks, as implemented by United Health Care of SAFECO Insurance.[45] Evans recommends Physician Based Group Insurance (PBGI) as a means of controlling costs; this system puts primary care physicians at financial risk for their patients by requiring that all costs of medical care ordered by the physician be paid out of funds prospectively allocated for such care.[46] The strategy as a whole, however, depends both on competition between similar systems on the basis of their ability to offer similar benefit packages at competitive prices, and on competition among altogether different health care packages. Enthoven claims that encouragement of competing provider groups establishes "...a framework within which providers can offer very different values, depending on the tastes of the patients served."[47] The premium charged by a provider group would thus be related to its ability to control costs, while the group still provides the services that consumers desire.

Proponents of this approach have suggested ways to remove the numerous obstacles to the development and successful operation of alternative delivery systems. These obstacles include the market power and domination of existing providers and provider groups; the cost or charge-based reimbursement under FFS, which provides no consumer incentive to search for lower cost forms of care; the employer-centered provision of a single type and level of health insurance, which prevents consumer choice of alternative health plans; and the difficulty of obtaining the capital financing and enrollees necessary to start alternative health plans.

Perhaps the primary barrier to the development of alternative delivery systems is the prevalence of employer provision of a single health insurance plan to all employees.[48] Like cost sharing enthusiasts, those advocating provider reorganization would weaken the employer link to health insurance by limiting or eliminating the tax subsidy of employer-provided health insurance benefits. Health insurance is typically offered as a perquisite of employment, and if the employee has any decision to make regarding health insurance coverage, it is to maximize the total salary and benefit package when choosing a job. Under existing arrangements, insurers compete with each other to offer the most comprehensive set of benefits to each employer while minimizing the cost of the total benefit package. Employers are assumed to act as relatively informed buyers in this purchase, attempting to maximize benefits at minimum cost.

Both the consumer sovereignty advocates and the proponents of provider competition identify the consumer as the best judge of what insurance to buy. Multiple choice proposals would both increase consumer participation in decision making and increase the opportunities for competitive alternatives to develop. If the employer continues to pay the full costs of employee choices, existing tax law encourages employees to maximize their income by electing the most comprehensive and expensive level of coverage regardless of their perceived need. Conversely, offering fixed-dollar employer subsidies to each employee would make the employee aware of and responsible for the fiscal effects of his choice of coverage. If the employee elects a level of coverage costing more than the fixed contribution, the difference must be paid out-of-pocket. Ideally, this out-of-pocket payment would not be deductible for tax purposes from total income, as it is under current law. If the employee elects a level of coverage costing less than the fixed contribution, the difference should be returned to the employee through rebates. This rebate should not be subjected to income tax if the employer-paid subsidy is not taxed. These steps eliminate any tax incentive to choose a higher level of insurance coverage than is perceived by the employee to be necessary. They would, however, produce fundamental irregularities in the income tax structure if cash income from rebates were excluded from gross income.

It is conceivable that the employer contribution could vary on the basis of such factors as the demographic characteristics, social class, or income of the employees in order to make the subsidy actuarially fair. It is important, however, that the subsidy not vary with the choice of the level of coverage and that the election of a more expensive form of care not be implicitly or explicitly rewarded. With that provision, then, proponents of this reform approach argue that fixed-dollar employer subsidies in conjunction with multiple choice of health plans and a limit on the tax subsidy available to health insurance would result in fundamental changes in the medical care financing and delivery system.

Multiple choice by employees is currently mandated in areas that have a federally qualified HMO. The "dual choice" option, however, is not aggressively marketed to employees, and many areas are still unserved by HMOs. Moreover, some established HMOs do not seek federal qualification. The existing dual choice option has therefore had little impact. Regulations require that federally qualified HMOs offer certain benefits. This requirement may reduce the effects of multiple choice where HMOs do exist and may inhibit the development of HMOs. As McClure has stated, "In order for consumers choosing efficient plans to be rewarded, multiple choice arrangements must allow competing plans some flexibility to establish benefits and premiums they believe consumers will find attractive. . . . *Effective market forces are impossible if all consumer benefits and premiums are fixed.*"[49] The major successful implementation of multiple choice currently in operation is the Federal Employees Health Benefits Program (FEHBP). FEHBP has, however, not been a particularly striking model of cost containment, although it does prove the administrative feasibility of employer-provided multiple health plan choice.

Multiple choice and alternative provider systems could result in a two-tiered system of medical care that divides the poor, who will of necessity choose low coverage, from the relatively affluent, who will choose higher levels of coverage. On the other hand, it may result in a two-tiered system that separates the relatively healthy from the relatively sick, as low cost medical care develops for low risk individuals and a high cost system develops for high risk populations—a dilemma that present forms of employer-provided group insurance do not create. The latter system could be prohibitively expensive for the high risk population, particularly if tax subsidies for the purchase of health insurance are eliminated.

Proponents of systemic reorganization rely on the experience of HMOs in areas of the country where they have a relatively large market share as an analogy for nationwide HMO success. The Minneapolis-St. Paul region is often cited to demonstrate the potential impact of alternative health plans on cost and utilization.[50] Moreover, a recently completed study demonstrated that the costs in a prepaid health plan in Seattle were lower than costs in a competing FFS plan. The study also found that the similarities between the two plans regarding access to care were more striking than the differences.[51] While studies have generally demonstrated lower hospitalization for PPGP enrollees than for those individuals covered by conventional insurance, it is unclear why this difference occurs and whether it has any effect on the local FFS market. Existing studies have not conclusively demonstrated that this lower utilization is not due to enrollee differences through self-selection, a process in which less healthy individuals elect more comprehensive coverage.[52] If self-selection and enrollment of a relatively healthy population is, in fact, the explanation for lowered hospital utilization in HMOs, then the total effect of HMOs on hospital utilization may be minimal, and the end result may be to encourage development of a high cost system of care for high risk populations and a lower cost system for low medical care utilizers.

In addition to doubts about the efficacy of programs for organizational restructuring, questions arise about the likelihood that the preconditions for successful reform on such a massive scale can be met. Proponents of competitive alternatives acknowledge that it will take time for this competition to develop. In fact, it is estimated that if current circumstances continue, only 10% of the population could be covered by HMOs by 1990,[53] up from the current 4% enrollment rate. The capital needed to support the fledgling HMOs has been difficult to raise, and attempting to attract enrollees who are accustomed to the established FFS system is expensive. The existence of these barriers does not imply that reform outcomes would be less preferable than the current system; they only suggest that it is highly questionable whether the final form of a medical care system incorporating organizational competition will closely resemble the vision of its advocates.

C. The antitrust approach

The application of antitrust law to the problems of the medical care system is the third approach to reform. Similarities underlie the assumptions about antitrust initiatives and the alternatives discussed earlier in this essay, including a generalized preference among procompetitive advocates for market allocation mechanisms in medical care. The policies prescribed to increase competitive behavior, however, differ. The reformers previously discussed assume that consumers, medical care providers, and financiers are reacting rationally to perverse economic incentives. Thus, restructuring financial systems and altering the reimbursement systems would allow competition to develop on the basis of price. The advocates of antitrust have a different conception of the problem. They contend that collusive behavior on the part of established medical providers prevents the emergence of competition in the market for medical care.

Antitrust law places singular emphasis on the benefits of competition. Havighurst has stated that "antitrust doctrine leaves very little room to ask whether competition is a good or bad thing. The law presumes that it is the most desirable way to organize and carry on any form of economic activity that Congress has not made exempt from the antitrust laws."[54] The antitrust preference for competition above any other goal implies that any cost containing effects of physician or medical system organization should be rejected if the effects are brought about through a lack of competition or by the domination of the market by a particular group. "Antitrust laws were created and have been enforced to prevent marketplace participants from colluding to disrupt an otherwise effective market. The aim of antitrust interventions is to maintain a competitive market, which is viewed as the ideal."[55]

While responsibility for antitrust enforcement rests with both the Department of Justice and the Federal Trade Commission (FTC), it is the FTC that is most actively involved in studying the medical market. The FTC is concerned with activity that potentially violates section one of the Sherman Act, which prohibits contracts, combinations, and conspiracies in restraint of trade, and with violations of the Clayton Act.[56] Under its enabling legislation, the FTC is authorized to conduct investigations of possible violations of both Acts.[57] "The primary enforcement tool is the 'Cease and Desist Order,' enforceable under threat of civil penalties, court injunctions and contempt citations. . . . The FTC also enacts trade regulations and industry guidelines, recommends Congressional legislation, and seeks to influence other government agencies."[58]

The FTC's ability to initiate antitrust action in the medical care field was enhanced recently by two Supreme Court rulings. In 1975 the Supreme Court in *Goldfarb v. Virginia State Bar*[59] determined that the "learned professions," including the medical profession, were not exempt from the antitrust laws.[60] In 1976 the Court ruled in *Hospital Building Co. v. Trustees of Rex Hospital*[61] "that hospitals were sufficiently involved in interstate commerce to warrant federal application of the antitrust laws."[62] The FTC is presently investigating the medical profession to determine if antitrust violations are present, and whether these violations, if present, have been responsible for medical cost inflation. Aspects of that investigation include the anticompetitive impact of the American Medical Association (AMA) ban on physician advertising;[63] the effect of provider influence on the accreditation of medical schools and the consequent control over the supply of physicians;[64] the inhibiting effect of established providers on the growth of physician groups and HMOs;[65] and the anticompetitive impact of physician domination of third-party reimbursement mechanisms.[66]

Fundamental conflicts exist between the traditional practice of medicine and the ideal of antitrust proponents. As Havighurst explains,

> The dominant premise of profession-sponsored reforms in the financing and delivery of medical care—that is, in the economic organization of care—has been that the public should look to the profession rather than to the individual competitive behavior for solutions to any problems that exist. Traditional antitrust doctrine, however, rejects the premise that industry-wide groups can serve as unbiased arbiters of price, quantity, quality, and other economic matters, and demands instead that decisions on such matters be made on a decentralized competitive basis, by producers whose ability to further their own interests is checked by the need to satisfy consumers. Moreover, this principle applies even when it is unclear that market forces can be immediately or totally effective.[67]

Antitrust will support the development of competitive alternatives that are not collusive and do not dominate the market. Antitrust standards, however, will likely be applied to the medical industry when physicians attempt to exercise their market power through boycotts of medical groups, restrictions on how physicians sell their services, prescription of payment methods, or domination of utilization review through insistence on peer review.[68]

Havighurst contends that existing financing mechanisms have developed in response to the demands of the profession. "The greatest obstacle to third-party cost containment," he asserts, "is the willingness, even eagerness, of doctors to act collectively to halt, dilute, co-opt, or capture any cost-containment measures that they find objectionable or threatening."[69] The power of organized medicine, in Havighurst's opinion, lies in "the implicit threat of boycott facing any plan which departs from accepted practice without professional approval....Removal of that threat should permit competition finally to stimulate insurers and others to develop more effective cost-containment measures."[70] These cost-containment alternatives, however, are themselves acceptable only if they are not collusive in nature. This is particularly applicable to provider domination of third-party payment plans. In recognition of the power that physician groups and medical societies can wield over markets, the FTC's Bureau of Competition in April 1979 "...recommended to the Commission that it propose a trade regulation rule to divest organized medicine of control over various health care financing plans."[71] This proposed rule would probably affect not only the Blue Shield physician payment plans but also emerging financial arrangements that either are controlled by physicians or include a large proportion of the physicians in a community. Antitrust law requires opposition to provider control of the market even when that control is alleged to have a beneficial impact on prices. Havighurst suggests that "the insight that the effect on competition, not prices, is the crucial issue will be particularly relevant in deciding whether to adopt a rule governing profession-sponsored IPAs [Individual Practice Associations]," one form of physician controlled organization that the rule would probably address.[72] He concludes that applying antitrust law to IPAs is reasonable. "The IPA," he contends, "is simply a way of reorganizing the monopoly's internal operations so that the profession can better protect itself against both government intrusion and competitive developments,"[73] regardless of the apparent effects on price.

The antitrust proposals have some immediate potential for implementation. Unlike other procompetitive reforms, they require no explicit legislative initiative. In fact, if evidence of antitrust violations is present, antitrust action is mandated. Moreover, since antitrust actions can be instituted at a state level, as well as by private citizens, competitive reform through antitrust need not await action by federal agencies.

In considering antitrust potential in the medical industry, however, it is useful to raise issues of the feasibility and desirability of antitrust action. Conceptually, an analysis of the Oregon State Medical Society actions in the 1930s and 1940s suggests that the antitrust laws may play a potentially effective role in increasing competition in the medical industry by reducing the market power of medical stakeholders.[74] Antitrust litigation may also be applicable, and possibly effective, in the case of provider domination of medical school accreditation and the AMA ban on physician advertising, if the adverse impact on competition of these provider activities can be demonstrated. Both of these examples involve national policies promulgated by the Liaison Committee on Medical Education and the AMA. It is possible, therefore, to concentrate antitrust action on identifiable national targets. Arguably, however, antitrust litigation is unlikely to have an appreciable impact on collusive behavior by physicians in individual communities. The absolute number of physicians, physician groups, and medical societies and organizations suggests that the national impact of a few antitrust lawsuits may be minimal. Alternatively, if antitrust litigation does have a pervasive impact on physician behavior in groups, the fear of an antitrust violation may have a paralyzing rebound effect, thereby inhibiting the development of alternative medical plans.

Similarly, proposed trade regulation rules to prevent provider control of payment plans are unlikely to be effective because of the decentralized nature of the medical care system, the many potential sources of violations, and the limited resources available to spend on enforcement activities. The competitive preference of antitrust proponents is premised in part on the failure of current regulations to alleviate the problems of the medical care industry. The conventional regulatory critique is partially based on the difficulty of constraining a decentralized industry characterized by a large number of diverse provider institutions. Yet antitrust rulemaking appears in that sense subject to the same critique as command and control regulation.

Additionally, efficiency questions aside, the agency's lack of resources and threats from Capitol Hill combine to dilute the likely impact of antitrust approaches to medical system reform. The ultimate impact of antitrust actions will depend on the resources available to the FTC, its ability to target those resources effectively, and the ability of providers to fight antitrust litigation or to ignore FTC trade regulation rules.

Even if capable of implementation, it is also questionable whether antitrust is the sensible response to the problems of the medical industry. While competition may be a desirable means to an end, it is not obviously an end in itself in the medical care industry. Medical care is not a good that should be allocated solely by the market. Even more than other procompetitive approaches, antitrust actions are committed to competition for its own sake, with less regard to its impact on costs and the atmosphere of medical practice. Rather than forcing the FTC to attack the medical care system in the name of idealized competition, the antitrust debate should perhaps return to the legislative arena, where Congress can decide whether the peculiarities of health economics require that some aspects of medical care be exempt from the antitrust laws.

IV. Conclusion

The health policy arena is politically unbalanced, with concentrated provider interests juxtaposed against the diffuse interests of consumers. This imbalance alone would imply little or no sustained interest in cost containment or structural reform. The increasing role of the government as financier and purchaser of medical care, however, has concentrated its interest in controlling costs in the medical sector. The health care industry is increasingly alert to the presence of that new player. Like the Voluntary Effort by the hospital industry,[75] procompetitive proposals are efforts to preempt government cost-containment strategies. All of the major reform approaches are politically volatile. The role of government in controlling medical costs and changing the patterns of financing and delivering care generates intense ideological struggle. This type of political dispute typically continues until legislative stalemate is broken by major political-electoral realignments.

National health insurance and hospital cost containment have indeed been stalemated health issues. The position of the Reagan Administration in early 1981, however, is clear. As President Reagan stated in his Inaugural Address, "In this present crisis, government is not the solution to our problem; government is the problem."[76] The preliminary Reagan economic program intends to phase out federal regulation of the medical industry: "If competitive forces are to restrain costs, free entry into health care markets is essential."[77] The new administration preference for free market, private sector initiatives, coupled with the new Republican majority in the Senate, could well break the national health policy deadlock. On the other hand, it could merely be the articulated rationale for reducing the regulations that constrain the profits of some parts of the health care sector, with real competition receiving only nominal support.

Procompetitive proposals represent one class of responses to the worrisome directions American medicine has taken in the past decade. Changes that would enhance the market structure in the long run, however, do not provide solutions to the immediate crisis. The encouragement of alternative delivery mechanisms would not solve immediate problems with geographic maldistribution of medical resources. The possible attainment of a long-run market equilibrium would not solve current cost problems. Even if "equilibrium" were possible, it would be slow to evolve[78] and, until it did, there might be significant underinvestment in health care by relatively uninformed consumers. One must wonder whether we as a society would be willing to tolerate the effects of consumer miscalculations in their consumption choices regarding levels of coverage under, for example, restructured delivery systems. *Caveat emptor* can hardly be casually applied to medical care.

Finally, procompetitive proposals are not themselves cost-containment strategies, although cost containment is frequently cited as the expected result of increased competition. In fact, should market allocation in health care dominate, total expenditures on health could be higher than the current levels, although public costs may be lowered. To the extent that they merely shift costs from the government health budget to the private sector, the fiscal gains are socially illusory.

It is not the purpose of this article to reject all features of procompetitive proposals. Competitive health plans, multiple health plan choice, provider and consumer cost consciousness, and antitrust activity all may have some place in a larger strategy to rationalize the medical care system. Each of the proposals has some advantages in terms of increasing consumer choice and altering the balance of power between existing actors. As an approach to universal medical care system reform, however, competition alone is inadequate. In fact, one could argue that the most technically feasible way to both rationalize the medical care system and reduce total societal expenditures on health would be to nationalize a public budget for health care and to pass the total costs of medical care through the political budgetary process.[79] Total societal costs might actually be reduced by increasing the program costs to government, as long as public authority is, as in Canada, adequately increased. The centralization of regulatory and allocative decisions could well result in a more suitably restrained form of American medicine. That, however, is a discussion about the alternatives to procompetitive proposals, rather than the problems of procompetitive proposals, and is therefore beyond the scope of this article.[80]

Notes

1 U.S. Department of Health, Education & Welfare, *Health United States: 1979*, at 184 (Public Health Service Pub. No. 80–1232 1980) (table 64).

2 Gibson, "National Health Expenditures, 1978," 1 *Health Care Financing Rev.* 1 (Summer 1979).

3 See P. Starr, "Transformation in Defeat: The Changing Objectives of National Health Insurance, 1915–1980," *Am. J. Pub. Health*, 72: 85 (1982). This article's ideas have fuller expression in a new book. P. Starr, *The Social Transformation of American Medicine* (1982).

4 Gibson, *supra* note 2, at 26 (table 5).

5 Section 106 of the Internal Revenue Code of 1954 provides that employer contributions to an employee's accident or health insurance plans for personal injury or sickness are not included in gross employee income. I.R.C. § 106. Mitchell and Phelps found, by comparison of the magnitude of this tax subsidy with the loading cost of insurance, that "the extent of the tax subsidy is greater than the cost of insurance," effectively giving negative net loading rates. Across all income classes, they found that, at the time of their study, this tax subsidy accounts for 16.7% of the cost of premiums. B. Mitchell & C. Phelps, *Employer Paid Group Health Insurance and the Costs of Mandated National Health Coverage* 17 (1974), cited in K. Davis, *National Health Insurance: Benefits, Costs and Consequences* 16 (1975). Obviously, as a perquisite that is not included in taxable income, the provision of health insurance by the employer is worth more to the employee than an equal contribution to income, which must be discounted by the employee's marginal rate of taxation. Therefore, employees are implicitly encouraged to accept more health insurance coverage, even at the expense of wages, because health insurance retains its full face value. This benefit is worth more to the high income employee than to the low income employee due to the graduated rate of taxation.

As noted in the text, in addition to insurance exclusions from gross income, one-half of private expenditures, up to $150, on personal health insurance is deductible from personal income, and all personal health expenditures, including any remaining health insurance costs, above 3% of adjusted gross income are deductible from personal income. I.R.C. § 213(a). Mitchell and Vogel demonstrate that these latter two provisions constitute a national program that provides partial financing of health expenditures for all taxpaying Americans. This Internal Revenue Service health plan includes an unusually broad definition of what constitutes a medical expense, see I.R.C. § 213(e), and "has a deductible proportional to income and a coinsurance rate that decreases with income." Mitchell & Vogel, "Health and Taxes: An Assessment of the Medical Deduction," 41 *S. Econ. J.* 660, 665 (1975). Despite the income-related deductible of this program, the total effect is a regressive financing mechanism, with substantially larger benefits for high income taxpayers. See chapter 11 of this volume.

6 See generally *Tax Expenditures for Health Care: Hearings Before the Task Force on Tax Expenditures and Tax Policy of the House Comm. on the Budget and Subcomm. on Oversight of the House Comm. on Ways and Means*, 96th Cong., 1st Sess. 16 (1979) (statement of Emil M. Sunley).

7 See P. Starr, *supra* note 3, at 86.

8 See C. Schultze, *The Public Use of Private Interest* 2–4 (1977).

9 *Report of the President's Commission for a National Agenda for the Eighties* 78–79 (1980).

10 See, e.g., Christianson & McClure, "Competition in the Delivery of Medical Care," 301 *New Eng. J. Med.* 812 (1979) (constructive competition helped reduce hospitalization, contain costs, improve access to medical services, focus consumer attention on consumer satisfaction, increase consumer choices and information); A. Enthoven, "Rx for Health Care Economics: Competition, Not Rigid NHI," 59 *Hospital Progress* 44

(Oct. 1978) (although health services market not structured to fit competitive model, restructuring possible to yield more competitive benefits).

11 Huff, "A Little Healthy Competition," *Washington Post*, Aug. 26, 1980 § A, at 19, col. 4.

12 See Demkovich, "Competition Coming On," 12 *Nat'l J.* 1152 (1980); Demkovich, "New Congressional Health Leaders—The Emphasis Is on Competition," 12 *Nat'l J.* 1093 (1980).

13 Patient cost sharing devices are proposed as ways to make the consumer more conscious of the costs of medical care demand decisions, without putting the consumer at risk for the full cost of medical care. Deductibles require that consumers pay full costs of all medical care up to some dollar limit, beyond which the public or private insurer pays in full. Copayment is a consumer utilization fee, charged at such time that medical care is utilized for each service subject to copayment provisions. Coinsurance requires the consumer to pay some portion of the total costs incurred. For an excellent discussion of the effects of cost sharing, see M. Barer, R. Evans & G. Stoddart, *Controlling Health Care Costs by Direct Charges to Patients: Snare or Delusion?* (1979) [hereinafter cited as *Controlling Health Costs*]. For a discussion of the administrative feasibility of cost sharing proposals under national health insurance, see Conrad & Marmor, chapter 11 of this volume.

14 Under "fee for service" (FFS) payment, providers are paid on the basis of identifiable, billable procedures performed. This reimbursement may be on the basis of the costs incurred by hospitals, or the charges made by physicians. Most medical care is currently paid for on a FFS basis. This payment method implies that providers can increase their total revenues by increasing the number of procedures performed, knowing that they will be reimbursed for their costs or charges by the patient or the patient's insurer. Because the provider does not often suffer losses from ordering superfluous services, implicit incentives exist under FFS to provide medical services without regard to the costs incurred.

15 Prepaid Group Practice (PPGP) is an alternative payment mechanism intended to address the lack of provider cost awareness under FFS reimbursement. As under insurance, the enrollee pays a fixed capitation rate, and is entitled to medical benefits as needed. Unlike insurance, the enrollee is contracting with an organization that not only finances medical care, but that also accepts responsibility for the delivery of care. The PPGP employs or contracts with providers who provide medical care to the defined, prepaid enrolled population. PPGP revenues are not open-ended. They are a function of the total number of enrollees, not of the number of procedures performed. PPGP is an umbrella term, and encompasses a number of alternative financing and delivery mechanisms, including the Health Maintenance Organization (HMO), Individual Practice Association (IPA), and Foundation for Medical Care (FMC).

16 See A. Enthoven, *Health Plan: The Only Practical Solution to the Soaring Costs of Medical Care* 94 (1980).

17 These competitive conditions include: free exit and entry into the market by providers; costless transactions; perfect information on the part of consumers; voluntary purchases by the consumer; limitations on consumer resources requiring that each purchase be traded off against another; inability of producers to exercise market power over consumers or over other providers; absence of collusive behavior by producers; payment of full costs of production of goods or services by producers; and the absence of externalities associated with the provision of the good or service.

18 P. Samuelson, *Economics* 462 n.12 (10th ed. 1976).

19 A. Enthoven, *supra* note 16, at 1–12.

20 See K.J. Arrow, "Uncertainty and the Welfare Economics of Medical Care," 53 *Am. Econ. Rev.* 941 (1963).
21 Although only an estimated 18 cents of every health care dollar pays for actual physician-provided services, doctors influence the expenditure of a much greater portion of that dollar because of their ability to "determine who goes to the hospital, how long they stay, and what will be done for them while they are there." Relman, "The Allocation of Medical Resources by Physicians," 55 *J. Med. Educ.* 99, 99 (1980).
22 See Marmor, "Regulatory Choice in Health," in *Issues in Health Care Regulation* 310–317 (R. Gordon ed. 1980).
23 See *id.* at 13.
24 See text accompanying notes 13–15 *supra*.
25 One or more of these broad procompetitive approaches has influenced several recent legislative initiatives. During the 96th Congress, particularly the first session in the summer and fall of 1979, when the Carter Administration's Hospital Cost Containment Act of 1979, S. 570, 96th Cong., 1st Sess., 125 *Cong. Rec.* S2187 (daily ed. Mar. 7, 1979), began to flounder, a number of legislative alternatives to regulatory medical care cost containment arose. Senator Durenberger introduced The Health Incentives Reform Act of 1979, S. 1968, 96th Cong., 1st Sess., 125 *Cong. Rec.* S15699 (daily ed. Nov. 1, 1979), which provided for a specified fixed dollar amount of deductible employer contributions to health insurance plans with contributions in excess of that amount to be included in employee gross income and, therefore, taxable. The bill mandated a choice of multiple health plans for employees, who then would receive rebates for choosing plans less expensive than the employer contribution. See Staff of the Joint Comm. on Taxation, 96th Cong., 2d Sess., *Descriptions of Proposals to Restructure the Incentives for Coverage under Employer Health Plans* 16–17 (Comm. Print 1980).

The Health Cost Restraint Act of 1979 was introduced by former House Ways and Means Committee Chairman Al Ullman. H.R. 5740, 96th Cong., 1st Sess., 125 *Cong. Rec.* H9970 (daily ed. Oct. 30, 1979). It embodied the same provisions as the Durenberger bill and, also, contained provisions concerning HMO reimbursement under the Medicare program that were designed to encourage Medicare recipients to choose enrollment in prepaid group plans rather than FFS. See Staff of the Joint Comm. on Taxation, 96th Cong., 2d Sess., *Description of S. 1968 and Other Proposals to Restructure the Incentives for Coverage under Employer Health Plans* 12–13 (Comm. Print 1980).

Representative Martin introduced the Medical Expense Protection Act of 1980, H.R. 6405, 96th Cong., 2d Sess., 126 *Cong. Rec.* H532 (daily ed. Feb. 4, 1980), which would have created a "Catastrophic Automatic Protection Plan," funded by general revenues and coinsurance. H.R. 6405, 96th Cong., 2d Sess., reprinted in *National Health Insurance: Hearings Before the Subcomm. on Health of the House Comm. on Ways and Means*, 96th Cong., 2d Sess. 230 (1980). The Plan mandated for families with incomes of less than $10,000 a deductible of $300, plus 20% of the income in excess of $4000, and a deductible of $1500, plus 20% of income in excess of $10,000, for families with incomes of more than $10,000. In addition, the Plan disallowed employers the tax deduction available for qualified health insurance plans unless they offer this coverage to employees. See *id.* See also *National Health Insurance: Hearings Before the Subcomm. on Health of the House Comm. on Ways and Means*, 96th Cong., 2d Sess. 164 (1980) (statement by Representative Martin).

Representative Jones introduced a bill, H.R. 3943, 96th Cong., 1st Sess., 125 *Cong. Rec.* H2722 (daily ed. May 4, 1979), which would have amended the Internal Revenue Code to disallow an employer's business deductions for costs of premiums of specified employee insurance contracts and mandated catastrophic coverage for health care expenses over $2000 or 15% of the employee's average adjusted gross income. See *National Health Insurance: Hearings Before the Subcomm. on Health of the House Comm. on Ways and Means*, 96th Cong., 2d Sess. 27 (1980) (statement of the American Hospital Association).

The Comprehensive Health Care Reform Act was introduced by Senator Schweiker. S. 1590, 96th Cong., 1st Sess., 125 Cong. Rec. S10656 (daily ed. July 26, 1979). It would have amended the Public Health Service Act of 1977, Pub. L. No. 95-83, §§ 102–104, 105(b), 106, 107, 91 Stat. 383–86 (codified in scattered sections of 42 U.S.C.), and established standards for qualified employer health benefit plans, including catastrophic coverage, and conditions under which employer contributions to employee health insurance could be deducted by employers and excluded from gross income by employees. The bill also mandated a multiple health plan choice for employees and a fixed dollar contribution by the employer, with rebates available to employees choosing less expensive plans. See Staff of the Joint Comm. on Taxation, 96th Cong., 2d Sess., *Description of S. 1968 and Other Proposals to Restructure the Incentives for Coverage under Employer Health Plans* 10 (Comm. Print 1980).

Representatives Gephardt and Stockman introduced The National Health Care Reform Act of 1980, H.R. 7527, 96th Cong., 2d Sess., 126 *Cong. Rec.* H4683 (daily ed. June 9, 1980), which would have limited the tax subsidies for employer contributions to health insurance plans; provided tax free rebates to employees selecting health plans costing less than the fixed dollar contribution; provided tax credits for the private purchase of health insurance not through the employer; mandated a catastrophic level of coverage; replaced retroactive, reasonable cost reimbursement with prospective premium payment; repealed existing regulatory structures such as Certificate of Need and Professional Standards Review Organization; mandated health plan choice under Medicare; and provided vouchers under Medicaid.

26 See Feldstein, "The High Cost of Hospitals—and What to Do About It," 48 *Pub. Interest* 40 (1977); Feldstein, "A New Approach to National Health Insurance," 23 *Pub. Interest* 93 (1971); Seidman, "Income-Related Consumer Cost Sharing: A Strategy for the Health Sector," in *National Health Insurance: What Now, What Later, What Never?* 307 (M. Pauly ed. 1980).

27 See note 5 *supra*.

28 A tax expenditure is a provision in the tax code that is intended to "achieve a particular purpose, claimed to be desirable, other than the measurement of net income under an income tax." Surrey, "Tax Incentives as a Device for Implementing Government Policy: A Comparison with Direct Government Expenditures," 83 *Harv. L. Rev.* 705, 707 (1970). Proponents assert that tax incentives encourage the private sector to participate in social programs and that tax incentives are simple and involve less government intervention. See, e.g., 115 *Cong. Rec.* S5329–30 (1969) (statement of Senator Percy), quoted in Surrey, *supra*, at 716. Surrey, on the other hand, argues that any tax expenditure could be replaced by a direct expenditure. A tax incentive will have some legislative appeal partially because of the asserted advantages of tax expenditures and partially because of the structure of the legislative process—the House Ways and Means Committee and the Senate Finance Committee consider all tax proposals. When tax proposals, however, concern indirect program outlays, as opposed to revenue gathering, consideration by these committees of these proposals

defeats the committee system of distributing congressional expertise and affects the administration of the program. See Surrey, *supra*, at 728–29. Professor Surrey, in his criticism of tax expenditures, further notes that their costs are uncontrollable, unpredictable, and largely hidden in foregone revenues rather than in budgeted outlays. See *id*. at 729–31. Moreover, tax incentives, in general, are intrinsically inequitable in a positive, progressive income tax system. See *id*. at 720–25. For a complete discussion of tax expenditures, see S. Surrey, *Pathways to Tax Reform* (1973).

29 See Feldstein & Taylor, "The Rapid Rise of Hospital Costs," in *Council on Wage & Price Stability Staff Report*, Jan. 1977, at 66–67 (well insured consumers choose more expensive medical care than those "not so well insured").

30 Insurance should protect against large losses that are very unlikely to occur—that is, an expensive event that will occur in only a few cases. In such a case, the extent of the risk is so great that very few individuals could afford to suffer the risk, but the likelihood of the event occurring is so small that the pooled risk is minute—and consequently inexpensive—through a risk-sharing mechanism. According to Arrow, "if the costs of medical care are a random variable with mean m, the [ideal insurer] will charge a premium m, and agree to indemnify. . .for all medical costs." Arrow, *supra* note 20, at 960 (emphasis in original). Thus, actuarially, a fair insurance premium will simply be the projected total cost of health care to the population at risk, divided by the number of people in that population. See *id*. at 959–60. Because of administrative costs, or "loading costs," incurred in the provision of insurance, however, the cost to the individual will be higher than the expected benefits from insurance. In spite of this, risk aversion in the face of potentially severe or catastrophic costs causes individuals to insure. The institutionalization of risk-bearing through insurance serves to relieve much of the economic uncertainty associated with accident and disease. Health insurance, however, does not fit the ideal model of insurance. So-called "moral hazard" is present when the consumption of an insured good is altered by the possession of insurance. The implication is that there is a relatively high elasticity of demand or considerable consumer discretion regarding demand decisions. It is this tendency to over-utilize medical services because of prepayment through insurance that concerns cost sharing proponents.

31 A. Enthoven, *supra* note 16, at 19.

32 See generally M. Feldstein & E. Allison, *Tax Subsidies of Private Health Insurance: Distribution, Revenue Loss and Effects* 16 (Oct. 1972) (Health Care Policy Discussion Paper No. 2, Harvard Center for Community Health and Medical Care, Program on Health Care Policy).

33 *Controlling Health Costs*, *supra* note 13, at 111.

34 Roemer, Hopkins, Carr & Gartside, "Copayments for Ambulatory Care: Penny-Wise and Pound-Foolish," 13 *Med. Care* 457, 464 (1975).

35 A. Enthoven, *supra* note 16, at 34–35.

36 See B. Vladeck, *The Market vs. Regulation: The Case of Regulation* 4 (May 22, 1980 as revised June 13, 1980) (paper presented at the *Symposium on Health Care Regulation and Competition: Are They Compatible?* Project HOPE Institute for Health Policy Study). Ironically, if consumers *do* make coverage decisions on an economic basis, based on their assessment of the likelihood of needing care, adverse self-selection consequences may result.

37 McClure, "An Analysis of Health Care System Performance Under a Proposed NHI Administrative Mechanism," in *Effects of the Payment Mechanism on the Health Care Delivery System* 12 (1977) (U.S. Dept. of Health, Education, and Welfare, Public Health Service).

38 See Conrad & Marmor, chapter 11 of this volume, pp. 223–230.
39 See W. Lynk, "Regulation and Competition: An Examination of the 'Consumer Choice Health Plan'," *J. Health Pol., Pol'y & L.* 6: 625–636 (1982).
40 *Controlling Health Costs, supra* note 13, at 115.
41 A. Enthoven, *supra* note 16. See also Enthoven, "Consumer-Choice Health Plan" (pts. 1–2), 298 *New Eng. J. Med.* 650, 709 (1978); Enthoven, "Cutting Cost Without Cutting the Quality of Care," 298 *New Eng. J. Med.* 1229 (1978).
42 McClure, "On Broadening the Definition of and Removing the Regulatory Barriers to a Competitive Health Care System." 3 *J. Health Pol., Pol'y & L.* 303 (1978).
43 Elwood, Anderson, Billings, Carlson, Houghberg & McClure, "Health Maintenance Strategy," 9 *Med. Care* 291 (1971).
44 H. Frech & P. Ginsburg, *Public Insurance in Private Medical Markets: Some Problems of National Health Insurance* 58 (1978).
45 Moore, "Cost Containment Through Risk-Sharing by Primary-Care Physicians," 300 *New Eng. J. Med.* 1359 (1979). See also Moore, Martin, Richardson & Riedel, "Cost Containment Through Risk-Sharing by Primary Care Physicians: A History of the Development of United Health Care," 1 *Health Care Financing Rev.* 1 (Spring 1980).
46 Evans, "Physician-Based Group Insurance: A Proposal for Medical Cost Control," 302 *New Eng. J. Med.* 1280 (1980).
47 A. Enthoven, *supra* note 16, at 67.
48 A. Enthoven, "Consumer-centered vs. Job-centered Health Insurance," 57 *Harv. Bus. Rev.* 141 (1979).
49 McClure, *supra* note 42, at 307.
50 See Christianson & McClure, *supra* note 10, at 812–18.
51 "Comparisons of Prepaid Health Care Plans in a Competitive Market: The Seattle Prepaid Health Care Project—Research Summary", cited in *National Center for Health Services Research*, NCHSR Research Activities (Jan. 1981).
52 Luft, Feder, Holahan & Lennox, "Health Maintenance Organizations," in *National Health Insurance: Conflicting Goals and Policy Choices*, at 129, 130 (Feder, Holahan & Marmor eds., 1980).
53 Office of Health Maintenance Organizations, United States Public Health Service, "Projections for HMO Development, 1980–1990" (1980), cited in A. Miller & M. Miller, *Options for Health and Health Care: The Coming of Post-Clinical Medicine* (forthcoming 1981).
54 Havighurst, "The Antitrust Laws, the Federal Trade Commission, and Cost Containment," 56 *Bull. N.Y. Acad. Med.* 170 (1980).
55 Drake & Kozak, "A Primer on Antitrust and Hospital Regulation," 3 *J. Health Pol., Pol'y & L.* 328, 330 (1978).
56 Sherman Antitrust Act, ch. 647, § 1, 26 Stat. 209 (1890) (codified at 15 U.S.C. § 1 (1976)); Clayton Act, ch. 323, § 1, 38 Stat. 730 (1914) (codified at 15 U.S.C. § 12 (1976)).
57 Federal Trade Commission Act, ch. 311, § 5, 38 Stat. 717 (1914) (current version at 15 U.S.C. § 45(a)(2) (Supp. III 1979)).
58 Avellone & Moore, "The Federal Trade Commission Enters a New Arena: Health Services," 299 *New Eng. J. Med.* 478 (1978).
59 421 U.S. 773 (1975).
60 See Avellone & Moore, *supra* note 58, at 478.
61 425 U.S. 738 (1976).
62 Drake & Kozak, *supra* note 55, at 340; see 425 U.S. at 744–47.
63 Avellone & Moore, *supra* note 58, at 479.

64 *Id.* at 480.
65 *Id.* at 481.
66 *Id.* at 482.
67 Havighurst, "Antitrust Enforcement in the Medical Service Industry: What Does It All Mean?," 58 *Milbank Memorial Fund Q.* 89, 96–97 (1980).
68 Havighurst & Hackbarth, "Enforcing the Rules of Free Enterprise in an Imperfect Market: The Case of Individual Practice Associations" 18–19 (Sept. 25–26, 1980) (paper presented at *A Conference on Health Care—Professional Ethics, Government Regulation, or Markets?*, American Enterprise Institute). See also Leibenluft & Pollard, "Antitrust Scrutiny of the Health Professions: Developing a Framework for Assessing Private Restraints," 34 *Vand. L. Rev.* 927 (1981).
69 Havighurst, "The Role of Competition in Cost Containment," in *Competition in the Health Care Sector: Past, Present, and Future* 299 (W. Greenberg ed. 1978).
70 *Id.* at 313.
71 Havighurst & Hackbarth, *supra* note 68, at 6.
72 *Id.* at 15.
73 *Id.* at 26.
74 Goldberg & Greenberg, "The Effect of Physician-Controlled Health Insurance: United States v. Oregon State Medical Society," 2 *J. Health Pol., Pol'y & L.* 48 (1977).
75 In 1977, in response to the threat of President Carter's hospital cost containment legislation, the hospital industry developed the Voluntary Effort, a program to voluntarily lower hospital costs without the pressure of publicly mandated cost containment.
76 *N.Y. Times*, Jan. 21, 1981, § B, at 1, col. 1.
77 Office of Management and Budget, *America's New Beginning: A Program for Economic Recovery* 6–22 (Feb. 19, 1981).
78 See Bovbjerg, "Competition Versus Regulation in Medical Care: An Overdrawn Dichotomy," 34 *Vand. L. Rev.* 965 (1981).
79 See Marmor, Wittman & Heagy, chapter 3 of this volume.
80 For an exploration of such alternatives, see *National Health Insurance: Conflicting Goals and Policy Choices*, *supra* note 52; A. Miller & M. Miller, *supra* note 53.

Index